Privatization
and
Educational
Choice

CATO
INSTITUTE

PRIVATIZATION AND EDUCATIONAL CHOICE

MYRON LIEBERMAN

ST. MARTIN'S PRESS
New York

First published in the United States of America in 1989

Printed in the United States

ISBN 0-312-02799-0

Library of Congress Cataloging-in-Publication Data

Lieberman, Myron, 1919–
  Privatization and educational choice / Myron Lieberman.
    p. cm.
  Bibliography: p. 351
  Includes index.
  ISBN 0-312-02799-0—ISBN 0-312-02845-8
  1. Public schools—United States. 2. Privatization—United
States. 3. Private schools—United States. 4 Educational
vouchers—United States. 5. School, Choice of —United States.
6. Education—United States—Aims and Objectives. I. Title.
LA217.L542 1989
371′.00973—dc 19   88–7801

For Wally and Jess, and the memory
of my sister Elinor.

Contents

List of Tables

Preface

In 1986 I published *Beyond Public Education,* a book that argues that the educational reform movement in the United States is essentially a futilitarian effort. Nothing that has happened since then has led me to change this conclusion; if anything, subsequent developments have led to widespread albeit not unanimous agreement with this point of view.

In that book, my contention was that schools for profit could avoid the obstacles that frustrate conventional school reform. Although this conclusion still seems valid, I have come to realize that such schools are not the only way, or necessarily the best way in all circumstances, to utilize the for-profit sector to provide educational services. This realization was partly a consequence of a more intensive analysis of the privatization and educational choice movements. Eventually I recognized a need to assess educational reform from a broader perspective than characterized earlier publications. For example, discussions of educational choice typically treat it as an isolated phenomenon and rarely consider the underlying social forces that generate pressures for more differentiation among products and services.

This book, then, constitutes an effort to relate educational improvement to the privatization movement and to certain broad social changes as well as to circumstances within the field of education itself. Regardless of whether readers agree or disagree with my resolution of various issues, the book is intended to generate discussion of several neglected issues in educational policy and practice.

Acknowledgments

In writing this book, I was helped by several people over a two-year period. With apologies to anyone inadvertently not mentioned, I would like to express my appreciation to the following persons for various courtesies, criticisms, and suggestions related to the manuscript:

Gregory Anrig, Educational Testing Service; Marc Bendick, Jr., Washington, D.C.; Mark Blaug, London, England; David D. Boaz, Cato Institute; Alan Campbell, ARA Services; John Chubb, Brookings Institution; James S. Coleman, University of Chicago; Bruce S. Cooper, Fordham University; Larry M. Cuban, Stanford University; Stanley M. Elam, Phi Delta Kappan; David F. Englehardt, Independent School Management; John Esty, National Association of Independent Schools; Michael Farris, Home School Legal Defense Association; Arnold Fege, National PTA; Milton Friedman, Hoover Institution; Nathan Glazer, Harvard University; Don Hendricks, American Learning Corporation; Albert O. Hirschman, Princeton University; Glenn A. Hogen, Sylvan Learning Corporation; Robert P. Inman, University of Pennsylvania; Thomas H. Jones, University of Connecticut; Ted Kolderie, University of Minnesota; Robert Lytle, Birmingham, Michigan; Jacob B. Michaelsen, University of California at Santa Cruz; Russell Miller and Michael Ward, Huntington Learning Centers; Caroline More, Eagle Forum; Charles O'Malley, U.S. Department of Education; Samuel H. Preston, University of Pennsylvania; Robert L. Smith, Council for Private Education; Robert M. Veatch, Georgetown University.

None of these people received a complete copy of the final draft, and several expressed disagreements with the text made available to them. For this reason, as well as others, and although the assistance received is often reflected in the manuscript, I am solely responsible for the content.

Privatization
and
Educational
Choice

1

The Significance
of Privatization and
Choice for Education

This book is an effort to explain what must be done to improve elementary and secondary education in the United States. In view of the thousands of publications devoted to this subject, let me begin by pointing out why this one differs fundamentally from the overwhelming majority and on a smaller but significant scale from the rest. I shall then provide an overview of the topics to be discussed and the intended audience for this book.

Most other publications on educational reform (hereinafter referred to as "conventional approaches") either accept the existing governance structure of public education or would increase producer control of it; the latter category includes proposals to "increase teacher autonomy," or "empower teachers," or otherwise weaken teacher accountability to parents or school boards. In my opinion, educational reform cannot be achieved through these conventional approaches.

Such approaches emphasize the need for better school

boards, more qualified teachers, higher teacher salaries, strong antidrug measures, more homework requirements, the elimination of superficial courses, and strengthening student discipline, to mention just a few staples in the reform reports.[1] For the most part, the actions required would be taken at the local level. The argument to be made here, however, is that any of the local actions required cannot be widely successful under our present system of education.

Essentially, the inability of local school boards to implement needed reform is due to three kinds of factors. One kind is encompassed in the decision-making structure of education. This structure includes but is not limited to the statutory provisions governing pupils, teachers, administrators, school board members, and support personnel; the ways funds for education are raised and distributed; and the legal requirements governing a broad range of educational and administrative affairs.

The second major set of factors blocking reform are the interests that would be adversely affected by it. The reformers typically rely on a vast uncoordinated effort by legislatures, governors, school boards, chief state school officers, institutions of higher education, teacher unions, foundations, and a host of other parties to work for common policies regardless of how the policies would affect each group's interests. In addition to neglecting the role of interest groups, reform efforts also ignore the tremendous importance of the short-range view to most political and educational leaders and their much greater personal stake in the appearance of reform than in the reality of it.[2] What is to be done?

My view is that contrary to conventional reform proposals, the only ways to improve American education are to (1) foster private schools that compete with public schools and among themselves and/or (2) foster for-profit competition among service providers within the public school system. Such competition might be structured at the state, school district, school, department, grade, and/or teacher level; as I see it, competition at any one of these levels could be beneficial under certain circumstances.

Both of these proposed ways to improve education require "privatization." As used herein, the term denotes transferring activities conducted by public employees to the private sector. The activities transferred may include the funding as well as the actual delivery of services; in this analysis, however, the emphasis is on the delivery of educational services.

The relationships between privatization and educational choice are an integral part of my analysis. "Educational choice" refers to choices made by students and/or parents. In some contexts "educational choice" denotes only choice of school, public or private. But it can also refer to choice of program, course, or teacher. These various choices have very different ramifications; for example, choice of public or private school has financial implications that are not present in choice of teachers or courses within a school.

Privatization and educational choice may or may not be interrelated in practice. A school board that contracts out education of the disabled to a for-profit company is privatizing education; educational choice is not involved if the students are required to use the contractor's services. If educational choices are restricted to options within public school systems, we would have "choice," or some versions of it, without privatization.

Nevertheless, there are strong reasons to consider privatization and choice in the same analysis. The extent of privatization may limit choices. For instance, under current circumstances at least, parents cannot choose to provide their children with a denominational education in a public school. One of the crucial issues to be explored is the extent to which privatization is essential to provide the kinds of choices parents and students wish to make. In addition, privatization has significant implications for the cost, variety, and quality of educational services provided in response to choice mechanisms in public and private schools. Finally, the politics of educational choice is greatly affected by whether the choices are available in the private sector. In brief, we must consider the specifics of choice from the provider as well as the consumer side in order to assess the potential of choice policies. Choice of subjects or teachers within public schools differs more than it resembles choice of school, public or private. Treating such widely disparate modes of choice as substitutes for each other can only lead to hopeless confusion.

The distinction between educational choice and vouchers should also be noted to avoid a potential source of confusion. Vouchers are defined as entitlements that may be used to implement educational choices. Usually voucher plans envisage public financial assistance to attend a school of choice, but they could be used for other purposes as well. For instance, vouchers might be used to pay for a course instead of enrollment as a full-time student. Most forms of educational choice, such as choice of subject or teacher, are implemented without vouchers, but vouchers to cover the costs of education at a private school are the primary objective of the educational choice movement. Partly for this reason, my discussion of educational choice emphasizes voucher issues. Such issues have received a great deal of attention over a long period of time. I discuss them here because previous discussions are deficient. For instance, the literature on educational vouchers typically ignores the distinction between nonprofit and for-profit schools. In my analysis, the distinction is crucial to the resolution of several basic issues in both privatization and voucher controversies.

The Modes of Privatization

Educators often view privatization as synonymous with educational vouchers or tuition tax credits. In fact, however, privatization can be implemented in a variety of ways, some of which receive little or no attention in educational analysis. These ways include:

1. Contracting (with independent contractors)
2. Vouchers
3. Load shedding
4. Franchising
5. Subsidies to nongovernmental suppliers

6. Voluntary service
7. Sale of government assets
8. Construction or purchase of public facilities with leaseback arrangements

Although the various forms of privatization will be discussed in more detail later on, a brief explanation of them here will help to clarify the discussion.

Contracting out of public services is defined as the contractual utilization of nongovernmental entities to provide or help to provide public services. "Nongovernmental entities" can be companies, partnerships, individuals, nonprofit organizations, and/or independent contractors, whether for-profit or nonprofit. The test is whether the persons providing the service are school district employees. If they are and are also acting in that capacity, their services are not contracted out.

Contracting out applies to support services as well as instruction. In other words, the concept applies to any activity required to provide education. Furthermore, the contractor need not be a for-profit company or an individual entrepreneur. Nonprofit organizations can and often do contract with public agencies to provide services. We cannot assume, however, that the outcomes of privatization are the same for both nonprofit and for-profit service providers. On the contrary, the distinction vitally affects some of the most important issues discussed in this book.

Vouchers are government payments to consumers or on behalf of consumers who may use the payment at any institution approved by government for the purpose of the voucher. Thus in both contracting out and vouchers, government pays the service provider; under a voucher plan, however, parents choose the service provider.

Ordinarily, vouchers are assumed to be pieces of paper that can be used like cash or as a credit toward a purchase approved by the government; food stamps illustrate this point. In education, however, vouchers are typically envisaged as a credit to be claimed by a school. The parents would choose the school, and the school would apply for the payment according to procedures established by statute and/or regulations.

Load shedding refers to government withdrawal from both funding and providing a service. Although there is very little popular or academic support for educational load shedding at this time, my analysis will suggest some reasons support is likely to increase in the future.

A *franchise* is an arrangement whereby a private organization is awarded monopoly privileges to provide a service. For example, a school district may allow McDonald's the right to operate the school cafeteria for a stipulated period of time. Unlike vouchers, the consumer does not necessarily use funds provided by government to pay for the services.

Subsidies are government payments or credits to producers to minimize or eliminate the costs to service users. In effect, tax exemptions for nonprofit schools are subsidies. Education tax credits may also be considered to fall within this category of privatization.

Voluntary service is simply the provision of service by parents or other volunteers. Home schooling and the presence of Planned Parenthood representatives in sex education courses illustrate this form of privatization.

The sale of government assets is a transfer of property rights to tangible assets from government to the private sector for an agreed upon price.

Leaseback arrangements are the construction or purchase of public facilities by private parties who then lease the facilities to public agencies under mutually agreed upon terms. An example is a school district that cannot get voter approval required to build a new school and arranges for private construction—after which the school leases the facility at a rental amount agreed upon prior to construction.

In terms of relevance to public education, these forms of privatization vary widely. It would be premature, however, to dismiss any of them as irrelevant to education. Religious history provides an illustration of the possibility of a basic change in attitudes toward privatization. In some countries religion was formerly a state affair. Governments forced individuals to accept the state religion, and state-supported schools fostered adherence to a state-supported religion.

Today, however, religion has been left to individual decision and support in many of these countries. Although important differences still exist on the matter, the American people as a whole clearly support the privatization of religion; this support is frequently expressed as support for "separation of church and state." In terms of our categories of privatization, the separation of church and state is an example of load shedding—that is, government withdrawal of support as well as provision of service.

Many persons who support the privatization of religion oppose the privatization of public education. This is not necessarily an inconsistency. It may make sense to support privatization in one field and oppose it in another, such as education. Support or opposition should not be based on a preconceived idea that "privatization" is good or bad. Instead, we should look to *what* is being privatized and why. We should also consider how privatization is being implemented, since one way may be worthy of support but other ways may not.

The Privatization Movement

Whatever one's attitude toward privatization, it is a major economic and political movement in the United States. There are a number of reasons why this is so. First, a number of foundations and policy institutes are actively encouraging it. The Reason Foundation, a free enterprise oriented foundation that has supported research on privatization for several years, publishes an annual report on privatization. Its 1986 report lists the following foundations, policy institutes, and research organizations as active in the privatization movement:

Academy for State and Local Government
Adam Smith Institute-USA
American Legislative Exchange Council
Cato Institute

Center for the Study of Market Alternatives
Citizens for a Sound Economy
Council of State Governments
Council on Municipal Performance
Heartland Institute
Heritage Foundation
International City Management Association
Manhattan Institute for Policy Research
National Center for Privatization
National Center for Policy Analysis
Political Economy Research Center
Privatization Council Inc.
Reason Foundation
Sequoia Institute
Urban Institute
Privatization Research Organization, Public Management
Center, Baruch College, CUNY[3]

In addition, university departments, such as those de-voted to health care or transportation, and various centers not devoted primarily to privatization frequently sponsor research and service activities on privatization issues. Else-where, university centers with a broader agenda, such as public policy or public administration, are also active on privatization issues. In addition, the Reason Foundation's annual survey lists eight trade associations that are ac-tively promoting privatization as well as several others less systematically involved. Journals devoted exclusively or substantially to privatization have also been established re-cently—*Privatization Review, State and Local Govern-ment,* and *Fiscal Watchdog.* Furthermore, articles about privatization have become commonplace in a wide range of journals. Influential mass media have also devoted increasing attention to privatization developments; be-tween November 2, 1985, and January 20, 1986, at least twenty-six articles on privatization appeared in *The New York Times, Washington Post,* and the *Wall Street Jour-nal.*[4]

Significantly, the privatization movement is not confined

or even centered in the United States; it is worldwide in scope, with the "privatizers" achieving greater influence in all geographical areas. Although the most publicized developments have been the expansion of the private sector in the Soviet Union and the People's Republic of China, a trend toward privatization is evident in every continent and within nations of widely different political systems. This is not to say that the trend toward privatization characterizes every nation or that it may not be halted or even reversed in some nations; on the other hand, there is no question that we are witnessing a worldwide trend toward private instead of government service delivery.[5]

What are the reasons for the growth of the privatization movement? One is the allegedly greater efficiency of the private sector; the case for regarding this reason as relevant to public education will be considered in subsequent chapters. In the context of privatization, however, "increased efficiency" is not just a fiscal concept. Instead, it should be viewed as a response to widespread dissatisfaction with government services; the belief that the private sector can deliver services more economically is only one factor underlying the growth of privatization.

This growth has an intellectual base in the "public choice" approach to government decision making. Simply stated, public choice theory asserts that the behavior of politicians and bureaucrats can be explained by the same principles that govern behavior in private economic affairs. In the latter, persons generally act so as to enhance their self-interest. According to public choice theorists, public officials also act in this way: They act either to get reelected or to enhance their pay, perquisites, and status. These motivations, not an abstract devotion to the public interest, are said to dominate political as well as economic activity.[6] Needless to say, this view of public affairs is consistent with our recent widespread disenchantment with political leaders and public services. It may also help to explain the growing interest in using market systems to deliver public services that are funded by government.

The public choice framework has its critics, but it is

widely recognized as an important perspective from which to analyze the conduct of public officials. The perspective does not assume that a calculus of self-interest determines all decision making by public officials. Nevertheless, it does offer a rational explanation for our persistent inability to solve longstanding social problems by means of government services. To put it in the educational context, public choice theory suggests that the obstacles to educational reform may be inherent in government delivery of services. Obviously, if this should be the case, policies that do not privatize education are bound to fail. The fact that public choice theory is at least as applicable to public education as to any other public service gives this possibility added significance.

Privatization also has roots in studies of the political role of interest groups. Such groups are often viewed as manipulating our political processes to their own advantage but to the public's disadvantage. By having certain decisions made in the political instead of the economic system, privatization seeks to avoid such subordination of the public interest.

As we shall see, privatization faces vigorous intellectual as well as political opposition, at least in the United States. Proponents and opponents agree on the dangers of ideological rigidity and the importance of evaluating proposals on the basis of their specific features and circumstances. Unfortunately, as evidenced by the way they consistently disagree over just about everything else, partisans on both sides tend to ignore this advice as soon as they have given it.

At any rate, neither the broad arguments for nor against privatization are equally applicable to all its forms, or to specific proposals within each category. Assessing privatization proposals in the context of public education often turns out to be an extremely complex task. In many cases the complexity results as much or more from the difficulties of assessing the status quo as from the uncertain consequences of privatization. Understandably, persons strongly critical of the educational status quo are more willing to run the risks of changing it. For this author at least, the deficiencies of public education are less acceptable than are the uncertain ones of changing our educational system. There is, however, a critical difference between accepting policies despite risks that are understood and accepting them because of failure to understand the risks in the first place. Essentially, in this book my objective is to provide a broader understanding of privatization issues, not to convert readers.

To Whom Is This Book Addressed?

The intended audience for this book has perhaps only one common characteristic: an interest in improving elementary and secondary education. Within this large and diverse group, I hope to reach the leaders who are especially situated to act on or influence the issues discussed herein. Realistically, this means state leaders, because education is primarily a state responsibility in the United States; while changes are needed at the local level, such changes are usually dependent on system changes at the state level. Consequently, my analysis is addressed to state leaders with the power to implement such changes.

In this respect, the analysis differs from reform proposals that envisage parents and taxpayers persuading their local school boards to initiate needed reforms. Later on I shall suggest some actions at the local level that might improve matters, but I emphasize the limited effectiveness of such action more than its potentially beneficial outcomes. Local action is essential to improving education, but such action must focus primarily on support for changing our system of state regulation, financial support, and governance of local school districts.

Similarly, federal officials can influence but not effectuate the needed system changes. Federal leverage on states and local school districts consists of making funds available if recipients adopt certain policies or practices. As federal funds for education decline, as compliance with federal mandates or incentives is difficult to monitor, and as federally sponsored policies are the most difficult to enact or change, this approach offers little prospect for achieving education reform. In short, if system change is needed, the movers and shakers will be found primarily among political and educational leaders at the state level.

Despite the importance of state leadership, my target audience is a much broader group. Business leadership is becoming increasingly concerned about the effectiveness of our educational system. If that concern is to lead to improvement, it must be based on an accurate diagnosis of what must be done and by whom; such a diagnosis requires that business leaders understand both the underlying obstacles to educational improvement and the strategic role of state action in overcoming them.

School boards, school administrators, teachers, and parents are not in a position to achieve more than marginal improvements as matters stand. Often any improvements are achieved only by actions that result in marginal deterioration elsewhere—districts that hire good teachers or administrators from other districts improve their own situation by actions that weaken others. Nevertheless, there are compelling reasons for addressing this book to this wider audience. First, state leaders are unlikely to bring about the changes required without a significant measure of support from the educational community. Changes that are overwhelmingly opposed by local school boards, school administrators, teacher unions, and parents are much less likely to be implemented than changes that command some significant level of support among one or more of these groups. Eventually the educational community will have to confront the system issues either on its own initiative or, as is regrettably more likely, that of others. Whatever the circumstances, well-informed followers as well as leaders will be essential; it is hoped that the analysis will help to create both.

WHY REFORMS FAIL: AN ILLUSTRATIVE SCENARIO

Obviously, whatever school deficiencies exist have a past. In some cases erroneous policies were initiated decades or even generations ago. Others may have been initiated more recently. For whatever reason, educational authorities once deemed them to be the right course of action. A policy that is harmful now may have been the right one when it was initiated; the underlying circumstances may have changed. Or the policy may have been based on the best information available at the time; now, in the light of better information, a policy change may be needed. Unfortunately, change frequently turns out to be impossible under current circumstances. Let us see why this is the case.

Suppose you are a concerned parent who wants your school board to adopt two reforms widely advocated by educational reformers. First, you want to strengthen the mathematics curriculum. Second, you want to introduce merit pay for teachers (a system that pays good teachers more than average or poor ones).

For the sake of argument, let us assume that these changes should receive a high priority. Unfortunately, the incumbent school board does not share this view. You and a fellow citizen who shares your views therefore become candidates for the school board. One year after you became active on the issue, you and your colleague are elected to the school board.

About 94 percent of the school boards in the United States have five to nine members; there is an almost equal division among boards with five, seven, or nine members. Let us, therefore, assume that you now have two votes on a seven-member school board. Undaunted, you organize a caucus that elects two additional board members in the next election, which takes place two years after your own. It has been a long, hard struggle, but you are now the leader of a majority on the board committed to the reforms you seek.

Unfortunately, you are still unable to implement your proposed changes in the mathematics curriculum. Such implementation requires changing the district-adopted textbooks as well as retraining most of the mathematics teachers. Neither action is easy to accomplish. Any textbooks adopted by the board have to be included on a state-approved list. The textbooks you would like to adopt are not on the list. As the state textbook commission revises the list for each course every five years, you may have to wait several years before the mathematics textbooks are reviewed again. Since there is no assurance that the textbooks you prefer will be included on the new state-approved list, you decide to press for adoption of a less preferred series of mathematics textbooks and turn your attention to training your teachers to use them.

The teachers, comfortable with the current texts and uninterested in learning to use a new series, have been opposed to any change from the outset. Their union insists that any in-service training to use the new series effectively be provided during the regular school day at board expense. Needless to say, the disruption of regular classes may be quite expensive. After training is provided at board expense, the newly trained teachers may leave for better jobs. The older mathematics teachers may be nearing retirement, so there may be little return on any district investment in their in-service education. The new board members may also be committed to a sex education program that would require most of the board's discretionary funds. The upshot is that several years have gone by and your goal of improving the mathematics curriculum is not much closer to reality than it was at the beginning of your efforts.

Meanwhile, your plan to pay good teachers more than average or poor ones has encountered even greater difficulties. Again, let us pick up the course of events after you have achieved a board majority. Although four years have elapsed since you became an activist on the issue, you can do absolutely nothing about it until the collective bargaining contract with your teachers' unicn expires, which will be in two years. Salary incentive plans are a mandatory subject of bargaining, so you must bargain on your merit pay proposals before you can implement them.

Prior to the expiration of the teacher contract, you discover that your administrative staff does not really support merit pay for teachers. While that staff cautioned you that the teacher union would oppose it, it now becomes evident that they also oppose merit pay. The principals believe strongly that they will upset nine teachers for every one they recommend for merit pay. Your negotiating team responds very slowly and very cautiously to your request for some concrete proposals on the subject. Also, you discover that what concerns the administrative staff as much as anything is the fact that their teacher evaluations will be scrutinized intensively if merit pay is implemented. Consequently, you begin to appreciate something that was not apparent at the outset: Merit pay is a severe test of administrative judgment and competence. At bottom, administrators prefer to avoid this test, but they also wanted to avoid expressing this preference. After all, their tenure, salary raises, and promotional opportunities depend on the school board, so they have avoided open opposition to its policies. Nevertheless, their footdragging has become too obvious to be ignored.

In at least one respect the administration has advised you correctly: The teachers' union is adamantly opposed to merit pay. In fact, the union has privately and publicly emphasized that it will strike, if necessary, to force the board to drop its merit pay proposals. Moreover, while the entire agreement is being held hostage to this issue, the union has launched an aggressive campaign depicting you and your fellow board members of scheming to reward board lackeys and undermine the union by rewarding antiunion and nonunion teachers.

As the impasse drags on and your fellow board members become increasingly reluctant to insist on merit pay, you decide to make one last effort to resolve the issue. The effort consists of an off-the-record meeting with the union president alone in order to ensure candor.

Candor is what you get. The union president says flatly (but off the record) that the union is not overly concerned about merit pay for bootlickers or antiunion teachers. On the contrary, it is more concerned that merit pay would be implemented objectively. "If you award $3,000 more to ten

outstanding teachers, there will be ninety others who believe, rightly or wrongly, that they deserve it as much or
more than the recipients. They will come to me as union
president and ask me to do something about it. What can I
do? I'm not going to tell them the $3,000 was awarded
fairly and they have no case. That's not the way I got to be
a union representative and it's not the way I'll continue to
be a union representative."

You ask why the union can't agree to merit pay with an
appeal procedure for teachers who regard themselves as
unfairly passed over. The union president points out that
such appeals would place the union in the middle of a battle between union members. The union would either have
to support the teacher who is appealing or the teacher(s)
who allegedly did not deserve merit pay as much as the
appellant—a no-win situation for the union. The only way
to avoid it is to avoid merit pay, at least in cases where
local administrators are responsible for deciding who receives it.

"Do not forget," the union president continues, "the
union is a political organization. It's controlled on the basis
of one person, one vote. Union members aren't interested
in large rewards for a few members. They are interested in
more for themselves, not rhetoric about the need to reward
the better workers. That stuff is for kids, not teachers.
Think of my situation as if I were a political leader, which I
am essentially. Political leaders are concerned that no small
group of constituents be perceived as benefiting excessively
compared to others. I have the same problem with merit
pay, except that the small group of constituents receiving
excessive benefits is not a geographical or separate interest
group.

"I have several other objections," the president continues, "but let me ask you a question. How will you know
whether merit pay is 'successful'? You might be able to ram
it down my throat, although I doubt it; after all, no other
school district in the area has it, and you're going to look
worse every day holding out for something that is not included in any other contract in the area. Sure, the idea

seems like common sense, but when we hit the bricks, the parents aren't going to support you. They'll be much more concerned about getting their kids back in school than about merit pay. Most people don't work under merit plans anyway. But my question is this: What do you expect to gain from all this that is worth the headache—and when do you expect to get it? The headache is now—I doubt whether you will even be around when it comes time to evaluate the plan in a way we could both accept."

You were going to say that the benefits would be visible immediately as teachers worked harder to receive the additional cash. Now this response seems unrealistic, perhaps even naive, so instead, you thank the union president for being candid and depart. The futility of what you are (or were) trying to do seems so obvious—why was it not obvious before you had wasted all this time and effort? And if you could just get your hands on the prestigious educational reformers who had peddled this snake oil from one end of the country to the other, you would tell them a thing or two. Unfortunately, your immediate problem is how to abandon merit pay without antagonizing your supporters and appearing to have knuckled under to the union. The union president comes to the rescue by suggesting that the board and the union accept the contract without merit pay but with an agreement to appoint a joint committee to study the problem and submit their recommendations before the next contract negotiations. The same education reporters who naively believed the union really feared favoritism treat this like a statesmanlike compromise, and the issue never comes up again.

The preceding scenario is intended to illustrate the rationale that underlies my analysis. To begin with, my analysis treats the interest group stake in reform (or in blocking reform) as just as important as the educational policies to be initiated, changed, or terminated. Furthermore, conventional approaches assume that the changes required can be made within the existing governance structure of education.[7] This assumption is not explicit, but it is a logical inference from their neglect of governance issues. In contrast, the approach adopted here assumes that a laundry list of educational changes is inadequate for two reasons. First, without basic changes in the way educational decisions are made, it is virtually impossible to implement them, regardless of their merit. Second, even if the proposed changes could be implemented, it would soon be necessary to eliminate or modify many of them. Consequently, we would soon find ourselves in a situation similar to the one in which we find ourselves today.

Let us bear in mind what is at stake here. Suppose that by waving a magic wand we could effectuate the agenda recommended by the reformers. Several recommendations make no sense and/or are inconsistent with each other, but let us assume that all embody the best thinking on the issues currently available. Over time, and not much time at that, we would want to change or eliminate some of the policies. New information, new technologies, new careers, new educational and economic demands, new civic and cultural developments, new demographic situations—all would require changes in our educational system. As our scenario suggests, however, it would be practically impossible to effectuate them.

This is not idle speculation. Most recent reform proposals are not new. Many are simply reiterations of policies proposed decades, even generations, ago. In my opinion, many of these policies will never be implemented under our existing governance structure, but let us waive the point. Instead let us assume that at some point in the future, near or remote, the proposed reforms have been achieved. For conventional reform, this would be the end of the matter. Yet a critically important question is left unanswered: What can and should be done to ensure that the system does not deteriorate again? Clearly, our existing system of education is inadequate protection against deterioration; we already have it. Of course, no system can guarantee good results in all cases and situations, but what will prevent slippage if improvements are made?

Conventional approaches have no answer to this question because they have never raised it. What is needed, however, is an educational system that will generate continuous improvement, either in educational outcomes or in our efficiency in achieving them. As education analyst Ted Kolderie has suggested, the basic issue is not how to improve the educational system; it is how to develop a system that seeks improvement.[8]

To illustrate, Americans who study the Japanese educational system usually reach two conclusions about it. One is that the system is extremely successful in meeting the objectives of literacy and academic competence. The other is that Japanese education is characterized by an emphasis on competition and testing that would supposedly be undesirable, not to say intolerable, in the United States.[9] I do not intend to advocate this emphasis here but simply to comment on one aspect of it. If we do not rely on frequent testing and public awareness of results, what should we rely on to maintain the pressure on all concerned to get the job done effectively? In the reform literature, specific proposals simply do not come to grips with this issue. To resolve it, we need to change our decision-making system in education. At least, that is a possibility to be explored in the following chapters.

From this perspective, we can fairly assert that educational reformers show a pervasive bias in favor of the status quo. At first glance the assertion seems paradoxical, even contradictory. Minimally, a "reform" is a proposed change: How can reformers be charged with supporting the status quo? The bias in favor of the status quo, however, refers to the bias in favor of the existing decision-making structure of education. The reformers are trying to change policies that cannot be changed within a governance structure that is taken for granted. In this respect they are like the critics who point to deficiencies in the federal budget but are silent on the budget-making process that underlies those deficiencies. Analogously, it will be argued that educational reform must focus on the educational policy-making process itself, not the specific policies emerging from the process.

The Plan of This Book

The modes of privatization have different utility and political prospects from state to state. In many states, however, the most promising approach to privatization in the near future will be through purchasing instructional services from independent contractors instead of teachers. Consequently, chapter 2 is devoted to the rationale for contracting out, its development in other public services, and its advantages and disadvantages, both generally and in public education. Chapter 3 continues this discussion by focusing on two issues that are critical to all forms of privatization: comparative costs and the evaluation of outcomes. Chapter 4 is devoted to previous efforts to contract out instruction and to issues that must be resolved to do so more effectively in the future. These issues illustrate again the fact that effective action at the local level usually requires changes in the state framework for education.

Chapter 5 opens up the discussion of educational choice. Proposals to empower parents to choose the schools, public or private, that their children will attend are considered first. After explaining why my analysis will be limited to voucher plans, the chapter sets forth the argument that educational vouchers would result in educational improvement. This argument is essentially an illustration of the voice or exit controversy that has dominated policy analysts in recent years.

Chapter 6 focuses on the competition issues raised by voucher proposals. It first discusses the potentially negative effects of the competition anticipated to result from voucher plans and then probes whether competition would really result. The suggestion is that the nonprofit status of private schools would be a major limiting factor in this regard. This possibility leads to consideration of the role of schools for profit in voucher plans.

In chapter 7 I take up four additional independent arguments for vouchers. My objectives are to explain their rationale, their implications for voucher plans and for policy. Chapter 8 is devoted mainly to a political analysis of voucher plans and an assessment of their chances for enactment.

Chapter 9 raises the broad issue of whether privatization in education will develop as a cottage industry or as a large-scale enterprise. Experience in education and in other fields, especially the health industries, is cited to show that both approaches are likely to emerge, depending on the particular activity that is privatized. The possibilities of franchising certain kinds of educational services are also explored in this chapter.

Chapter 10 is devoted to load shedding—proposals that government withdraw support as well as provision for education. The home schooling movement is analyzed to illustrate the possibilities in this neglected mode of privatization. The conclusion is that load shedding has much greater potential than is commonly realized, especially if its substantive and tactical flexibility are clearly understood and there is adequate recognition of demographic and social changes affecting load-shedding issues.

Chapter 11 analyzes the ethical and professional issues raised by privatization in education. These issues do not simply emerge as a consequence of privatization; they often constitute barriers to it when they are perceived as not being subject to satisfactory resolution. Because certain issues frequently arise under different modes of privatization, they are considered generally, not in the context of any specific way of privatizing. The analysis then concludes by suggesting a rationale for privatizing education that is ignored in the field of education but widely accepted outside of it.

Most emphatically, this analysis is not presented as an infallible guide to educational improvement. It is presented to suggest the policies that offer the best chance of improving education, but "the best chance" may not even be a fifty–fifty one.

Two Caveats

The chapters that follow recommend a more significant educational role for privatization, competition, and profit-making organizations in the field of education. The recommendations apply, however, only to certain circumstances; frequently it is impossible to say how widely these circumstances prevail or can reasonably be made to prevail.

One additional cautionary note cannot be overemphasized. This is the danger of applying a double standard, or an unrealistic standard, to the policies recommended. For example, reliance on for-profit organizations to perform a service does not guarantee that the service will always be provided satisfactorily. No approach ensures perfection, and no approach should be unacceptable because it fails on occasion. The policies proposed here may or may not make sense, but they should not be held to a standard that is impossible for any policy to meet. Our options are not between policies that are always successful and policies that are not. It is between two or more policies, each with some desirable and some undesirable consequences—and often with some unknown ones also. Formulating sound policy is difficult in any case; it is hopeless if the standards for evaluating the status quo tolerate a variety of undesirable consequences while those for evaluating proposed changes tolerate none.[10] I will return to this problem later, but sensitivity to it is essential throughout this analysis.

2

Should Government Buy or Make Education?

We begin with a simple question that has perhaps several complex answers. Should governments (primarily states and school districts) buy education? Or should they make it? Before attempting to answer this question, let me first try to clarify it.

At a personal level, the ubiquity of the buy-or-make decision is taken for granted. Eat in or eat out, wash one's dirty clothes or take them to a laundry, repair a garment or leave it with a tailor—such decisions are made every day. Likewise, there is widespread recognition of the fact that companies face similar decisions on a daily basis. Should company reports be printed in-house or contracted out? Should cleaning and custodial services be provided by employees or contractors? Should employees be asked to work overtime or should an independent contractor be asked to provide temporary help? Should the company have guards or should it hire a security agency that will in turn employ the guards? As in personal life, corporate (and public agency) make-or-buy decisions are pervasive. While a particular decision may be controversial, the need to make them frequently is not.

When governments are involved, the decision is inherently political as well as economic. This dual nature of the decision often complicates it in ways that do not arise, or are not so critical, when the decision is made by individuals or companies. Although contracting out always has economic consequences, government officials often subordinate such consequences to political ones. For this reason, the political dimensions of contracting out public services are at least as important as the economic ones.

I do not mean to suggest that make-or-buy decisions in the private sector are always purely economic ones. Corporations as well as individuals sometimes make these decisions on noneconomic grounds. In fact, the greater the economic consequences of an economic decision, the more likely it is to involve political considerations of some kind.

From a legal standpoint, the make-or-buy decision involves the distinction between employees and independent contractors. Although the distinction can be difficult to make in borderline cases, it is usually clear in practice. Employees are subject to the control and direction of the employer; independent contractors are employed to provide a service, but they exercise a high degree of independence in doing so. If you hire a secretary to work in your office, he or she will ordinarily be an employee. On the other hand, if you employ a secretary to perform secretarial services in an office he or she owns, and the work is performed without your on-site supervision, the secretary is an independent contractor.

In brief, both employees and independent contractors perform services under contract; if the individual(s) performing the services have legal control over how the service is to be performed, they are independent contractors. If the service buyer controls both what is to be done and how, the persons performing the services are employees.

In some situations, individuals will perform services as employees at certain times and as independent contractors at others. An example outside the field of education illustrates this possibility. Public transportation companies often experience severe employment problems as the result of their rush-hour needs. If they use employees to cover rush hours, the companies may be forced to pay the employees for unnecessary layover time. Or because the use of their employees may require excessive overtime pay, companies may employ independent contractors to perform rush-hour services. Regular company employees may be allowed to bid on contracts for rush-hour services as independent contractors. If successful, they serve as regular employees at certain times and as independent contractors at others. As we shall see, similar possibilities could arise in education.

The Make-or-Buy Decision in Public Education

Let us first consider the make-or-buy decision from a state perspective. Public education is a state function in the United States. As noted previously, the states establish most of the legal and operational framework for education. Also, the states provide more school revenues than either the federal or local governments; in fact, the state share is roughly equal to the federal and local share combined.

Clearly, therefore, the states are buyers, not makers, of educational services. As buyers, however, the states have adopted policies that buyers elsewhere try to avoid. Most buyers are better off if there is competition among their vendors, whether we buy automobiles or haircuts, houses or hospital services. When we sell our own services, we may welcome monopoly status for ourselves, but not for our vendors. Nevertheless, as buyers the states have established a monopoly (public schools) and in effect buy educational services only from the state-created monopoly. To be sure, its supporters contend that there are valid reasons why public education is an exception to the general rule. Yet the burden of proof is on them. On its face, it appears to be an inefficient way to procure educational services.

This conclusion appears also to apply to local school districts. At the local level, virtually all school districts utilize both employees and independent contractors. Independent contractors, however, are utilized primarily to provide non-instructional services, such as transportation, legal and medical services, data processing, security guards, maintenance services, and labor negotiations. On the other hand, school districts are much more likely to make instead of buy instructional services. One exception occurs when school districts do not include all the grade levels. In such cases, the districts often contract with other districts to provide the required grade levels of instruction. Another common practice is to use independent contractors to provide instructional services for students who are severely disabled (blind, mentally retarded, deaf, and so on). It is often impractical, especially in smaller districts, to provide instruction for such students because the specialized teachers, facilities, and equipment needed are prohibitively expensive if used by only a small number of students. Generally speaking, however, school districts prefer to make rather than to buy instructional services. In fact, the make option is largely taken for granted; the buy option is considered only when some unusual situation renders the make option especially impractical.

The preceding discussion might be criticized on the grounds that school districts are legally agencies of the state governments. That is, the states control school districts to whatever extent the states deem desirable. For this reason, states are not buying education from independent contractors. Instead they are making it through their agents, the local school districts.

It can be conceded that local school districts are agents of the states, not independent contractors. Nevertheless, the agency relationship here is very different from the agency relationship in an employment context. States do not control local districts in the same sense as employers control employees. State control over local school boards exists—indeed, such control underlies my contention that local districts are frequently unable to act effectively. Nevertheless, such state control is not tantamount to state production of educational services.

In summary, then, public education does not share a consistent approach to make-or-buy decisions. One reason is that voters are characterized by inconsistencies on the same issues. As taxpayers, voters want to spend as little as possible for education. As educational consumers, especially in their role as parents, voters want government to pay for whatever services the parents might wish to use. In other words, the citizen's role as consumer conflicts with the citizen's role as taxpayer. Individuals relate to these roles in various ways; even the same individuals relate to them differently over time. Parents who support higher school taxes while their children are in school may oppose such taxes when their children have left school.

Regardless of the criterion of consistency, it should not be assumed that a consistent approach would always lead to contracting out or would never lead to it. The problem is the absence of any rationale or policy to guide specific decisions. In view of our enormous expenditures for public education ($184 billion, or $4,538 per pupil in 1987–88), this policy gap merits thoughtful consideration.

Contracting Out: Some Caveats

In terms of our previous terminology, contracting out is the "buy" decision. In common usage, however, the phrase "contracting out" often gives rise to some erroneous assumptions. One is that employees are not under contract. Another is that employees are always replaced when contracting out occurs. This is not necessarily the case. The legal status of the persons performing the work may change from employee to independent contractor while there is no change in the physical composition of the work force. We must be careful to distinguish what contracting out means from the consequences that may or may not occur in contracting out situations.

It is also essential to avoid rigid assumptions about what can or should be contracted out. Legal considerations aside for the moment, it might be possible to contract out the entire operations of a school district. At the other extreme, employees might provide all services needed by a district. Between these extremes, there is an extremely broad range of possibilities. Specific support services, such as pupil transportation, or specific instructional services, such as remedial instruction, might be contracted out. Or certain functions that cut across subject lines, such as management or achievement testing, might be contracted out. In other words, contracting out is an extremely flexible practice. I would not exclude the possibility of contracting out district operations in toto in special situations, but this possibility is not my major concern or objective.

CONTRACTING OUT BY LEVEL OF GOVERNMENT

Before considering the policy issues involved in contracting out by school boards, let me comment on the practice in other government services. Because contracting out is a common practice at all levels of government and in virtually every type of public service, a detailed summary would be impractical; on the other hand, a few highlights may help to clarify some issues that arise, or would arise, in the educational context.

Contracting Out at the Federal Level

Although the federal government uses all forms of privatization, contracting out is undoubtedly the largest in dollar value. The federal government contracts out an enormous number of services, from the operation of one-person postal stations to complex defense installations and services all over the world. It would require volumes merely to list the services involved, but they include such diverse activities as ship repair, hospitals, maintenance, personnel recruitment, data processing, operation of correctional and detention centers, transportation, and research in scores of fields. Indeed, it has been estimated that expenditures for contracted services amount to approximately one-fourth of all federal expenditures.[1]

At the federal level, privatization was vigorously advocated in the 1983 report of the Privatization Task Force of the President's Private Sector Survey on Cost Control.[2] Widely known as the Grace Commission (after the chairman of the executive committee, J. Peter Grace), the task force recommended various privatization measures that it estimated would result in federal savings and increased revenues of over $28.4 billion over a three-year period. Although the procedures and conclusions of the Grace Commission have been severely criticized, the widespread attention paid to the commission's report has undoubtedly led to increased support for privatization.[3]

For example, the commission recommended legislation to ensure that the federal government does not embark on any new ventures that can be carried out just as well by the private sector. Significantly, legislation introduced in the U.S. Senate in 1987 provided that with certain exceptions, "an executive agency may not start or conduct any commercial activity in the executive agency to provide goods or services for the use of or in behalf of the agency if such goods or services can be procured from any responsive and responsible profitmaking business concern."[4]

The recommendations of the Grace Commission were devoted entirely to federal agencies. Partly for this reason, the President's Commission on Privatization was established in 1987 and submitted its report in March 1988. The report recommended strengthening parental choice in education. It also recommended that ". . . private schools should be able to participate in federal programs providing educational choice to parents." In explaining these recommendations, the commission suggested that the following governance patterns might emerge:

1. Private schools declining government assistance and regulation.
2. Private schools accepting government assistance and related regulation.
3. Public schools with choice programs.
4. Public schools not participating in choice programs as a result of local decision.

The report also emphasized the importance of "civil rights guaranteed by the Constitution" and of ensuring "that any system of assistance to private institutions not violate the constitutional clause prohibiting any establishment of religion."[5] In view of its failure to give equal emphasis to the importance of protecting the free exercise of religion, the report did not support privatization as unequivocally as might have been expected from its auspices. On the other hand, given the fact that the commission included prominent Democrats as well as Republicans, its unanimous support for choice and privatization in education is impressive.

Contracting Out at the State Level

States as well as local governments have been contracting out a wide variety of services in recent years. Perhaps the most highly publicized state efforts have been private operation of state prisons, but many prison operations have been contracted out for a long time: food and health care, education and job training, work release, and juvenile detention are examples. In any event, few if any state services have not been affected by privatization in one way or another.[6]

At this time, the most important state activity relating to contracting out is their legislation on the subject. Local governments, including school boards, can contract for services only within the parameters set by state law. These parameters can apply to the invitation and bidding procedures, avoidance of conflicts of interest, duration of contracts, bonding and performance guarantees, compliance with affirmative action policies or policies relating to minority contractors, flexibility in accepting bids that are not the lowest in dollar amounts, adherence to prevailing wage or minimum wage requirements, and so on. Restrictive legislation on some of these matters can have major negative effects on contracting out.[7]

State collective bargaining laws are also very important considerations. About thirty-five states have such laws covering at least some state or local public employees. In most states that have enacted such legislation, contracting out of work that is or might be performed by employees represented by a union is a mandatory subject of bargaining. In these states school boards ordinarily must give notice of intent to contract out and bargain on it. Inasmuch as the unions are usually opposed to such action, they will often do their utmost to prevent it, especially if some employees would lose their jobs or benefits or if the union would lose members. For our purposes, however, the important point is that state statutes and judicial decisions control whether a school district is required to bargain on contracting out. The situation varies widely, even among states with bargaining statutes.[8]

Contracting Out at the Local Level

At the local level, a wide variety of public services are contracted out. In 1986 the Local Government Center (LGC) of the Reason Foundation noted about 28,500 instances of local and state privatization.[9] Table 2.1 shows the services contracted out by local governments in 1987. The figures in the table are based on questionnaires sent to every city with a population of 5,000 or more and every county in the United States, with a 19 percent response rate. School districts were not included in the survey, so the table substantially understates how much contracting is done by local governments.

TABLE 2.1

SERVICES CONTRACTED OUT

Which services has your government contracted out in the last five years? Which services does it plan to contract out in the next two years?

Cities with 5,000 or more population and all counties in the U.S., 19 percent response.

PERCENT OF RESPONSES TO QUESTION

Service	Last five years	Next two years
Administration (e.g. legal, accounting, payroll, collections)	36	30
Airports	11	10
Buildings or grounds (including trees or plantings)	43	47
Child care or day care	5	5
Data processing	31	22
Elderly or handicapped	12	10
Fleet or vehicle maintenance	21	27
Hospitals, health care, or emergency services	16	13
Housing or shelters	5	6
Parking lots or garages	7	10
Public safety or corrections	7	10
Recreation, parks, convention halls, stadiums, or cultural activities	19	21
Solid-waste collection or disposal	59	56
Streets and roads (including snow removal)	29	30

PERCENT OF RESPONSES TO QUESTION

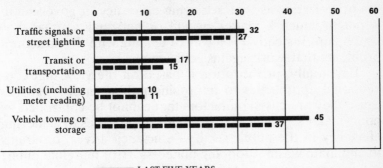

SOURCE: Reprinted, by permission of the publisher, from *Privatization in America* (New York: Touche Ross, 1987), p. 10.

Overall, our nation spends more for education than for any other local public service. It is therefore somewhat surprising that the interest in contracting out has largely ignored education—and education has largely ignored the growing interest in contracting out. Undoubtedly, the governance structure of education helps to explain its isolation from the privatization movement. Mayors, city managers, and city councils are typically responsible for a wide range of municipal services. They are therefore much more likely to be exposed to the theory and practice of contracting out. Their publications, organizations, conferences, and political activity are also likely to touch upon the subject.

In contrast, school boards and administrators tend to be preoccupied with instructional services; as a result, they receive relatively little information regarding contracting-out developments. Not that contracting out per se is unknown; as previously noted, most school districts do contract out some support services. Nevertheless, as discussed, the prevailing attitude in public education is not to contract out unless there is no alternative. Municipal officials tend to be more receptive to the practice. This difference in attitude understandably leads to differences in the attention paid to alternative ways of delivering public services. The rationale for privatization is that achieving efficiency in government is not so much a matter of will or personality or ad hoc leadership. Instead, it is a way of dealing with the structural problems that work against efficiency.

Essentially, privatization is based on the view that conventional approaches to improving public services fail because they are based on factors that cannot be controlled by policymakers. This is why orthodox approaches to achieving efficiency in the public sector—efficiency drives, programs to eliminate waste, dropping unnecessary or marginal public service programs, or spending limits on public officials—are bound to fail. In the long run, they are unsuccessful because they do not affect the incentives or the means to reduce public expenditures.[10] For example, when spending limits are imposed, public officials do not cut "the fat" or "the waste," or the unnecessary or marginal programs. They cut the most visible and popular programs in order to rally public opinion against the limits. Campaign promises to introduce "business practices" in government fail to materialize because businesspeople elected to government office behave like politicians, not businesspeople—just as politicians who go into business behave like businesspeople, not politicians. Similarly, attempts to institute other methods of government efficiency encounter pitfalls of their own that destroy their effectiveness in the not so long run.

It should also be emphasized that the proponents of privatization do not regard contracting out as a panacea for all government ailments. In fact, some privatizers are fearful of contracting out and see no long-range advantage to it. Furthermore, even the most partisan advocates of contracting out agree that it is not the proper method for all public services. At the same time, the most partisan opponents of the practice concede that it is necessary under certain conditions. In effect, this means that the feasibility of contracting out in education is not necessarily similar to its feasibility in other public services. Experience from other fields can be helpful in education if we are also sensitive to any differences that might be relevant to contracting out issues. Needless to say, it is for the reader to decide whether my analysis satisfies this important criterion.

Efficiency and Management Incentives

Management incentives under contracting out differ from the incentives that motivate public managers.[11] The differences are conducive to greater efficiency under contracting out, at least if the contractors are for-profit organizations. For-profit contractors generally try to operate as efficiently as possible. Their incentives to be efficient are their need to avoid losing market share to competing contractors, who could provide the service for less if they are more efficient, and their desire to maximize profits.

These incentives contrast markedly with those of public officials, who typically do not share in the savings generated by increased efficiency. For this reason, they have less incentive than for-profit managers to foster or demand efficiency in the operations they manage. As a matter of fact, public officials may have strong incentives to be inefficient. This happens often when the public employees under their supervision are politically influential. Public management may tolerate inefficiencies that benefit those employees in exchange for the political support the employees provide.

Another dimension of this argument concerns pensions and retirement benefits. Some groups of public employees (police, firefighters, teachers) are very influential politically. Public officials may foster political support from these groups by approving excessive pension benefits for them. As such benefits do not raise taxes immediately, they are often approved without protest or even the knowledge of most taxpayers. By the time the excessive nature of the pension benefits becomes widely known, the public officials who voted for them have left public service, thereby avoiding completely any accountability for their actions.[12]

To appreciate the differences in incentives between public and private managers, let us suppose the public services had been contracted out. In that case, management would have had strong incentives to oppose the excessive pension costs. Acceptance of them would immediately have depressed the value of the company's stock, including any shares owned by management. For this reason, managerial opposition to these costs would be immediate also.

The rationale for contracting out also emphasizes the importance of incentives to innovate. The lure of rewards and the concerns about competition lead private sector managers to develop and introduce more efficient services and products and/or more efficient ways to provide and sell them. Public management, which doesn't have to worry about competition, lacks this incentive to foster innovation.

Economies of Scale

From an economic point of view, the most efficient scale of production depends on the nature of the service. Large-scale production of automobiles is much more economical than small-scale production. At one time books were produced by scribes and there was no alternative to small-scale production. The development of the printing press made it possible to produce books on a larger and more efficient scale.

Clearly, the economies-of-scale rationale is applicable to public education. School districts vary in size. Many districts will not be the optimum size from an efficiency point of view, for providing instruction, pupil transportation, or whatever. Contracting out, however, can help provide solutions to this problem. If a school district is too large for efficient service, it can be subdivided. If the district is too small, a contractor can achieve optimal size by also selling its services to other nearby school districts. As I hope to show, economies of scale are an important consideration in virtually all modes of privatization.

The Job Redundancy Issue

An important reason for the greater efficiency of the private sector is its greater freedom to fire employees who are no longer needed. To fully appreciate the importance of this reason, we must first recognize its role throughout our economy.

About 20 million workers change jobs every year in the United States. About half change voluntarily.[13] The other half do so involuntarily—they are fired, or their business fails. Offhand, this appears to be a source of great instability, and in a sense it is. Nevertheless, involuntary terminations are not a disaster to our economy as a whole or to most of the workers who lose their jobs. Essentially, the reason is that the process that creates jobs is also the process of eliminating them. Airlines have generated an enormous number of jobs, but in the process they wiped out many jobs based on intercity bus transportation. New goods or services do not always eliminate existing jobs, but no economist challenges the view that job creation requires a significant amount of job destruction. Keep in mind, however, that the elimination of jobs is not the same as unemployment. A person whose job becomes redundant may find another position the same day.

For our purposes, it is essential to recognize the differences between job redundancy in the political system and in the economic system. In the latter, the process typically is regulated informally but effectively by the market. If the service you provide can't be sold at a price sufficient to maintain the enterprise, the jobs disappear. If a job is not needed to provide services, competitive factors and the search for profits result in elimination of the job.

What happens to redundant employees in the public sector? What serves the function of markets and competition as an incentive to terminate public employees who are no longer needed? Because redundancy in the public sector is a political issue, its economic aspects are frequently ignored; taxpayers, not public agencies, absorb the costs of keeping unnecessary employees on the public payroll. Although the taxpayer costs in particular cases or services may not be very large, the aggregate costs of keeping redundant employees on the public payroll are probably substantial.

Whether redundancy decisions are made on a political

or an economic basis is an extremely important matter. In the Soviet Union, most economic activity is state operated. Consequently, redundancy is resolved through its political instead of its economic system. The result is an extremely inefficient economic system. In Western Europe and the United States, 3 percent of the work force or less produces more food than the population can eat; in the Soviet Union, 20 percent of the labor force is on the land and shortages of agricultural products are chronic.[14] Indeed, as this is written, the political leaders of the USSR have announced plans to have redundancy decisions made on economic grounds by economic managers, with the government assuming responsibility for retraining and relocating redundant employees.

The reference to the Soviet Union may seem farfetched, but it is not. It is intended to underscore the fact that political control of employment decisions has economic consequences, and the consequences may not be economically desirable regardless of the political system involved. From this perspective, the teacher tenure laws are only one aspect of a much larger problem characterizing public education in the United States. These laws were enacted to protect individual teachers from arbitrary dismissal. Regardless of their intent, the laws unquestionably protect many incompetent and marginal teachers.[15] The critical point, however, is that the protection of such teachers is not the major problem created by the emphasis on teacher security. Most employees who lose their jobs involuntarily in the private sector are not incompetent. Their jobs were eliminated for reasons having nothing to do with their competence. On the other hand, eliminating teacher jobs (as distinguished from firing teachers for incompetence) is very difficult to do, even in the absence of tenure laws. Teacher job security in the United States comes at a price, and the price is an extremely inefficient educational personnel system. Contracting out would be much more likely to avoid this inefficiency, at least insofar as termination would be an economic instead of a political decision.

Of course, even if contracting out instruction avoids an

inefficiency, that would be only one of several factors to be considered in the make-or-buy decision regarding instructional services. To formulate wise policy, our attention should focus on all the consequences of the systems, not the outcomes of particular cases or issues. Regardless of whether teacher tenure is decided in the political or the economic system, we can cite horror stories that imply that the decisions should be made in the other system. We must also recognize that assessing the system consequences requires some assessment of individual cases. What is objectionable, however, is the preoccupation with individual cases without regard to the system costs of the remedy.

Avoidance of Bureaucracy

Providing services through the private sector minimizes the size of government bureaucracies. The more government provides services, the more government employees are needed to provide it, supervise it, keep records of it, monitor it, and so on.

Suppose that instead of food stamps, government-operated stores provided food to those deemed eligible for it. In the latter situation, the government would have to buy, store, insure, display, and transfer and account for the food. This would require a large number of additional government employees. In contrast, the use of food stamps enables the government to avoid being in the grocery business and thus to avoid expanding the number of government employees.

Actually, there are two dimensions of the bureaucracy issue. Contracting out requires fewer governmental employees to provide a service. On the other hand, it may also require an increase in regulatory personnel. Overall, fewer government employees are needed, but the regulatory issues should not be ignored. If contracting out instruction should increase, increased state regulation of contractors may also. Even now the contractors who provide services directly to children (e.g., bus transportation) are sometimes required to meet special requirements, such as having screened their employees for prior drug use or sex offenses. Of course, in addition to any special restrictions, school contractors must also comply with the regulatory measures applicable to business generally in their state.

Capital Outlays

School districts may wish to avoid purchasing expensive capital equipment, such as fleets of buses or vocational equipment or data processing facilities. Contracting out the relevant service may enable districts to avoid such purchases and contribute to increased efficiency in a variety of ways: prompt use of new equipment, predictable costs, and avoidance of sunk costs in outmoded equipment.

In some states, various tax limitations have made it difficult for local governments to raise money for construction. Local governments must often seek bonding authority, which may be turned down by the electorate or lead to bond issues that come on the market at an inopportune time. In many instances, therefore, private companies have built the needed facilities in conjunction with a management contract to operate them for a specified number of years.

To facilitate arrangements of this sort, states have found it necessary to change their statutes on municipal contracts, taxes, bonding, debt, and related issues. Although such changes were a response to noneducational needs, they may be suggestive of things to come in education. In fact, companies seeking to become contractors over a range of municipal services have emerged in recent years. That is, instead of being established to provide a particular public service, such as waste disposal, the companies are not service specific.[16] Given the fact that school districts also may be unable to finance school construction by conventional procedures, the possibility that schools may be built and operated under contract by the private sector is discussed in chapter 3.

Avoidance of Single-Supplier Problems

The arguments for contracting out emphasize the fact that it avoids single-supplier problems. Such problems fall into two categories: the effect on the service providers and the effect on the service users or receivers. Let us consider these problems briefly.

The employees of a monopolistic employer have more power to achieve concessions than employees in a competitive industry. A strike at one automobile plant is not a threat to car buyers as long as other companies can make and sell new cars. Because the strike will not be a threat to the consumer, employees must moderate their demands. If they insist on excessive salaries and continue the strike, they will be jeopardizing their own jobs. This would not be the case if the employees enjoyed monopoly status.

In education, the public is the ultimate employer. It would seem to be in its interest to avoid union/employee pressures based on the monopolistic nature of public services. In this connection, strikes by public school teachers are often extremely effective because no alternative supply of teachers is readily available.

Even if a service is not contracted out, a realistic possibility that it might be helps to keep employee demands at a reasonable level. Just as the threat of strikes often achieves concessions, the threat of contracting out may also achieve concessions by public sector unions. The failure of legislators and school boards to be more concerned about this issue points to a widespread inconsistency in public policy. In the private sector, public policy treats monopoly as undesirable and competition as desirable. Paradoxically, public policy does not adopt the same posture toward monopoly in the public sector, even in those services where competition is quite feasible.

The effects of single-supplier status on service users must also be considered. Public employees are not as likely to be responsive to citizen concerns as service providers who can be replaced from time to time. Significantly, many contracts to provide public services specify how complaints are to be recorded and processed. The data is subsequently used in decisions on contract renewal.

The responsiveness issue seems especially pertinent to education because a large share of school revenues comes from state governments. State aid is usually allocated to local districts on the basis of the number of students. Quality of service or responsiveness is not considered. Therefore, unless school districts establish other potential sources of supply, their reliance on a single noncompetitive source (their own employees) is bound to affect system responsiveness adversely.

Generally speaking, responsiveness issues are not as relevant to contracting out as they are to some other forms of privatization, especially vouchers. One reason is that under contracting out, the school district, not the parents, still chooses the service providers. Responsiveness issues will be discussed again in connection with proposals to strengthen parental rather than school district choice of service providers. Needless to say, however, school boards and school administrators seldom concede any private sector advantage in responsiveness. For one thing, the rhetoric of education emphasizes "meeting the needs and interests of pupils." In smaller communities, school board members frequently receive calls from parents—over rowdyism on a bus, a poor grade, failure to make a team, too much homework, too little homework, whatever. In such communities the school board functions as a group of ombudsmen as much as it does a policymaking body. As school district size increases, however, school boards cannot be as responsive to individual complaints and grievances. Efforts to ameliorate this problem by decentralizing governance or administration have not been very successful, partly because of the difficulties in establishing clear-cut lines of responsibility.

The fact is, however, that school boards are not especially responsive institutions. Even in small districts, the ability of the boards to be responsive is severely limited by state mandates and restrictions, such as collective bargaining, tenure, and textbook laws.[17] Indeed, since small districts often require more flexibility because of their limited resources, they often suffer more than large districts from state mandates.

Like most local governments, school districts seldom conduct market research or anything that could reasonably be equated to it. Responsiveness in school districts, as in public agencies generally, is usually directed at the politically influential or the most aggressive complainers. The fact that many citizens have deep concerns but lack the time or the temperament or the sophistication to articulate them is widely ignored.

Inefficient Public Sector Business Practices

All levels of government come under pressure to spend (obligate) their funds by a certain date or lose them. That is, funds are appropriated for expenses, usually on a fiscal year basis. If a government agency approaches the end of the fiscal year with excess funds, there is strong and usually irresistible pressure to spend the money so that it does not revert to the general fund or to another department that may not have been so efficient.

In the case of school districts, funds unspent by departments are usually available to other departments. If the district as a whole showed a surplus, the excess funds might be subtracted from its allocation for the following year. Regardless of how or to whom the excess funds are distributed, this common policy constitutes a strong deterrent against efficiency. School districts are just as likely to be subject to the policy, and to make sure that all the money is spent, as any other unit of government. Indeed many school boards would be embarrassed, not gratified, by a surplus. They would be in a weak position to deny employees wage increases or to object on cost grounds to various demands of their constituents.

The relevance of the issue to contracting out seems indisputable. The contractor does not lose the unspent funds; on the contrary, such funds can simply be held in reserve for contingencies or improvements in following years. That is, even if the excess funds are not distributed as profits, they can be used more efficiently in providing services because they do not have to be spent by an arbitrary date ("arbitrary" from the standpoint of efficient service). This advantage of contracting out is probably more significant than is generally realized.

Government restrictions also impair efficiency in purchasing services. Purchase may be limited to local firms. For legal reasons, it may be necessary to limit flexibility in the terms of a contract, so that it is impossible for bidders to make the best overall offer to provide services. Payment procedures may be so slow that firms fear cash-flow problems and are reluctant to bid.

Public Awareness of Service Costs

When services are provided by government, citizens have relatively little awareness of costs. Inasmuch as the revenues to pay for public services do not come primarily or at all from service users, the relationships between costs and services are not widely understood. The more we separate those who pay from those who receive services, the more we foster unrealistic perceptions about both services and costs.

Under pressure from public employees and/or service users, public officials find it politically advantageous to increase both the services and the wages of the public employees who provide them. Because the required tax increases are only a small part of the entire public budget, public officials tend to vote for them for the political rewards they bring. Meanwhile, citizens who receive the services tend to underestimate their costs, often by a wide margin.

If services are privatized, however, the costs are more likely to be visible within the public budget. At first glance this seems implausible. Why expect citizens to know more about the cost of a service when provided privately, with no public access to the contractor's financial records, than when it is provided by a public agency whose financial records are open to public inspection?

Perhaps an analogy will help to answer this question. When you buy a car, you don't know the manufacturer's internal breakdown of costs. That is, you are not informed about how much of the sales price went into final assembly, transportation, research and development, insurance, advertising, and so on. You don't get this information partly because there's no way you could use it; you aren't likely to offer $250 less because the manufacturer's advertising costs were excessive.

Similarly, when you purchase a service, you ordinarily rely on the price of the service, not the service provider's internal breakdown of costs. Your protection is your ability to shift to another service provider. At the present time, however, we don't know the real costs of public education, nor are we protected from excessive costs by competition among service providers. As I will show in the next chapter, school district budgets simply do not provide accurate estimates of the costs of education.

If a service is privatized, however, all the costs must be identified. Contractors need to know all the costs in order to avoid a contract that neglects some costs that they must pay. Public officials need to know the costs in order to avoid contracts based on inflated cost estimates. Thus the dynamics of contracting out lead to more accurate estimates of the service costs. The same process applies to outcomes. Contracting out forces public agencies to be clear about outcomes. Otherwise it is impossible to know how adequate a service is.

THE CASE AGAINST BUYING PUBLIC SERVICES: AN OVERVIEW

Thus far I have outlined several arguments supporting decisions to buy educational services. These arguments have been general in nature; they do not take into account specific circumstances that might justify a different decision. For example, if there are no contractors, the theoretical advantages of contracting out cannot be achieved in practice. Just as it is important to consider the general arguments for contracting out, it is likewise essential to consider the general arguments against the policy.[18] After doing so I shall review briefly the evidence on contracting out public services other than education. The next chapter will come to grips with the issues that are especially pertinent to make-or-buy decisions in education.

A major criticism of contracting out is that it does not eliminate the use of political influence to maintain inefficient services. Contractors often contribute to political candidates with the expectation of being awarded a contract to provide services. Their activities can be just as harmful as public employee support for candidates who support employee interests. Undeniably, there is some validity to the criticism. Lobbying by contractors for contracts may be as serious a problem as lobbying by public employees and their unions for concessions that serve their interests.

Indisputably, the criticism has an empirical basis and is not to be taken lightly. In my opinion, no approach can totally prevent political leaders from rewarding their supporters in ways that are not in the public interest. Whether the underlying problem is more manageable under contracting out depends in large part on whether there is sole-source or competitive bidding. In the latter case it is much more difficult for any one contractor to gain an unfair advantage by means of political influence; the other contractors will be alert to the problem. They will have a larger stake in taking remedial action than citizens have in monitoring politically motivated concessions to public employees or public sector unions.

To what extent is there meaningful competition to deliver public services? The critics of contracting out emphasize how often only a small number of qualified bids are received on most contracts. Obviously, the likelihood of collusion instead of competition among bidders increases as their number decreases. Even when there is more than one bidder, the incumbent contractor is often able to manipulate the bidding and cultivate the key contracting officials to ensure that others are frozen out. In some cases cost-plus contracts have been negotiated; such contracts are often conducive to inefficiency because the contractor receives a percentage of the costs.

These criticisms do not undermine the rationale for contracting out. Instead, they point to some conditions that must be satisfied for it to be fully effective. If there is only one bidder, there is less competition than if several contractors bid.

Unquestionably, incumbent contractors tend to have advantages. It is also true that contractors sometimes submit extremely low bids to win initial contracts, anticipating that they will be able to recoup any losses in subsequent renewals. I have seen health insurers submit such bids, anticipating that they will be firmly entrenched at the next round of bidding.

It seems to me that whether public agencies are disadvantaged by this practice depends on the sophistication of public officials. Knowledge about a public agency is worth something. If a contractor is willing to pay for it by submitting a low bid, I see nothing wrong in the practice; it may be a recognition of the efficacy of competition, not a denial of it. We should be cognizant of the conditions under which contracting out is most effective, but this does not mean that it is necessarily undesirable if there is only one bidder. At least, if the only alternative is having the work performed by district employees, one outside bidder is preferable to none.

A related objection is that contracting out can lead to undesirable government dependency on contractors. This argument is hardly persuasive since it assumes that government dependence on a sole-source supplier is acceptable if the sole source is the government employees themselves.

The contention that government may become too dependent on contractors is often related to the possibility that a contractor may go bankrupt, thereby forcing government to provide services on short notice without adequate personnel or facilities. Although contractor bankruptcies do occur, any serious problems usually can be avoided by demanding appropriate information and financial guarantees from contractors.

A less frequent objection is that contracting out is contrary to the spirit of veterans' preference legislation. By removing positions from the public payroll, contracting out allegedly removes opportunities for veterans to be appointed to public positions. This objection, however, is unpersuasive for at least three reasons. First, veterans' preference laws have not, or should not, require inefficient modes of delivering public services in order to maximize the number of veterans on the public payroll. Second, contracting out does not necessarily require the dismissal of veterans (or even nonveterans) on the public payroll. Current employees frequently are allowed to remain in their positions and are replaced, if at all, only through attrition. Quite often employees can be transferred, reassigned, or induced to retire by special benefits. Finally, we cannot assume that more veterans are disadvantaged by contracting out than by government provision of service.

Corruption Issues in a Systems Perspective

Another line of criticism emphasizes the corruption, influence peddling, and kickbacks sometimes associated with contracting out. These practices weaken the argument that contracting out will result in greater efficiency.

Unquestionably, corruption can be a serious problem. One difficulty with the objection, however, is the lack of systematic data on it. Another is that it is often very difficult to draw the line between corruption and legal activities that also constitute policymaking for special interests. Suppose, for example, that although contracting out would be beneficial in a given situation, public officials do not utilize it because the unions involved have been instrumental in their election. Obviously, the public officials are not going to say this explicitly, but it would be naive to suppose that it does not happen.

Again, we must consider the issue from a systems, not an anecdotal, perspective. Whether public services are bought or made, public officials may subvert the process for their private gain. Under certain conditions, contracting out is more likely than direct provision to avoid this outcome; under other conditions, it is less likely to do so.

For example, school districts typically require competitive bidding to provide their milk requirements. The contracts are largely similar. It is quite clear what products and services dairies must provide and how much they are paid for these things.

The losing bidders are in a strong position to monitor the alleged reasons why their bids were unsuccessful. For this reason, corruption and kickbacks to get the contract are not so great a danger.

When it comes to instructional services, however, the analogy is not so persuasive. It is relatively easy to specify the amount and quality of dairy products; this does not hold true for instructional services. On the contrary, it is much easier to manipulate the description of the instructional services or the service providers in order to favor a particular bidder. Yet this hardly resolves the issue of which system or service is more vulnerable to manipulation for private gain. The reason is implicit in our previous discussion of public awareness of service costs. The dynamics of contracting out are conducive to greater specificity in describing the services being purchased. If only one district buys foreign-language instruction, it would be difficult to demonstrate favoritism in awarding the contract. If twenty-five districts in a metropolitan area do so, it becomes much easier to compare services and costs as a check against corruption.

To summarize, the subordination of the public interest to private interests must be viewed as a systems problem. In my twenty years of experience as a labor negotiator for school boards, the legal ways of doing this (for example, concessions to public employees in exchange for their political support) were vastly more harmful than the illegal ways, such as bribes and kickbacks. Of course, school district purchasing agents may have a different story to tell. Regardless, both ways of subverting the public interest raise legitimate questions to which we lack good answers.

Contracting Out Noneducational Services: A Summary of the Evidence

The foregoing objections to contracting out are by no means exhaustive. At this point, however, it may be more helpful to review the evidence on contracting out in fields outside of education. The next chapter will then take up several additional issues for and against contracting out instruction.

One cautionary note has been mentioned but bears repeating. We should not apply a double standard in evaluating the evidence on contracting out. Although anecdotal evidence may be suggestive, our underlying concern must be with systematic data. Furthermore, it should be recognized that whatever system is used to deliver services, there will be instances of inefficiency and poor quality.

The most difficult problem in assessing the evidence on contracting out is simply the sheer number of studies on the subject. In the United States alone there have been hundreds of such studies; worldwide there may have been thousands. Contracting out of virtually every public service, and at every level of government, has been studied somewhere. It was not feasible to analyze each study, desirable as that might have been. Instead, my comments will be based on publications that review a substantial number of studies and that are deemed representative of the research on the subject. Although my approach is not ideal, it reflects widespread albeit not unanimous agreement on the results of contracting out.[19]

In general, the research supports the idea that contracting out is often more efficient, or provides higher quality service, or both. Let me cite just one of several studies that supports this conclusion.

A study of 121 cities in the Los Angeles metropolitan area covered eight services: payroll preparation, road paving, residential refuse collection, tree maintenance, turf maintenance, traffic signal maintenance, janitorial services, and street cleaning. Comparisons were made only if at least ten cities provided the services directly and ten contracted out for them. The study found that with the exception of payroll maintenance, costs for the contract services averaged 54 percent less than direct provision by the cities. Service costs under contracting out were less because contractors (1) used less labor; (2) experienced less absenteeism;

(3) used more part-time labor; (4) employed younger workers; (5) fired more incompetent employees; (6) used more capital equipment; and (7) held managers responsible for equipment as well as personnel.[20]

Several summaries of the research in other fields reach similar conclusions. The research that does not is predominantly in the area of welfare and human services—job training, counseling, employment, and other services intended to change the behavior of service recipients in some way.[21]

One interesting summary concludes that the change from public to private service delivery results in greater efficiency because the change is usually made when the existing mode of delivery is noticeably inefficient. In fact, the study contends that changes from private to public sector delivery also show savings because the prior mode of delivery was highly inefficient. In other words, either mode of service delivery can become extremely inefficient; when this happens, a change is likely to show savings, regardless of whether the change is from public to private or from private to public delivery.[22]

This study may well explain some of the efficiency gains attributed to contracting out. It does not seem plausible, however, that it accounts fully for the savings in so many services and jurisdictions. Furthermore, the possibility of contracting out as an option may have forestalled a great deal of inefficiency in service delivery by public agencies; minimally, the point underscores the value of contracting out as an option.

Marc Bendick, Jr., an economist who favors increased federal spending on various social services, probably reflects a common if not the prevailing view. Referring to the results of a 1973 survey on contracting out, he comments:

> Where controlled evaluations have been undertaken, verifiable cost savings were observed, if not universally, more often than not . . .
>
> In extrapolating from these generally favorable findings to social welfare services, it is important to note the

nature of the services encompassed within this pool of experience. Contracted-out municipal functions are predominantly straightforward, immediate, measurable, monitorable, and technical in nature—such as refuse collection, data processing, and street light maintenance. As one moves from such examples to (relatively rare) examples of contracting out for more complex, undefinable, long-range and "subjective" services such as are characteristic of the social welfare field, the record of successful experience rapidly thins.[23]

Bendick's conclusions reflect the predominant view among the comprehensive surveys of contracting out. Inasmuch as the argument for contracting out is based on the advantages of market over political systems, we could expect research to support it widely, if the arguments are valid ones. Granted, some research supporting contracting out is sponsored by organizations already committed to it; this fact, however, does not justify automatic rejection of their arguments and data. For that matter, it is more significant that the only groups consistently opposed to contracting out are public employees and public employee unions. If their objections are valid, it is surprising how little research on the subject supports them. Such research does not show that contracting out is always beneficial; on the other hand, it frequently supports the practice even when the issues raised by unions are taken into account.[24]

Actually, the support for contracting out would be incomprehensible if the union objections to it were valid. For instance, American Federation of State, County, and Municipal Employees (AFSCME) publications emphasize that contracting out is less efficient than service by public employees. If this argument is valid, the taxpayer organizations and supporters of economy in government who support contracting out are badly mistaken. To this observer, it seems unlikely that the unions are more interested in cutting the government costs than their critics—especially when approximately 70 percent of the costs of local and state government are for employee wages and benefits.

Developments in the private sector also weaken union arguments against contracting out. Union efforts to restrict contracting out are often a major issue in the private sector. They are currently a major issue in the automotive industry, as automobile manufacturers seek to purchase parts from outside (often foreign) suppliers, instead of manufacturing the parts themselves. It would be absurd for the unions to argue that General Motors, Ford, and Chrysler really do not understand that contracting out is more expensive, and the unions involved do not make any such claim. On the contrary, they contend that for one reason or another, it is unfair for the companies to rely on the least expensive suppliers. Incidentally, this line of argument illustrates how semantics often dominates the discussion of these matters. In the automotive industry, the union argument is that the companies should not allow cheap foreign labor to undermine the wages and benefits of U.S. workers. Similarly, public sector unions allege that contracting out undermines the wages and benefits of public employees. In the public sector, however, the argument overlooks the fact that public employees generally receive higher pay and benefits than their private sector counterparts. This is indisputable, especially in education; total compensation for public school teachers averages 25 percent more than compensation for teachers in private schools.[25]

The opposition to contracting out by public sector unions also ignores the trend toward it in the private sector. For several years the proportion of the U.S. labor force engaged in the production of services has been increasing. Contrary to popular opinion, however, the change is not due to a larger proportion of the labor force being employed in retail or personal service enterprise. Instead, it is primarily due to the increasing proportion of workers who provide producer services; as one recent study notes, the growth in services is primarily a "transformation at the level of intermediate outputs." This transformation has resulted in the growth of specialized producer services, "both in-house (in the central administrative facilities of the corporation) and out-of-house (among producer service firms)."[26] Thus the service revolution is not simply a shift in the kind of work being performed; it also reflects a private sector trend toward contracting out instead of internal production of goods and services. In the long run, the economics of contracting out may overcome the opposition to it in both sectors.

3

Efficiency Issues
in Educational
Perspective

This chapter is devoted to various efficiency issues in contracting out, especially of instructional services. A preliminary statement of my assumptions and rationale may be helpful.

Generally speaking, approaches to privatization fall into two categories. One category emphasizes the ideological dimensions of privatization. Supporters of this view see privatization as much more than a management option; it is a way of diminishing the role of government, of enhancing the role of the private sector, and of avoiding inefficient government activities that would be difficult if not impossible to eliminate. Supporters in this category regard efficiency as important, but they tend to view it as intimately related to the functions of government, the role of our economic system, and the relationships between political and economic freedoms.

By the same token, privatization also has its ideological detractors. Some critics of privatization also do not separate the broader philosophical issues from the immediately practical ones. Whereas the supporters view privatization within a favorable philosophical framework, the ideological opponents view it within an unfavorable one. Although both groups agree that privatization proposals should be evaluated on a case-by-case basis, they seldom agree on the merits of specific proposals.

The other major approach to privatization analyzes it primarily as a management tool. In this context, efficiency issues are resolved without much regard to their philosophical implications. I shall label this group "the practical decision makers." To this group, contracting out does not raise any broad philosophical issues. If contracting out is a more efficient way to get the job done, so be it. To these people a decision on whether to contract out instruction is similar to one on whether to drive the car or take the bus to a football game. After all important practical considerations are taken into account, what is the best way to get there? There is no need to relate the decision to the role of public transportation. Similarly, practical decision makers might see no need to relate make-or-buy decisions in education to ideological issues.

In this chapter I shall discuss contracting out instruction primarily from the standpoint of practical decision makers. In doing so I do not imply that the ideological issues are unimportant, or that I have no views about them, or that the discussion can always avoid the broader issues. Instead, it is due to the fact that the major audience for this book are practical decision makers, not of ideological supporters or opponents of privatization per se. Furthermore, although efficiency issues are not the whole story, they are a large part of it. If we could reach a workable consensus on the efficiency issues, the ideological ones would be much easier to resolve.

Efficiency Issues and State Regulation

Arguably, at least, the efficiency argument for contracting out is much stronger in education than it is in most state and local public services. This is because state regulation of education is usually more detailed, more restrictive, and more conducive to inefficiency than it is in other public services. People not professionally involved in public education find it difficult to grasp the sheer volume of regulation or the myriad ways that it results in inefficiencies. Let me first outline the broad categories of statutory regulation before citing some specifics.

Regulation of Governance and Financial Procedures—State statutes normally govern eligibility for: school board election; board meetings; financial and business procedures; budget categories and budget schedules; board authority to contract; school district bond and insurance requirements; bidding procedures; power to appoint administrators, teachers, and support staff; and health and safety standards and procedures.

Regulation of the Educational Program and of Students—State statutes often prescribe: the minimum and maximum age for compulsory education; subjects to be taught; the student work day and work year; the choice of instructional materials; graduation requirements; maximum class size; vaccination and medical examinations; how to deal with disabled, migrant, and/or delinquent children; and so on.

Regulation of Teachers and Administrators—Statutes control: eligibility to teach or administer schools (often by grade level or subject); discipline and dismissal procedures; layoffs and recall; mandatory leave benefits; retirement eligibility, procedures, and benefits; duty-free lunch periods; seniority; and teacher evaluation.

Regulation of Support Staff—In general, state regulation of support staff (secretaries, bus drivers, custodians, cafeteria workers, groundskeepers, data processing technicians, and other support staff) differs in degree but not in kind from state regulation of teachers and administrators.

It is hardly possible to overemphasize one basic point about state regulation. Very little state regulation restricts what teachers teach, or how they teach. The vast majority of state statutes affecting teachers provide teacher benefits and were enacted at the behest of state teacher unions. They are restrictive, but the restrictions overwhelmingly apply to school management, not to teachers. When teachers are restricted in the classroom, it is usually an indirect result of a direct restriction on management. For example, if a state law restricts a district's choice of textbooks to those approved by a state textbook commission, the restriction on teacher choice derives from the restriction on management choice.

Although the amount and nature of state regulation varies enormously from state to state, some regulatory elements force districts to be inefficient everywhere. Let me cite just a few examples from California and New York simply to illustrate the tremendous variety of these inefficiencies.

First in California:

1. According to the California Education Code, "It is the intent and purpose of the Legislature to encourage, by every means possible, the reduction of class sizes and the ratio of pupils to teachers in all grade levels in the public schools and to urge every effort to this end be undertaken by the local school administrative authorities."[1] Although average class size in California's schools overall is among the highest in the United States, this statement of policy does not take into account the possibility that class size is often extremely low. Regardless, the next section of the Education Code penalizes school districts if their class size exceeds thirty in grades 1 to 3 and 4 to 8, or thirty-one or thirty-three in kindergarten.

There is no credible evidence that these limits have any relationship to educational achievement or productivity. Let us suppose, however, that adding another first-grade pupil to a class of thirty has a discernible negative effect on class members' educational achievement. To decide whether to split the class or to add another pupil to the existing one, we should compare the costs as well as the educational outcomes. The costs of splitting the class would perhaps be $40,000 (average salary plus benefits for an additional teacher). The underlying issue, however, is not the impact of the additional student on the class as a whole. It is whether spending $40,000 for an additional teacher is the optimum educational use of the money. It is not possible for a legislature, or anyone else, to make this judgment sensibly without understanding the district's other needs and resources. In the vast majority of cases, adding a pupil to a class of thirty would not result in any perceptible educational loss; failure to do so, however, would cost the district a substantial amount of money, which could be used more productively on other needs. Nevertheless, Sections 41375 and 41376 penalize a California school district for making the most cost-effective use of its resources.

Let me cite just one additional dimension to the inefficiencies resulting from the class size statute. Under California law, class size is a mandatory subject of bargaining between teacher unions and school districts. The bargaining law authorizes additions but not reductions in the statutory benefits of teachers. Thus in conjunction with the state's bargaining law, the class size statute forces school districts to begin bargaining on class size at a level that is already advantageous to teachers.

2. School districts cannot assign teachers to extra duty, even with the extra pay agreed upon by the union, against the teacher's wishes. I have seen cases in which teachers who had been employed partly because of their ability to handle certain extracurricular duties declined to perform such duties after receiving tenure. When the districts were unable to recruit individuals not on the regular staff to take the assignment, they were forced to overpay existing staff or drop the extracurricular activity.[2]

3. Any benefits provided full-time support personnel must be prorated for part-time employees. Thus if a school district increases vacation benefits for full-time cafeteria workers or bus drivers who work a full year, it must as a matter of law increase vacation benefits for such employees

who work four or even only two hours a day for only 180 days a year.[3] Not surprisingly, the legislation was enacted at the behest of the California School Employees Association (CSEA), the state union representing most noninstructional employees in the state. CSEA sought the legislation primarily to avoid internal conflicts between part-time employees seeking health benefits (a significant proportion of its membership) and regular full-time employees. The legislation was also intended to discourage part-time employment.

4. A specified minimum percent of school districts' operating budgets must be spent for teacher salaries. The minimum is 50 percent for elementary districts, 55 percent for districts including both elementary and secondary schools, and 60 percent for high school districts.[4] The effect of this legislation is to discourage school districts from introducing any changes that would reduce the proportion of their budgets devoted to teacher salaries. Districts that are able to operate satisfactorily while paying teachers less than their state-mandated share of the district budget are nevertheless forced to increase teacher salaries. In some cases the increases result in higher salaries than the teacher unions have already accepted. A private company would never try to become more efficient by requiring itself to be labor intensive.

5. If a district wants to suspend a teacher for as little as one day, the procedure that must be followed is the same as for firing a tenured teacher. The district and the employee each appoint someone to a three-member commission to conduct a hearing on the suspension. (The third member is a state-appointed hearing examiner.) If the school district loses, it must pay any compensation lost by the employee and the employee's hearing expenses as well.[5] Not surprisingly, only about one teacher in 10,000 is suspended annually in California.

California is supposed to be a leader in the school reform movement. Nevertheless, the California Education Code includes scores of such indefensible statutes, virtually all of which have been ignored by reform leaders in that state. In fact, some were enacted at their behest or at least without their overt disapproval. If California regulated garbage removal as it does education, its laws would prescribe what days garbage would be picked up, between what hours, the qualifications for the supervisors of garbage disposal, the standards and procedures for disciplining or firing sanitation workers, the insurance policies governing equipment and personnel, policies governing layoff and recall of sanitation workers, the size and safety requirements for sanitation department trucks, and so on. All these regulations would be imposed on a statewide basis, without regard to a community's economy or the citizens' wishes. Under such circumstances, it would be astonishing if garbage removal by public employees was even close to efficient.

To illustrate how pervasive state-mandated inefficiencies are, let me cite a recent development from New York. In 1987 the state enacted legislation that required school districts to provide training for teachers who did not meet regular certification requirements.[6] Under the statute, New York City could continue to employ teachers on emergency certificates, but such teachers could be required to teach only 80 percent of a normal teaching load. During the remaining time the school districts were required to provide the teachers with additional training to aid them in achieving regular certification. The school districts, therefore, lost 20 percent of the teachers' instructional time and also had to pay for their additional training. New York City school officials estimated the district's additional costs in 1987–88 would be about $25 million.[7]

Whatever the costs, they will not have contributed much if anything to better teaching in the city's schools. The reasons some teachers are not certified have nothing to do with their teaching effectiveness. Where additional training might be helpful, there is no assurance that qualified persons are available to provide it. The district recruited retired teachers to provide the training, but their qualifications do not necessarily meet the needs of the teachers they supervise. Once teachers acquire a regular certificate, they may seek teaching positions outside the state. And so on.

These specifics from California and New York illustrate how public education operates under a crushing burden of mandated inefficiency, that those who preach "educational reform" are often the ones most responsible for its absence, and that there is not the slightest let-up of legislation mandating inefficiencies.[8] As numerous as they are, however, the inefficiencies mandated by statute are probably outnumbered by those in collective bargaining contracts. Approximately 75 percent of the nation's public school teachers work under such contracts. In varying degrees, these contracts impose a wide range of inefficiencies on school districts; they restrict district flexibility in employment, assignment, transfers, scheduling, work day, work year, class size, and in a host of other matters. Although some school board leaders have become more outspoken against these restrictions, there is no reason to believe they can eliminate them, absent some form of privatization.

Realistically, there is no movement within public education to change its governance structure or operating procedures.[9] Although they are desperately needed, such changes are not even being discussed in our political forums. Even a rollback in teacher collective bargaining, which will happen as a result of judicial decisions if it happens at all, would not overcome most governance and regulatory obstacles to better education. Ideally, school board members are supposed to be public-spirited citizens who volunteer for public service in order to help children. In the real world, however, school board candidates have the same need for support as other candidates for public office. At the same time, teacher and support personnel unions have a larger stake in who is elected to the board than does any other group. Parents may be interested, but it is practically impossible or prohibitively expensive for most to try to change school district policies or practices. Furthermore, parental interest in school affairs wanes when their children graduate, whereas employee interests in school board affairs are permanent. In addition, as school board elections are often conducted separately from general elections, the political influence of teacher unions in those elections is greatly enhanced.

This analysis also applies to those school boards that are appointed instead of elected; usually the appointments are made by a mayor, who must be sensitive to the wishes of the public sector unions. Nor is the underlying argument weakened by the fact that, nationally, over half of school district revenues come from state governments. Again, the dynamics are the same—elected officials, primarily governors and members of state legislatures, frequently make legislative concessions in exchange for political support from unions.

The foregoing considerations underscore the potential importance of contracting out. Because the employees of independent contractors are not public employees, they are not subject to the statutes and collective bargaining contracts that cripple school management. Thus private contractors may be able to avoid both the statutory and collective bargaining sources of inefficiency in school district operations. Reforms that propose to "empower teachers" or "replace hierarchical structures with peer group control" or accord "professional autonomy" to teachers are ludicrous intellectually but devastating in their political and policy consequences. Such proposals are tantamount to prescribing the HIV virus to cure AIDS. The only question is how long the patient can survive these misguided prescriptions.

COSTS AND BENEFITS IN EDUCATIONAL CONTRACTING OUT

Do the preceding considerations establish a case for contracting out instruction? Objectively, the answer is "Not thus far." The analysis has shown that conceptually, contracting out instruction might achieve increased efficiency and/or higher quality education. In order to decide whether to make or buy education, however, school boards must be able to compare the costs and outcomes under each decision. These may not be the only relevant considerations, but they are obviously important. If school boards know the costs but not the outcomes, they would not be able to make an informed decision. Similarly, if they know the outcomes but not the costs, they would lack an adequate basis for their decisions. Knowledge of both costs and outcomes is essential because school districts should not necessarily choose the option that results in greater learning. If this option results in a very small increase in learning but requires huge additional resources, it will usually be less desirable. At some point, educational improvement is not worth the cost of achieving it.

Unfortunately, it is extremely difficult, perhaps even impossible in some cases, to ascertain either the costs or the outcomes of public education. For one thing, as previously noted, the costs are virtually always understated, often by substantial amounts. These understatements vary from district to district and state to state. In this analysis I can only illustrate some patterns of cost understatement; the actual amounts involved have to be ascertained from state and local data.

Local Costs Not Shown on School District Budgets

Some of the local costs of public education do not even appear on school district budgets. Let me first cite a simple example from my own experience. Most school districts are contiguous with local governments, such as cities, municipalities, or counties. It often happens that the local government tries to achieve a common labor relations position for all public employees within its borders; for example, it may not wish to give teachers an 8 percent salary increase if other public employees are receiving only a 5 percent increase.

In some areas, especially when the school district receives some funds from the local government, the latter provides negotiating services for the school district. Such services may include the time of a chief negotiator and members of the negotiating team, use of data processing facilities and personnel, and reproduction and communications costs incidental to bargaining. In large-city school districts, mayors and mayoral staffs may devote considerable time to school district bargaining. Such time is not shown as a cost of public education. Similarly, several municipal overhead costs are often not shown on school district budgets. These costs may be for legal, accounting, financial, or personnel services, to cite just a few. In some cases, such as the costs of school board elections, the understatements of the costs of public education are not relevant to cost comparisons of contracting out and direct provision of service. In other situations, such as school board utilization of the city's legal staff, the understatements are or may be relevant.

Costs Not Shown on Any Local Budget

In some states the state governments pay the contributions for teacher pensions. As a result, these contributions do not show up in the budget of either the school district or of any local unit of government.[10] Similarly, textbooks are sometimes provided by states at no charge or at a reduced charge to local school districts. These costs, especially the former, can involve substantial amounts relevant to cost comparisons.

In addition, the costs of state regulation of education (as distinct from the costs of compliance) are not included in estimates of the per-pupil costs of education. Unlike pension and textbook costs, the costs of state regulation would not normally affect comparisons between public and private provision. This is certainly true when states regulate educational activities regardless of whether they take place in public or in private schools. On the other hand, if one's purpose is to ascertain how much public education *in toto* costs the taxpayers, the costs of state educational agencies, and even of noneducational agencies that devote some of their resources to education, should be included.

Costs Not Shown on Any Budget— Local, State, or Federal

The market value of school district land and property is ordinarily not included in estimates of education costs. Economically, this makes no sense; nobody operates a business without factoring in the costs of land and buildings.

It is important to recognize that "cost" does not necessarily refer to initial cost. A school district may have acquired a school site fifty years ago for $1,000. Today the site may be worth $1 million on the open market. Conventional school finance would show the cost as zero, since the land is already paid for. Realistically, the cost to the community is the "opportunity cost"—the $1 million the district could get by selling the site at fair market value. We should not assume there are no costs merely because there are no cash outlays.

The largest opportunity cost systematically ignored in school finance is student time. This omission does not affect comparisons of public to private provision of educational services because the opportunity costs would be the same, regardless of whether a student was educated in a public school, a private school, or by a for-profit contractor. Opportunity costs are, however, relevant to several important educational policy issues, such as the maximum age for compulsory education or the desirability of subsidies to students in higher education. Needless to say, opportunity costs are closely associated with student age; a college student would ordinarily earn more than a first-grader if neither were in school.

Depreciation, of buildings or capital equipment or both, is routinely omitted from district budgets. The omission not only distorts the cost picture but is conducive to inefficiency. Failure to take depreciation into account often distorts comparisons of private to public school costs, even when the item is omitted from the financial statements in both sectors.

In economic terms, depreciation is the cost of using capital facilities or equipment. The depreciation costs of public education include the decline in the value of buildings and capital equipment. If the district builds a school, the costs should be prorated over the life of the school. Likewise, if it buys trucks or typewriters or computers, the costs should be spread out over the useful life of the equipment.

When this is not done, the costs are overstated when purchases are made and understated in other years. Quite often the outcome is excessive costs for repairs, with only lip service paid to preventive maintenance. Budgets may allow for repairs but not for replacement, so repairs are made until the building or equipment is beyond repair.

Recent developments in New York illustrate how and why the neglect of depreciation results in significant underestimates of the costs of public education. During 1986–87, the *New York Times* published several articles on the deplorable physical condition of New York City schools. These articles portrayed an appalling picture of deterioration and neglect. The articles asserted or quoted school officials as stating:

1. Many school buildings had not been painted in twenty years.
2. Holes in some classroom floors were large enough for students to fall through.
3. A school visited by Mayor Ed Koch had broken window shades, peeling paint and plaster, and no soap or paper for teachers or students.
4. Almost ten years were required to build a school; only one new school had been built from 1975 to 1987.
5. The schedule for painting schools was once every thirty-three years.
6. Most requests for repairs (for example, for broken windows) went unheeded for years unless the repairs were deemed an emergency.

7. The only way to have maintenance work done was to have a powerful political leader visit the school.[11]

How could such a situation arise? One reason is the time perspective of political leaders. Inevitably, their major concerns are focused on the next election or on their political careers generally. This generates enormous pressure to sacrifice long-range interests for immediate political advantage. In practical terms, it results in a political tendency to overspend on employee benefits and underspend on capital equipment and maintenance for public facilities. The benefits have an active, politically potent constituency; maintenance has only a diffuse public constituency that is unlikely to be effective in the budgetary process.

The politics of the New York City situation illustrate this point with unmistakable clarity. In 1982 Mario Cuomo barely defeated Edward Koch for the Democratic nomination for governor of New York. By all accounts, the all-out support of Albert Shanker, president of both the United Federation of Teachers in New York City and the American Federation of Teachers, was a critical factor in Cuomo's victory in the primary and in the general election for governor.[12]

In July 1986 New York enacted special state aid legislation for the New York City schools. The legislation provided $31 million in state aid. It specified, however—over the objections of Mayor Koch and the New York City Board of Education—that the aid could be used *only* for teacher salaries.[13] In view of the fact that the deterioration of the city's public school facilities had been widely known for years, it would be difficult to characterize the restriction as anything but a political payoff.

Although the physical deterioration of New York City schools may be exceptional, underfunding of maintenance needs is not. In 1987 the backlog of school repairs nationally was estimated to be $25 billion and was expected to increase rapidly as many schools built in the 1950s and 1960s require major repairs. The cost of meeting these needs is expected to be one of the most urgent problems facing state legislatures in the immediate future.[14] Whatever the outcome, it is not likely to include realistic treatment of the costs of educational facilities.

Unfunded Pension Costs

Another major cost that may not be shown on any budget is unfunded pension obligations. Typically, teachers pay a specified percentage of their salaries to a state teachers retirement system. The local school district and/or the state also contributes to the retirement system according to formulas set by the legislatures. Teacher and public agency contributions are invested, and the total revenues are available for payments to retirees.

Essentially, there are two different approaches to funding. One is "full funding"; under this approach, the funds contributed every year plus the anticipated earnings from investing prior contributions cover the costs of the anticipated obligations of the retirement system. The other approach is "pay as you go"; here the assets of the retirement system meet current obligations (if they can) and the states make up any shortfall. Some states have also added cost-of-living supplements from time to time to be paid from state, not local, funds.

Most teacher retirement plans are "pay as you go," and they often have substantial unfunded pension liabilities, regardless of whether the nonteacher contributions come from the local school district, the state government, or some combination of the two. Over the years the age of retirement and required number of years of service have been reduced. Benefits have been extended to spouses and children; disability and service-related handicaps have been liberalized. Meanwhile, beneficiaries' longevity has increased, so benefits must be paid over a longer period of time than was initially anticipated.

The extent of unfunded teacher retirement obligations varies widely from state to state. In some states it is not a problem, or at least not a serious one. In many others, however, it clearly is or will be. In some states the state teacher retirement system needed to add over $11,000 per teacher to their assets (1985–86) to be fully funded. These obligations amount to as much as $142 per resident of the state (the adult population minus those under eighteen years of age).[15] Furthermore, taxpayer obligations are increasing; in the near future we can expect several state financial crises from the underfunding. Regardless, the state teacher retirement systems are government agencies, and any shortfalls have to be made up by state governments. This means that the pension costs for teachers currently in service cannot be ascertained by analyzing either the state or the local school district budget, or both of them together. Insofar as such budgets do not show either future cost-of-living supplements or underfunded pension obligations, they understate the costs of public education.

To appreciate the importance of pension issues to contracting out, it is essential to recognize the difficulties of remedying the problems of excessive public employee pensions. Over the years most state courts have held that the pension benefits of public employees are contractual obligations of government; most state supreme courts have rejected the view that pension benefits are matters of legislative policy that can be changed by legislatures. In most states, therefore, it is legally impossible to reduce benefits for retirees and current employees, regardless of how much greater than anticipated the required payments turn out to be. At the same time, efforts to reduce benefit levels for new employees meet enormous resistance from public sector unions, including teachers'. Apart from their general opposition to reducing benefits, they fear that reducing benefit levels for new employees will weaken the union. Eventually the union would be divided between the new employees seeking to equalize pension benefits (thereby reducing the benefits that could be made available to the senior employees) and the senior employees seeking to add benefits to their existing ones.

Regardless of whether a state makes up a shortfall in contributions or adds a cost-of-living supplement, its additional contributions are not payments for current services. They are additional payments for services that have been rendered in the past. In pay-as-you-go plans, the cost figures for pensions are a mix of costs for present and for past services. To fully assess the costs of present services, we should deduct the costs for past services and add the unfunded pension obligations that will be owed to current employees. In effect, public school employees are being paid partly in cash and partly in promissory notes, but the cost figures show only the current cash payments to them or on their behalf.

Large unfunded liabilities have to be paid by future taxpayers; they are the big losers when political leaders increase retirement benefits without immediate appropriations or tax increases. Future teachers and students are also big losers. When the costs have to be paid, it becomes more difficult to increase or even maintain existing levels of public services.

Clearly, contracting out would tend to avoid most of these problems. Private employers have less incentive to conceal unfunded pension costs; even when they have such incentives, shareholders and the investment industry are likely to monitor the situation. The citizen who monitors public employee pension costs receives an insignificant benefit from detecting excessive pension costs; virtually all of the savings would go to other taxpayers. In contrast, shareholders may benefit immediately and substantially from information about unfunded costs. Such costs may lead to selling the stock immediately, since the future dividend stream would be reduced. For this reason, pension costs are monitored more carefully in the private sector, especially by large institutional investors.

Neglected Costs in Contracting Out

Unfortunately for policymakers, cost comparisons can and sometimes do overlook some significant costs associated with buying services. At least three kinds of costs are sometimes omitted. First, the costs of the process of contracting out—"transaction costs," to use the economists' term—are often omitted. Minimally, such costs include the process of preparing and advertising bids, evaluating offers to provide services, and negotiating and drawing up the appropriate contracts. Obviously, the nature of the service involved is an important cost factor. If the service requires substantial investment by the contractor or would idle district facilities, equipment, or personnel in the absence of a carefully crafted contract, transaction costs can be substantial. Resolving the parties' rights to terminate and the allocation of payments and costs on termination may also involve substantial transaction costs.

Although transaction costs should not be ignored, they are not likely to affect the desirability of contracting out in most situations. First of all, organizations of public officials have accumulated thousands of service contracts, many of them drafted by legal talent as good as any. For this reason, school districts that are contracting out a service do not confront a tabula rasa on which the first good contract must be drafted. Furthermore, whatever the transaction costs of the first contract, they are likely to be much lower for future contracts.

Like transaction costs, the costs of implementing rather than negotiating an agreement are sometimes overlooked. Such costs may be due to litigation, labor problems, contractor delay or failure, and a host of other unanticipated problems that turn out to be very costly, politically as well as financially.

Once negotiated and implemented, service contracts must be monitored, and adequate monitoring can involve significant costs. The basic issue is how the monitoring costs affect realistic comparisons of total costs. Outside of education, monitoring for contracted services typically range from 5 to 10 percent of direct costs. Obviously, omission of costs of this magnitude could lead to invalid comparisons. Sometimes public agencies do require private contractors to specify monitoring costs even while failing to consider the costs involved in monitoring the performance of its own employees. Quite clearly, valid comparisons include monitoring costs of both public and private service delivery.[16]

Overall, it is very likely that inclusion of the neglected

costs in cost comparisons would strengthen the case for contracting out. First, the most substantial costs that are frequently ignored, such as pension costs, are virtually always higher in the public sector. Second, the political pressures to underfund long-range needs, such as maintenance, are not as strong in the private sector. For example, I doubt whether private contractors in New York City have underfunded their maintenance needs to the same extent as the city's public schools. In other words, there appears to be less pressure in the private sector to conceal or minimize costs; if anything, the reverse is the case. The major exception seems to be the costs associated with corruption in awarding and monitoring contracts. These costs can be substantial, but they cannot be estimated accurately.

Studies indicate that contracting out is utilized most effectively when the service involved can be readily identified, measured, and evaluated. Refuse collection illustrates this. Is the refuse picked up by a certain time each day? How many complaints are there? Does the contractor respond within a specified time to complaints? Questions such as these can be answered in a relatively straightforward way. With education, however, it is more difficult to know what the outcomes should be, what they are, and how much weight to give them.

In the first place, schools have multiple objectives, such as literacy, computational skills, respect for others, patriotism, perseverance, creativity, and vocational/recreational/cultural skills. Unfortunately, there is no consensus on these objectives or on how much weight to give them, even when their desirability is not in question.

In addition, the technical problems of assessing the school contributions to these outcomes are virtually insuperable. Herbert J. Walberg, a leading scholar of school effects, has cited a number of major factors that influence affective, behavioral, and cognitive learning. First are the *student aptitude factors*. These include ability or prior achievement, as measured by the usual standardized tests; development, as indexed by chronological age or stage of maturation; and motivation, or self-concept, as indicated by personality tests or the student's willingness to persevere intensively on learning tasks.

Instructional factors include: the amount of time students engage in learning; and the quality of the instructional experience, including psychological and curricular aspects.

Environmental factors include: the educational climates of the home, the classroom social group, and the peer group outside the school; and use of out-of-school time (specifically, the amount of leisure-time television viewing).[17]

Clearly, some of these factors are largely or even entirely outside educators' control. In any case, it is frequently impossible to distinguish school from nonschool effects on most of the objectives of education. As Walberg comments:

> It seems ironic that schooling and other educative experiences which constitute such a large fraction of human time and which may have immense consumption and investment value, are so narrowly and poorly measured. Much more information is available on automobiles—for example, base price, accessory and maintenance costs; information on speed, safety, size and reliability; and ratings on style and handling. Comparatively little information of this kind is available on the costs and benefits of education.[18]

In addition to these difficulties, the opponents of contracting out assert that some of the objectives of instruction are not subject to measurement. Consequently, it is allegedly impossible to determine whether or not the contractor is performing adequately with respect to these objectives. On the other hand, if only the measurable objectives are specified in contracts, contractors will focus their efforts on them to the neglect of others that do not lend themselves readily to measurement. This would be undesirable.

Although these problems cannot be ignored, it is highly

debatable whether they constitute a valid argument against contracting out instruction. Indeed, some problems may even strengthen the case for it, although that may not be the intent of those raising the objection.

Granted, most of what we know about the outcomes of education is limited to what has been measured by tests. Furthermore, most tests measure verbal achievement and verbal skills. Although significant, this limitation neverthe-less should be viewed in perspective. People devote a large part of their time to verbal activities; a 1978 study found that the typical worker was involved in some type of read-ing for 141 minutes, or 29 percent, of the average work day. In addition, a great deal of leisure time is devoted to reading; for example, the mean time devoted to reading a newspaper the previous day was thirty-three minutes.[19]

Other studies show that an extremely wide variety of jobs require a high degree of reading competence. In fact, all types of workers placed a higher value on reading as a key to success than did high school students. Given the tre-mendous amount of time devoted to verbal activities, their importance outside the workplace, and the fact that verbal skills do not require substantial sacrifice of other educa-tional objectives, tests of verbal achievement are valuable albeit incomplete.

In any event, the most important issue is whether con-tracting out would fail because of evaluation problems or lead to a resolution of them. Contractors will naturally try to demonstrate that conventional operations are not as effective as contracting out the service. Their critics will try to identify negative outcomes that are ignored by the con-tractors. Thus the process of contracting out facilitates clar-ity and specificity with respect to both costs and outcomes. This outcome is independent of whether the contractors can provide equal or better service at a lower cost; what-ever the real costs of public education (or any aspect of it), contracting out will tend to show what they are. Public awareness of the costs is likely to help keep them to reason-able levels.

For all the rhetoric about nonacademic objectives,

schools and teachers rely almost entirely on tests of academic achievement to measure student progress. It hardly makes sense to allow public schools but not private contractors to ignore nonacademic criteria. Granted, education should have several objectives in addition to educational achievement. If, however, public school officials can't tell us the criteria used to evaluate progress on these other objectives, how do they know—how can they know?—whether the public schools are fulfilling them? And if the school officials themselves don't know, it's difficult to believe they regard the objectives very seriously. It is at least arguable that contracting out instruction would force school districts to come to grips with this issue.

Indeed, the assertion of behavioral and attitudinal objectives and the simultaneous absence of criteria to evaluate school performance on them is no accident. A criterion is a two-edged sword. It can be used to show progress—or it can be used to show lack thereof. Public schools, like public agencies generally, show little interest in developing criteria for evaluating their performance. In the absence of such criteria, school personnel are invulnerable; no matter how poorly students perform in any given area, it can be asserted that other objectives that can't be measured must be taken into account. In the meantime, the deficiencies are useful; for example, if students aren't learning, schools need more money for remedial programs, to attract better teachers, and to improve instructional materials.

Granted, it may be easier to compare public and private garbage removal or mail delivery than the outcomes of education. I think the difficulty is exaggerated, but whether it is or not is of secondary importance. We must ask ourselves why parents and taxpayers lack usable criteria for evaluating school performance and what can be done about it. Viewed in this light, the alleged absence of criteria for assessing educational outcomes is an argument for contracting out, not a reason to reject it.

I believe schools do have attitudinal and behavioral objectives, however poorly articulated they may be. The reason that schools do not ordinarily evaluate progress on these objectives is not the inherent technical difficulty of doing so. It is that no one has any stake in establishing the criteria necessary to do so.

Contracting out would provide the incentives for establishing such criteria. Contractors need to know how their services will be evaluated. School districts need to know whether contractors fulfilled district objectives. Consequently, the process of contracting out forces districts to define their objectives and specify the criteria for evaluating contractor success in achieving them.

Let us get down to specifics. Suppose we assume that public schools try to teach respect for others, patriotism, and good work habits, such as punctuality and perseverance. Although these attitudes and habits are distinct objectives, they are not "subjects" like mathematics or reading. Whether students learn these things depends on whether the teachers as a group and the school administration foster them. Although all teachers are responsible for helping to achieve these objectives, no individual teacher is held accountable for them. There is nothing necessarily wrong with this, since it may be practically impossible to disentangle individual teachers' contributions to the objectives. Yet it is still feasible to evaluate how effectively schools inculcate these habits and attitudes. The reason it is not done is not the technical difficulty of formulating the criteria to be used. The problem is managerial, not technical.

The foregoing analysis might be criticized as follows. Teachers have multiple objectives. If they are evaluated solely or primarily on the basis of objectives that can be measured, they will disregard the others. To avoid neglect of objectives not subject to measurements, we must avoid evaluation solely on academic criteria. Inability to measure nonacademic objectives should not lead us to adopt policies that will lead to ignoring them.

There is merit in the premise of this argument. If teachers are evaluated solely on specified criteria, they are more likely to ignore others no matter how important. Nevertheless, I regard the argument as weak. First, many of the nonacademic objectives of education, such as good work habits, are instrumental to the academic objectives. Even if these instrumental objectives are not measured directly, it is probably safe to assume that schools which show good academic results would show good nonacademic outcomes as well.

To the extent this analysis is valid, there is probably little to fear from contracting out. There is no reason why contractors would be less likely to foster the desirable habits and attitudes in question. These objectives are not so much a matter of expertise as they are of being clear about goals and being determined to achieve them. I see no basis for assuming public schools would do a better job than private contractors; if anything, the latter should be expected to perform better, since their livelihood will depend on performance.

Recent trends in school finance underscore this point. Over 50 percent of school revenues now comes from state governments. All that counts in the allocation of state aid is the number of pupils in various grade levels or categories, such as the disabled or non-English speaking. As state funds flow in regardless of performance on any criterion, there is no pressure on school districts to develop criteria for assessing performance.

In considering the difficulties of specifying instructional criteria, it is imperative to avoid a double standard of evaluation. It ill behooves public school personnel who lack criteria for accountability to demand that a contractor be held to higher standards. Initially, the same criteria that are used to evaluate conventional instruction can be used to evaluate instruction that is contracted out. Those who teach or allow teaching to go on in the absence of any criteria should not be allowed to block contracting out for this reason. Like public school personnel, contractors might prefer not to be evaluated, but they could hardly prevent school boards from doing so. No doubt contractors will propose criteria favorable to their efforts, but school boards need not accept them without change. Over time, especially if contracting out instruction becomes more common, the criteria can be refined and expanded. Furthermore, national and state organizations of school boards, school administrators, and teachers will provide feedback on contracting out in other school districts. In short, it is essential to visualize the development of contracting out over time, not to view it simply as a static and repetitive process.

In this connection, department stores provide some useful models for school districts. It is currently common practice for such stores to lease space to independent contractors. This may happen because certain product lines, such as large appliances, require services that store management is not prepared to provide. Or sometimes management wants to provide certain services, such as shoe repair, that do not provide an adequate return on investment; in such cases, lessees may be willing to operate at lower costs or be willing to accept lower returns. Sometimes leasing is used to introduce new products, or is required by vendors the store wishes to keep. Perhaps significantly, the major opposition to leasing comes from store buyers who would lose their positions if leases replaced direct store operation.[20]

Some of the reasons for department store leasing would apply to schools; some would not. We can also visualize reasons to lease school space that would not necessarily apply to the department store situation. For example, such leases might be the only way to avoid statutory or bargaining restrictions that impair the quality of service. In any event, the relationships among the school districts, independent contractors, students, and parents would be governed by the lease arrangements, just as they are in the department store situation; the leases spell out performance requirements, the application of store policies, dress codes, responsibilities for maintenance, and other potential sources of friction.

Private Ownership of Public Schools

Thus far we have assumed that school boards would be the agencies that would contract for instructional services.

Let us now consider a much different approach, albeit one that is gaining widespread acceptance in other public services.

In chapter 1 we noted the increasing resort to sale and leaseback arrangements in the public sector. Environmental Protection Agency (EPA) requirements have forced many public agencies to build waste disposal and water purification facilities. At the same time, public agencies have been limited by statutory restrictions on capital investment and voter resistance to the tax increases. For these and other reasons, local governments often contract with private companies that build a required facility and then lease it to the public agency for a stipulated period, at which time ownership may or may not revert to the public body. Frequently the lease also provides for the private operation of the facility. In some cases where the revenues come from user fees, the leases include profit-sharing arrangements between the owner-operator and the local government.

Although such arrangements are virtually ignored in education, sale/leaseback arrangements may be especially appropriate in school operations. The reason is that private owners of a school leased to a school district would be able to generate income that is lost under public ownership. This is apparent if we compare the profit-making potential of a school with a waste disposal facility. The latter has one service to sell. Depending on the lease arrangements, it may be able to sell its services to other local governments, but its potential for generating revenue will be limited to waste disposal.

Let us now consider a public secondary school, which is typically in operation only 180 days a year. On the days when it is used, most facilities may not be needed after the students have departed in midafternoon. Food facilities could be used as a restaurant or for take-out service. Meeting rooms, parking spaces, an auditorium, audiovisual and copying equipment, school buses, and perhaps several other facilities also could be used commercially.

Why are these facilities not rented when they are not required for school operations? Essentially, there are no personal incentives for school management to do so. On the contrary, school management would be criticized for competing unfairly with private business. Furthermore the "profits" would not go to management but to the school district—perhaps with the result that its tax revenues would be decreased because funds were available from these other sources.

Suppose, however, that a commercial company owns the facility and leases it to the school district for specific times. At other times the owners are free to use the school as a profit center. They can lease the kitchen facility for a restaurant or take-out service after school hours. They can rent space to hotels that need meeting rooms or organizations needing an auditorium. In other words, private sector owners would be able to generate the income in ways that school districts cannot.

Granted, school districts and other public agencies sometimes engage in such commercial efforts. Nevertheless, it would be unrealistic to expect the same outcomes, regardless of whether a public agency or for-profit company owns the facilities. If a private sector company seeking to earn profits owns a facility, we can expect much greater sensitivity to entrepreneurial opportunities. In contrast, if ownership is invested in a political body, as is the case now, facility utilization will be governed by a different set of incentives and a political, not an economic, calculus. Inasmuch as school districts can protect their interests in drawing up the sale and leaseback agreement, these arrangements should be at least as useful in education as in other municipal services.

As previously noted, there are problems with leasebacks; legal liability is a major one. The important point is that these problems are being solved every day in other public services. Furthermore, one of the problems in education may also turn out to be its biggest advantage: companies may participate because of the presence of secondary school youth while they simultaneously provide students with much-needed employment opportunities. In any event, many teachers might be entrepreneurs if circumstances were appropriate. As currently structured, education does not encourage or foster entrepreneurial talent; to be an entrepreneur, teachers are forced to leave the field. If and when this changes, we may see the emergence of educational leaders oriented more to the creation of value than to the redistribution of it.

4

Lessons from the OEO Fiasco

Our analysis to this point might be characterized as cautiously optimistic. Contracting out has been shown to result in significant savings and/or quality improvements under the proper conditions. Although the extent of these conditions in education is difficult to estimate, we certainly can expect them to exist in many areas. The major problem seems to be that as one moves away from readily observable and quantifiable services, the promise of contracting out is less encouraging. Another problem is the perception that contracting out instruction has been tried and has failed miserably as a means of achieving educational improvement. As one publication commented in 1975:

Performance contracting has been pronounced dead again, with the latest autopsy performed by the Educational Testing Service. Except for an occasional rumor that the deceased has been seen alive and well in Michigan, not many doubt the demise of the phenomenon that put private enterprise into the classroom a few years ago. What's surprising is how many people keep reopening the grave to see if the corpse is still there.[1]

To the extent that such an attitude still exists, it is likely to be based on experience with "educational performance contracting" in the early 1970s. This experience resulted largely from a series of contracts funded by the Office of Economic Opportunity (OEO) to improve reading and mathematics skills among disadvantaged children. Inasmuch as this experience was widely characterized as a test of contracting out instruction, it deserves a careful review.

As will soon be evident, every aspect of the OEO project was highly controversial. Although some discussion of the controversies is unavoidable, my purpose is not to resolve them. Rather it is to show what the project can tell us about contracting out instruction. After all, a great deal has been learned about contracting out since 1970, so we are better able now to assess our earlier experience with the process.

AN OVERVIEW OF THE OEO PROJECT[2]

The OEO was established in 1964 as the major federal agency to administer programs to alleviate poverty. At the time, federal strategy was to reduce poverty by improving the educational skills of disadvantaged youth. This strategy called for substantial federal support for programs of compensatory education. One such program was Head Start, the major federal program intended to enhance the school readiness of disadvantaged preschool children. As it turned out, however, Head Start was not very effective in improving the educational skills of disadvantaged minorities.[3]

In the late 1960s, however, a new and promising approach to the education of disadvantaged minorities developed in Texarkana, Arkansas. The Texarkana school district had contracted with Dorsett Educational Laboratories, a private firm, to provide reading and mathematics instruction. The contract provided that Dorsett would not be paid unless student achievement reached specified levels within a specified time. This feature led to the notion of "educational performance contracting"; as implemented in Texarkana, contractor compensation was based on student achievement. When early reports indicated that educational achievement was increasing dramatically under this contract, visitors from every state went to Texarkana to see for themselves what was going on; many were sufficiently impressed to launch their own educational performance contracts in 1970–71.

OEO representatives visited the Texarkana district in March 1970. In April the agency announced its intention to conduct experiments* in educational performance contracting; in these experiments, which were to be conducted in grades 1 to 3 and 7 to 9, private contractors were to be paid on the basis of gains in student performance in reading and mathematics, as measured by standardized tests. Thirty-one firms responded to the invitation to be considered for participation; eventually six firms were selected, based on their capability, experience, and proposed approach. Factors emphasized in selection were use of technology, student incentives, and use of paraprofessionals; firms that appeared to have the best chance of achieving high benefit-cost ratios were selected.

The school districts were chosen from a group of seventy-seven that expressed an interest in participating. These seventy-seven districts were screened on the basis of the following criteria:

1. At least 80 percent of the district population had poverty-level incomes, as defined by Title I of the Elementary and Secondary Education Act.
2. District students were below national norms in reading and mathematics.

---

*I have reservations about whether the term experiment should be applied to the OEO project, but as it has been used widely there is no point in fighting this semantic battle.

3. The district enrolled the required numbers of students in the grades covered by the study.
4. The district had recent, valid, and reliable test achievement data so that it was feasible to assign students to experimental and control groups.
5. The absence of any problems that might interfere with the experiment.

Twenty-two districts reflecting a reasonably good geographical and demographic distribution met these criteria. After four withdrew during negotiations, the remaining eighteen were assigned, three to each contractor. Within each district, the most deficient students in the most deficient school were designated as the experimental group, and the school with the next most deficient student population was designated as the control group. The experimental group consisted of the students to be taught by the private contractors; the control group, in theory a group of equal achievement at the beginning of the school year, continued to be taught by regular teachers. Arrangements were also made to take into account transfers out of the participating schools.

Despite a host of difficulties, the project got underway in the late summer of 1970. At the beginning and end of the 1970–71 school year, Battelle Laboratories, an independent testing and analysis organization under contract to OEO, tested the students in both groups. Using each grade at each site as a unit of comparison, the test results showed that the experimental groups scored better than the control groups in 28 cases, or 13 percent of the total number of comparisons. In 60 cases—28 percent of the total—the students in the control group scored higher than the experimental group. In 124 comparisons—59 percent of the total—there was no significant difference between the two groups. As Battelle Laboratories summarized the outcome:

There is very little evidence that performance incentive contracting, as implemented by the technology companies at the 18 school districts in this study for a period of one year, had a beneficial effect on the reading and mathematics achievement of students participating in the experiment, as measured by a standardized achievement test.[4]

As a result of this negative evaluation, educational performance contracting virtually disappeared. Districts that had been contemplating similar projects dropped their plans to do so; districts that had contracts usually did not renew them. For our purposes, however, the issue posed by the OEO project can be formulated this way: Assuming that the negative results of the experiment were accurate, what were the reasons for them? More precisely, were the reasons for the negative results inherent in contracting out? Or were they primarily situation-specific reasons that could reasonably be avoided in other efforts to contract out instruction?

Although my answer to these questions does not depend on the experiment's deficiencies, it will be useful to discuss them briefly. In most cases, the deficiencies are indisputable; what is controversial is the extent to which they impaired the significance of the results.

One goal of the project was to ascertain whether contracting out could improve the reading and mathematics skills of students deficient in these areas. On the other hand, the experiment was also designed to test the use of student and teacher incentives. As previously noted, Battelle Laboratories stated its major conclusion in terms of "performance incentive contracting." As a Brookings Institute study points out,

A fundamental shortcoming of the performance contracting experiment concerned confusion over the basic goal of the enterprise . . . the underlying concept of performance contracting could have been tested in two quite different ways: either to determine whether private firms with 1970 vintage technology could teach better than traditional schools, or to determine whether economic and contractual incentives would in the long run encourage better teaching and would therefore be a preferable means for local school boards to purchase educational services than the current procedures. There was confusion about these two partially incompatible objectives from the outset.[5]

Actually, more than two incompatible objectives undermined the experiment from the outset. As Charles Blaschke, a knowledgeable participant, pointed out:

Many school boards view performance contracting as a vehicle for introducing merit pay into public education, especially if contractors are permitted to reward their employees on the basis of student performance. At the same time, since most contractors utilize differentiated staffing, efficient practices by school systems during turn-key phases must also follow similar staffing patterns. . . .

While most guidelines of federal programs (for example, Elementary and Secondary Education Act Title I) require equality in terms of comparable inputs, such as facilities or student teacher ratio, performance contracting introduces the concept of equity of results. . . .

A proper analysis of the Office of Economic Opportunity experiment must separate contracting as a technique of experimentation from that of a technique of instruction.[6]

These comments highlight several basic points. First, they underscore the fact that at least some school districts viewed the project as a means of introducing or testing incentive plans for students, teachers, and/or parents. In and of itself, there was nothing wrong with this. It must be emphasized, however, that contracting out per se has no inherent relationship to incentive systems for compensating employees. The two concepts are separate and distinct. For example, if a bus company contracts to operate a school bus system for profit, it does not *necessarily* follow that its drivers (who may still be district employees) will be paid on an incentive basis. Of course, a school district could require a contractor to use an incentive pay system for its employees or for district employees covered by the contract. In such a case, however, we would have a contract to test an incentive system; the incentive system, not contracting out, would be the subject of the test. This point is especially crucial because the incentive systems sought to be implemented in the OEO experiment were certain to arouse widespread teacher opposition. It was as if a hospital contracted with a company to administer a drug that had never been effective and that would arouse intense opposition from doctors—and declared afterward that contracting out was a failure.

Blaschke's comments also reveal another fundamental distinction between the OEO approach and the normal practice in contracting out. In the OEO project, it was assumed that after the companies had demonstrated the success of their approach, the entire operation would be "turnkeyed" over to local school districts. That is, it was envisaged that district management would incorporate successful approaches on a day-to-day basis. Using contracting out in this way has little in common with proposals to use private contractors on a regular basis to provide services. About the only thing the two ideas do have in common is that in both cases there is a contract with a private firm. The differences, however, are fundamental.

First of all, the OEO approach had little relevance to the efficiencies of contracting out. With a contract for only one year, contractors are not likely to invest in the capital equipment, training, and other costs associated with a long-range investment. The contractors in the project did make some investment in these areas, but hardly what would be expected in a multiyear contract that had the possibility of renewal. Second, although contracting out might be useful as a way to test procedures that can be incorporated by the public agency, that is not its basic rationale. To some extent, it is actually inconsistent with it. Ordinarily the goal of contracting out is to achieve efficiencies that are not available under direct provision of services by a public agency. Viewing contracting out as a way to identify practices that can be incorporated by public agencies is a crippling limitation on its use, even experimentally.

This point highlights another example of the goal confusion characterizing the OEO project. After pointing out that the cost differences between experimental and control schools did not appear to affect the outcomes one way or another, Gramlich and Koshel point out: "One of the initial goals of the project, progressively abandoned as it ran its course, was to see if performance contracting companies could teach more cheaply than the control schools."[7]

This comment illustrates the extremely limited applicability of the OEO project. Contracting out can be the clearly preferred mode of service delivery solely on cost grounds, without any improvement in student achievement or service effectiveness. Suppose, for example, that in dealing with brain-damaged children, no type of instruction results in greater student achievement. Suppose also, however, that whatever is the maximum achievable level of student achievement, private contractors can achieve it for half the cost of public delivery, with no negative side effects. It would be ridiculous to argue that contracting out is a "failure" merely because there is no improvement in student performance. This conclusion would make sense only if costs were totally irrelevant in choosing delivery systems.

If we want to find out whether contracting out can bring about the same or higher levels of educational achievement but at a lower cost, we should not add costs intended to test whether the use of incentives can increase educational achievement. Inasmuch as either hypothesis could be valid while the other was not, combining the two in the same experiment results in conclusions that may not be valid for either hypothesis. When more goals are built into the experiment, the conclusions about any particular goal become even more suspect.

Teacher Union Opposition In choosing school districts to participate, OEO tried to select districts without problems that would interfere with the project. In retrospect, it is difficult to see how the agency could have selected districts more problematical than some of those selected.

One of the sites was part of the New York City school district. In 1969 the district had experienced the longest and most divisive teacher strike in the history of American education. The major issue in the strike was an effort by predominantly black community school boards to replace white teachers supported by the union with black teachers supported by the board.[8] Coming as it did less than a year after an unprecedented racial confrontation in the city's schools, the teacher union leaders perceived the OEO project as a way for the school board to have its way. As with most of the other districts the OEO chose to participate, the union was not consulted prior to the contract; participation was treated as a fait accompli. Not surprisingly, this particular site turned out to be a disaster area. As one study describes it:

There were also a few sites where extraordinary difficulties occurred, much beyond anything that might have been anticipated beforehand and sometimes so serious as to make the test results next to meaningless. The worst was the Bronx. In the late sixties the New York City school system had moved toward a decentralized, community-controlled system that had antagonized its strong local teachers' union, the United Federation of Teachers. This union, a chapter of the American Federation of Teachers, was as opposed as its parent to performance contracting, and its president, Albert Shanker, announced on the radio that he believed the OEO Bronx program to be illegal and threatened action to prevent its continuation. The teachers in the experimental schools took this cue and were continually at loggerheads with the contractor, Learning Foundations. There were reports that they threw some of the Learning Foundations equipment out of second-story windows and told students to throw away their parent questionnaires. Discipline in the junior high schools involved in the experiment became so bad at one point early in the fall that all testing and instruction were halted and a full-time policeman had to be stationed in one of them. Instruction could only be resumed when the president of Learning Foundations, Fran Tarkenton, at that time also quarterback of the New York Giants football team, was able to rally community support around the project. Even so, records from the project are very incomplete. The tests at the end of the school year were given in a ballroom a few blocks from the school and a new form of attrition was introduced as students walked from the school to the testing room. Moreover, some of the ninth grade control students were not post-tested because the school principal assigned Battelle a testing date that was after the school year was over, the parent questionnaires and student information cards were never filled out, and the project director kept very poor records of who was and who was not in the program. Fortunately, this experience was out of the ordinary.

The situation in Hartford and Philadelphia was almost as disorganized.[9]

Contract Errors and Miscalculations Every evaluation of the OEO project agreed that the contracting process was too brief, with serious errors and omissions on all sides as a result. As Gramlich and Koshel point out, "Performance contracting became a hot educational issue in the early months of 1970, and in its haste to take advantage of this opportunity, OEO rushed precipitously into the planning of the experiment."[10]

A brief chronology may help to explain just how inadequately all parties were prepared for the experiment. OEO representatives visited the Texarkana district in March 1970. By April the agency decided to launch the experiment and advertised for contractors on April 27, 1970. At this time, it sent requests for proposals (RFPs) to over twenty firms and also negotiated a contract with Educational Turnkey Systems to provide management support services. Within two months OEO selected the six contractors and the eighteen participating school districts; most of the contracts were signed by mid-July 1970, at which time OEO sent RFPs on the evaluation to approximately fifty companies. This contract was awarded in August to Battelle Memorial Institute, which began conducting the pretests two weeks later.

All of the parties encountered major problems as a result of their lack of preparation. The contractors had very little time to hire teachers and to establish lines of communication with school officials and local teachers. Equipment and instructional materials did not always arrive in time, necessitating changes in programs and materials. School district officials had to identify the students to participate in the project, explain and hopefully gain the support of teachers and administrators in participating schools, and employ a project director and two aides. It appears, however, that most teachers and principals were not informed about the project until they returned to school in the fall.

Battelle Institute, the contractor responsible for testing and evaluation, was also severely handicapped by the lack of time. Almost 30,000 students in six grades at eighteen sites had to be tested within weeks after Battelle was awarded the contract. As the institute had no previous experience in such large-scale testing operations, the arrangements to test students at the beginning of the school year were frequently inadequate, for both experimental and control students. Battelle itself noted disciplinary problems, overcrowding, excessive heat, student disruptions, and even a fire drill during a pretest; in some cases it was necessary to retest students a few weeks later.

Ordinarily, when a contractor undertakes a project with substantial indeterminate costs, there is provision for payment on the basis of actual expenses plus a percentage to allow for some profit. Such contracts are highly susceptible to abuse; if profits depend on the amount of expenses, it will be in the contractor's interests to run up the expenses. Intensive auditing can minimize the risks of abuse, but some risk is always present.

For whatever reasons, all of the OEO contracts were on a fixed-fee basis. This turned out to be a major mistake from any point of view. Unanticipated problems leading to unanticipated expenses not only rendered participation highly unprofitable, but ultimately led to lengthy litigation as contractual deficiencies became apparent to all parties. In addition to underestimating their costs and overestimating their ability to achieve educational improvement, the contractors naively accepted an "all-or-nothing" system of payment; they received no payment at all for students who did not advance at least a full grade beyond normal expectations. Such a clause is likely to encourage contractors to concentrate their efforts on the students who were most likely to fulfill the payment conditions. Although it is impossible to determine whether this happened, it is an example of the poor drafting that characterized the contracts.

A General Accounting Office (GAO) study of the OEO project listed several major additional deficiencies.[11] It pointed out that the bidding procedures for the management support contractor provided only "token acquiescence to requirements for competition"; the RFP was drafted in such a way that it rationalized the selection of two contractors who had already been negotiating with OEO for the contract. OEO did not apply the RFP criteria to the selection of contractors, none of whom had the experience specified in the proposal. In addition, some did not meet the standards of financial responsibility required by federal procurement regulations. These regulations were also violated in other ways; for example, changes in the RFP were not incorporated in it in a notice sent to all bidders. Five of the six firms did not provide a repayment bond as required in projects of this sort; such a bond was especially needed because the payment provisions allowed substantial payments prior to the definitive determination of the amounts due. The GAO also concluded that two of the six contractors did not meet the conditions of financial responsibility required by federal regulations.

The GAO report also listed several major deficiencies in project implementation. For example, no attention was paid to the amount of time students in the control group received instruction in reading and mathematics. Obviously, failure to control this variable might have discredited all the conclusions—differences between the experimental and the control group that were attributed to incentives (or the lack thereof) might have been the result of differences in instructional time. Whether or not this particular oversight affected the outcome, it was typical of the sloppiness at every phase of the project. The procedure for selecting the experimental and control groups was seriously flawed; the racial composition was different in seven of the eighteen sites and unknown in four others. Personnel were often hired just a few days before the project was to begin and even afterward, in some cases. The contracts with the school districts were inconsistent with those with the contractors; the former stated the contractor was responsible for the testing, the latter stated that the districts were responsible for it. Regardless, the test guidelines were frequently violated. Initially the results were to be evaluated on a site-by-site basis. In this way, it might have been possible to evaluate the performance of the different contractors. Instead, the results were aggregated. Furthermore, although the project was supposed to test different instructional approaches, all the contractors changed their approaches throughout the year; it would have been impossible to draw any valid conclusions about their approaches even if the data had not been aggregated.

Implications of the OEO Project for Contracting Out

OEO's report on the project, released in June 1972, states:

The results of the experiment clearly indicate that the firms operating under performance contracts did not perform significantly better than the more traditional school systems.

Thus while we judge this experiment to be a success

in terms of the information it can offer about the capabilities of performance contractors, it is clearly another failure in our search for means of helping poor and disadvantaged youngsters to develop the skills they need to lift themselves out of poverty.[12]

The GAO report flatly asserted that the OEO's conclusions were not justified: "Because of a number of shortcomings in both the design and implementation of the experiment, it is our opinion that the question as to the merits of performance contracting versus traditional educational methods remains unanswered."[13]

Essentially, it is not necessary to decide whether the deficiencies of the OEO experiment affected the test results. Even if the results were unimpeachable in every way, they would not affect the case for contracting out, for instruction or anything else. One reason relates to the limitations of the experiment.

According to the Battelle evaluation:

First, the analysis evaluated performance incentive contracting *as implemented by the six technology companies involved in the study.* The evaluation makes no pretense of generalizing results and conclusions to the effectiveness of performance incentive contracting in general. . . . Indeed, the obtained outcomes for the six companies involved in the study could be different if they were to implement their program in a different way as a result of experiences gained during the experimental year.

Second, the analysis evaluated performance incentive contracting as implemented *for a period of one year.* The evaluation makes no pretense of generalizing results and conclusions to the effectiveness of performance incentive contracting implemented for more than one year.

Finally, the analysis evaluated performance incentive contracting *using a standardized achievement test* as the basis for assessing program impact. The evaluation makes no pretense of generalizing results and conclusions to the effectiveness of performance incentive contracting using some other method of assessing program impact.[14]

Actually, the OEO project was neither an adequate nor a comprehensive test of incentives, whether for students, teachers, or contractors. In addition, the project shed no light on the effects of incentive systems not approved by OEO and the participating school districts. In any event, subsequent events have discredited any rejection of contracting out instruction on the basis of the OEO project. Today private contractors are providing instructional services for school districts in such areas as remedial reading, foreign languages, education for the disabled, and teacher training.[15] The "experiment" that proved it couldn't be done has turned out to be irrelevant.

In retrospect, the irrelevance of the OEO experiment to contracting out seems obvious. Why was it not obvious in the early 1970s? To answer this question, it is essential to understand the origins of the project. In 1970 there was much more opposition to school integration than there is today. There was also a great deal of concern among federal policymakers over both the persistence of de facto segregation and the educational deficits among disadvantaged minorities. These problems were seen as closely interrelated. School districts were frequently caught in a dilemma between legal mandates to end segregation and local political opposition to integration. Much of the opposition was due to the perception that black students' lower educational achievement levels would have a negative effect on white students if integration took place. Reading and mathematics skills were not only important in their own right but they were the primary, if not the only, academic skills that had been tested nationally. For this reason, they were a natural focus for the early efforts to contract out instruction.

Understandably, the OEO's concern was not to test contracting out per se. It was how to improve the reading and mathematics skills of disadvantaged minorities, especially blacks. Apart from this, OEO had no interest in educational contracting out. The possibility that contracting out instruction might have been a better way to provide educational services in general, or to students who were not disadvantaged and performing poorly, was not an underlying concern. This is not a criticism of OEO; it was not primarily an educational agency. Furthermore, there was nothing wrong with the OEO objective; it was a worthy one. On the other hand, the educational problems it sought to resolve were—and still are—largely intractable to remedial treatment. In effect, therefore, the OEO selected the most difficult student population in the most difficult problem area—and then, "failing" to show significant progress in one year, abandoned the effort. I cannot criticize the abandonment, especially after the way the project was initiated; what should be criticized is the contention that the OEO project is evidence that contracting out instruction won't work.

What the OEO project really demonstrated was not the inability of the for-profit sector to contribute to improving public education; it was how federal spending for educational research is dominated by short-term political considerations and is, therefore, largely a waste of money. Needless to say, however, the opponents of contracting out took full advantage of their opportunity to discourage any wider interest in the subject. Like the youngster who murdered his parents and then pleaded for mercy because he was an orphan, the teacher unions did everything possible to block or sabotage the project; then, having contributed so much to its demise, they pointed to the latter as proof that union objection to contracting out had been right all the time. In the antimarket environment of public education, this argument was persuasive.

Overcoming Union Opposition to Contracting Out

As we have seen, the major opposition to contracting out comes from the employees and/or the unions that represent them. Can this opposition be overcome or neutralized?

Three basic principles should guide school management on this issue. One is that no special interest group should be permitted to block an action that is in the district's interest. Occasionally it may be impossible to adhere to this principle, but it is better to recognize a violation of it than to rationalize it away. The second principle is to deal fairly with employees who are adversely affected by contracting out. What this requires in any specific situation may be controversial, but it should not be interpreted to give employees or their unions veto power over proposed changes.

The third principle is not always recognized, but it is critical from a strategic point of view. The principle is that union and employee interests are not identical, and the differences can sometimes be used to neutralize union opposition to contracting out. On this issue, there is much to be learned from the way Margaret Thatcher's government in Great Britain has facilitated privatization.[16] From the outset it has sought not merely to neutralize employee opposition but to gain employee support for privatization. To achieve this objective, it has offered employees a variety of benefits; for example, employees have had opportunities to buy stock at a deep discount in companies taking over former government enterprises. Similarly, to overcome management opposition to privatization, incumbent management often remains when the enterprise is privatized. In many instances even the unions that opposed privatization ended up purchasing a substantial number of shares in the new companies—as did large numbers of union members.

By and large, the specifics of the British approach are not applicable to public education in the United States; the underlying philosophy and attitude, however, are quite relevant. It is especially critical to recognize that the union's underlying interests are not necessarily identical to those of the employees. This is especially evident when the work is contracted out to a nonunion employer. Even when the contractor's employees are or can be unionized, they may come under the jurisdiction of a different union. For this reason, the union representing school district employees is likely to oppose contracting out regardless of the union status of the contractor's employees.

When employees would be adversely affected by contracting out, there is no conflict between union and employee interests. In many situations, however, employers can satisfy employee interests in ways that do not accommodate the union's. For example, in order to overcome employee opposition to contracting out, the employer may offer early retirement, severance pay, and/or transfers on conditions highly favorable to its employees. In some situations employers can assure employees against layoffs and depend on attrition or voluntary departures to carry out the commitment. In contrast, union staff who rely on dues income for their livelihood will accord preservation of the union a higher priority than the employees protected against loss of income.

In some cases union opposition to contracting out may be perceived as contrary to employee interests. Suppose that school boards in a given area propose to contract out instruction in a field in which they are unable to recruit enough teachers. Some teachers in the fields of shortage may feel that with extensive use of paraprofessionals and technology, they can meet district needs as contractors instead of as employees. The teacher unions in these districts, however, will be concerned about the precedent and the loss of dues-paying members. Even if the local teacher unions are not concerned, their state and national affiliates are likely to oppose such a development.

Of course, in any such situation, the unions would be denying teachers an opportunity to promote their own welfare by providing services as contractors instead of as employees. For this reason, the union's position would be difficult to defend. It is impossible to predict how often such situations will arise; the underlying issue is the extent to which contracting out will be a cottage industry or be the outcome of large-scale contracting in which contractors operate entire schools or even districts.

In the normal course of events, the union will be adversely affected by contracting out, at least in the short run. Although it would always be desirable to have union approval (if it can be achieved without excessive concessions), it will usually be withheld, except under heavy pressure. Such pressure may include benefits that are contingent upon acceptance of contracting out. The benefits may apply to employees not affected by contracting out as well as those directly affected by it. Efforts to overcome union and/or employee opposition could include one or more of the following provisions:

1. The employees remain on the district payroll but work pursuant to arrangements between the contractor and the district. This is a common procedure in certain types of support services.
2. As part of the contract, the contractor may be required to employ district employees on a preferential basis. The preference may be limited to a certain time (for example, up to five years). The district may supplement the contractor's payments. Some type of joint payment often occurs when employees would lose pension or health insurance benefits if forced off the district payroll.
3. Severance pay and/or maintenance of health insurance benefits might be considered to ease the transition.
4. Liberalized early retirement might be made available in certain situations.
5. Transfers or reassignments might ensure continuous employment without loss of pay or benefits for employees who would otherwise suffer from contracting out.

Of course, the savings achieved by contracting out over time must take into account the transition costs and the costs of contract monitoring. The important point is to analyze the circumstances to see what can and might be done to mitigate employee/union opposition.

Undoubtedly, salary and pension problems can be a major obstacle to contracting out instruction. Teacher salary schedules reward years of service. Although significant savings might be generated without loss of quality by using part-time and/or younger teachers, teachers with many years of service will be strongly opposed to a new system that does not pay as much for longevity. Pension issues often exacerbate the salary problem. Teachers are members of state teacher retirement systems, which usually base pension payments on the number of years taught and the average salary of the final one to three years. As a result, teachers within a few years of retirement may oppose contracting out because it jeopardizes their anticipated level of pension benefits. One question is whether such teachers can be retained as district employees until retirement or can be bought out without giving up the economic advantages of contracting out. Obviously, the answer will vary with such factors as the age of the teaching staff, but the issue has to be considered carefully.

Pension problems illustrate the point that the most difficult aspect of contracting out is its impact on public employees. On the other hand, it is not desirable to maintain an inefficient delivery system because some employees will be disadvantaged by change. In chapter 2 we noted the enormous costs of political bailouts for redundant public employees. The problem is not temporary government support to ease a transition; it is that all too often, the transition is not made in the public sector.

On the other hand, there is no clear-cut standard for government to apply in resolving situations of inefficiency or redundancy. How much protection or compensation should be accorded public employees when more efficient ways to deliver services eliminate or reduce the need for their services? In practice and in the absence of any economic guidelines, the question is answered on a short-term political or bureaucratic basis: How would a proposed cut affect reelection prospects or bureaucratic objectives? The result is a substantial tilt toward inefficiency in public employment. Essentially, we have to find ways to use the savings from more efficient procedures to gain the support, or at least neutralize the opposition, of public employees adversely affected by such procedures.

The Role of School Management in Contracting Out

Unlike teacher unions, school management has no reason to oppose contracting out as an option to be exercised when circumstances warrant. In fact, school management has strong reason to resolve any close calls in favor of contracting out. Let us see why this is so.

In conventional operations, school management hires staff: teachers, principals, custodians, bus drivers, cooks, and so on. On the other hand, management also is responsible for evaluating these employees. Inasmuch as no one likes to admit having employed incompetent employees, especially if there is a political cost to the admission, there tends to be a management bias in favor of favorable evaluations. When the legal and practical difficulties of terminating incompetent employees are added to the inherent management bias in their favor, the outcome tends to favor the employees over the service consumers. Teacher rhetoric notwithstanding, public schools suffer much more from pro forma evaluation, or none at all, than from unjustified negative evaluations.

The conflict of interest in employment situations is only one example of a broader conflict that limits the effectiveness of school management. On the one hand, it is the producer of educational services; on the other, it is also responsible for representing the consumers of the services. Although widely ignored, this conflict of interest constitutes a serious problem in efforts to improve education.[17]

Suppose, however, that management had no direct responsibility for hiring employees. Would it not be in a better position to evaluate their performance objectively? Not having any stake in their employment, management would probably be more candid in expressing its conclusions about service quality. Also, since it would need less time for its producer activities (for example, hiring teachers), management would also have more time for its consumer responsibilities, such as evaluating services and educational outcomes.

To some extent, therefore, contracting out would help management minimize the conflict inherent in being both the producer and the consumer of educational services. Management can focus on evaluating the services rendered under less political pressure to justify the results. Nor would bias resulting from the employment of individual employees simply be replaced by bias resulting from selection of a contractor. (This could happen if there was sole-source bidding and school management was clearly responsible for selecting the sole source.) When bidding is truly open and competitive, management is less likely to have a political stake in a favorable evaluation of the services received.

Furthermore, there is an important difference in the two situations. In conventional operations, management must evaluate each individual employee. Under contracting out, however, management can focus on service outcomes; evaluation of employees is likely to be the contractor's responsibility. Granted, in some cases it may be difficult, even impossible, to evaluate a service without some attention to the performance of individuals. Nevertheless, despite some overlap, the focal points are different. Education is excessively oriented to evaluation of inputs and simultaneous neglect of outcomes. Contracting out could help redress this imbalance.

Whether contracting out saves management time, and how much time, obviously depends on several factors. Nevertheless, contracting out clearly has the potential to save a great deal of management time. Because they are public agencies, school officials are required to approve many items of little or no practical significance. For example, to avoid approving purchases that have not been considered, school management has to devote many hours to plowing through minutiae of no importance whatsoever to the educational program. Contracting out could help to minimize some of these problems. If the competitive process provides assurance that the overall cost is reasonable, there is no reason why management needs to be involved in the details of providing the service.

In a 1982 survey board members indicated that they spent about forty-five hours a month on board business. Asked how they would like to devote more time, 19 percent said curriculum-related matters, 12 percent said policy matters, and 9 percent said visiting schools. When asked how they could save time, 13 percent—the highest of any time-saving option—preferred reducing the number of board meetings.[18] None of the other options even questioned whether boards could make better use of their time by contracting out some of the services they manage to the private sector.

In considering these possibilities, it must be emphasized that contracting out is not an abdication of management responsibilities. Instead, it is another way of fulfilling them. Furthermore, contracting out does not imply that the public agency can safely ignore what happens after a contract is signed; as will be discussed shortly, contract management, including an adequate reporting system, should be considered an integral part of the process.

The Allocation and Distribution of Instructional Time

The prospects for contracting out instruction may depend on school district willingness to restructure the allocation and distribution of instructional time. While there is good reason for such restructuring in any case, contracting out could stimulate and benefit from it.

To illustrate, districts short of mathematics and science teachers might contract with companies instead of individuals for instruction in these areas. With a contract to provide services, the companies would be able to recruit teachers and tutors from a variety of sources: retired college and public school teachers, college students, individuals in the private sector, and so on. Changes in the allotment and distribution of instructional time might enable or greatly facilitate the use of these resources. Instead of providing mathematics instruction an hour a day, five days a week, arrangements might be made to provide two to three hours twice a week. Such arrangements would enable contractors to provide instructional service to several districts in the same area.

To appreciate the potential of such arrangements, it must be recognized that individual school districts frequently lack the scale to utilize certain specialists effectively. It is prohibitively expensive for a district to employ teachers for only ten students who want to study any particular subject. There are two choices: not to offer the subject at all or to have it taught by nonspecialists. Districts willing to restructure instructional time to take advantage of economies of scale could avoid this dilemma.

There is ample educational reason to do this. The existing allocation and distribution of instructional time, especially in secondary schools, are not based on any educational reason or rationale. This is evident from comparing the ways instructional time is allocated in colleges and high schools. In typical high schools, students attend five classes every day for almost an hour a day. In college, total classroom instruction is usually reduced to fifteen to eighteen hours a week, in subjects that are taught only two to three times a week. Obviously, the students do not change that much from high school in the spring to college in the fall; if they do not have to attend class for the same subject five days a week in college, they probably do not need to do so during their high school days. In any case, the more flexibility school districts show in scheduling instruction, the better their chances of finding individuals and companies willing to provide it.

Invitations for Bid and Requests for Proposal[19]

Regardless of the services involved, the possibilities for contracting out will vary widely from district to district and region to region. Even so, school districts can investigate the possibilities at a relatively low cost. To see how, it is necessary to understand the differences between an invitation for bid (IFB) and a request for proposal (RFP). With an IFB, the service sought and the conditions of delivery are specified, and contractors compete largely on the basis of price. An RFP allows more flexibility and requires negotiation between the district and contractor before an agreement is reached. When a district is getting into a new area, and it is not clear how services can be provided most efficiently, RFPs are preferable. Table 4.1 summarizes the differences between IFBs and RFPs.

Assume there is a shortage of calculus teachers. Districts could jointly request proposals from potential contractors. The RFP should include essential data, such as the number of students who would study calculus, their location, and the beginning and ending dates of instruction. Contractors might be asked to submit proposals that require the students to assemble at a given location and/or proposals that envisage instructors going out to the participating districts. Instead of district personnel drawing up plans, potential contractors can suggest ways and means of delivering the services efficiently.

John Tepper Marlin has provided a useful comparison of IFBs and RFPs. Most school boards are somewhat familiar with the two procedures because they have already had to contract for products and services. Nevertheless, boards may lack the experience needed to decide which approach to use for instructional services. Although IFBs may be useful in certain situations, RFPs will probably be utilized more in contracting for instructional services. Until contracting out instruction becomes more widespread, it is especially important to foster a wide variety of approaches to the practice.

CONTRACT MANAGEMENT UNDER CONTRACTING OUT

As a result of collective bargaining, most school boards understand the concept of contract management. In the la-

TABLE 4.1

INVITATION FOR BID (IFB) VS.
REQUEST FOR PROPOSAL (RFP)

	IFB	RFP
Sealed bids (IFB) or offers (RFP) always opened at a public meeting; response becomes a binding contract; usually award made after bids or offers are agreed without further dialog	Yes	No
Candidates may be eliminated on quality grounds	Yes	Yes
Among qualified candidates, preference given to more qualified candidate even though price is higher	No	Possibly*
Pricing is the main basis of the award	Yes	No
Commonly a follow-up conference for negotiation after bids or offers are received and before award is made	No	Yes
Most commonly used for purchase of commodities	Yes	No
Most commonly used for purchase of professional services	No	Yes
Competition a factor; federal antitrust laws apply	Yes	Yes

*Preference given to a more expensive bidder only if the candidate is sufficiently superior. Award should always be made to the qualified offeror whose proposed services are most advantageous to the contracting government agency.

SOURCE: Reprinted, by permission of the publisher, from John Tepper Marlin, *Contracting Municipal Services: A Guide for Purchase from the Private Sector* (New York: Ronald Press, 1984), p. 72.

bor relations field, it refers to the fact that labor contracts
are not self-executing. Management must designate officials
who understand the contracts, monitor employee and union
adherence to them, confer regularly with union representatives, and maintain adequate records to protect management's interests in case of a dispute and in order to propose
appropriate changes in successor contracts.

Contract management is also essential when services are
contracted out. Designated management officials must
monitor contractor performance, note complaints and
problems, maintain liaison with contractors, and apply
what is learned to negotiations on successor contracts. The
time and resources required to do these things should be
considered a cost that must be offset by savings resulting
from contracting out. Experience with other municipal services indicates that the costs of contract management will
run about 5 to 10 percent of the amount of the contract;
obviously, what would be an acceptable cost will vary from
contract to contract.

It is not feasible to explore the gamut of contract management issues here. Fortunately, there are several useful
publications on the subject, including at least one comprehensive "how-to-do-it" manual that is an invaluable resource.[20] The following discussion, therefore, is intended
only to illustrate how various concerns about contracting
out can be resolved in the contract itself.

Complaint Procedures

An issue that must be resolved under contracting out is
whether the contractor or the school district will handle
complaints. This issue does not arise when a management
support service, such as data processing, is involved, but it
can be very important when the services directly affect students, parents, or others in the community. If complaints
are made to the district, there is a danger of interposing a
level of administration between the contractor and the public. If made to the contractor, there is a danger that the

responsible public officials may not be fully aware of problems associated with contractor performance.

A partial solution is to encourage citizens to express their concerns in whatever way is most convenient for them, but to require that the district be notified of all complaints and their resolution in timely fashion. As in the labor relations field, complaints should be reviewed carefully for significant patterns and for negotiating needed changes in the contract. Furthermore, contract monitoring should include some calls or visits to ensure that the contractor followed up on complaints promptly. Legislative bodies such as school boards play an important role as ombudsmen; contracting out should be handled in a way that does not impair this role. This does not mean, however, that districts can or should simply wait for complaints to be made. Districts can conduct surveys or interviews to ascertain how various parties feel about the services the contractor provides.

As previously noted, one of the objections to contracting out is that it renders public agencies vulnerable to undue pressure from contractors. For example, a municipality might have sold all of its street-cleaning vehicles after contracting out this service. Subsequently, when the city must resume direct service because of contractor failures, the city would be in an untenable position. It could not rush out and purchase a new fleet of vehicles and employ a new staff to use them. Yet the alternative might be to accept undesirable deficiencies or changes by the contractor in midstream, as it were.

Again, the point is not to deny the danger of such an eventuality. Rather it is to emphasize that the danger can be avoided by the way the contract for services is drafted. The contract may provide that the capital equipment be owned by the district or left in place for a certain time after termination. Or it may specify liquidated damages in case of default, with the amounts covering district costs for restoring adequate service. In other cases, the contractor will be using district employees who remain on the district payroll. Again, in drafting the contract, the district should always raise the question of what happens if contract termination becomes necessary. The OEO contracts did not cover termination procedures adequately, and the termination costs were the subject of extensive litigation. Good drafting would have avoided at the outset this litigation.

Low Bid Versus Best Bid

State legislation regulates most elements of contracts for services resulting from competitive bidding. As a result, school districts in some states are required to accept the lowest or "lowest responsible" bid, even though another bid may be preferable when quality of service and/or contractor history are taken into account. Sometimes statutory language is ambiguous and sometimes it is silent on the issue, but the way the issue is resolved has important implications for contracting out.

If a school district must accept the lowest bid, there is an obvious danger that other important criteria will be neglected. Of course, bids are bids to provide something, and the "something" is supposed to be spelled out in the IFB. On the other hand, since it is virtually impossible to specify all the criteria that should be considered, IFBs may omit some that would change the outcome. Indeed, we can cite this as another example of the greater efficiency of the private sector. Private companies are not as restricted as are public agencies in purchasing services; private companies are free to contract for the optimum arrangement, without being restricted arbitrarily by "the lowest price."

Contracting Out and the Improvement of Public Education

The educational reform reports pay no attention to contracting out as a means of improving education. Furthermore, the omission is not explained. It might be due to deliberate rejection of its potential to improve education.

More likely it is due to failure to consider the issue, a failure that might be explained in many ways. Whatever the explanation, what is the future of contracting out in public education?

In my opinion, this question cannot be answered with a high degree of confidence. There are approximately 15,000 school districts in the United States. They differ in size, resources, leadership, regulatory environment, student enrollment, socioeconomic breakdown, political structure, and just about every other dimension that comes to mind. At the same time, a wide variety of developments in the private sector, in other public services, and in the media could conceivably affect interest in and resort to contracting out in education. Under the circumstances, it seems futile to try to quantify the future of contracting out in education.

Three basic considerations, however, suggest a much greater resort to educational contracting out in the next decade. One is that the educational reform movement is not achieving any basic improvements in public education. As this conclusion becomes more widely expressed and accepted, interest in other approaches is likely to grow.

The second critical point is that other efforts to privatize education will continue to encounter massive resistance from all of the major interest groups associated with public education. The National Education Association (NEA), the American Federation of Teachers (AFT), the American Federation of State County and Municipal Employees (AFSCME), the National School Boards Association (NSBA), the American Association of School Administrators (AASA), the National Association of Secondary School Principals (NASSP), the National Association of Elementary School Principals (NAESP)—all are opposed to education vouchers and tuition tax credits. Their opposition, even in conjunction with other organizations opposed to family choice, may not always be successful; the enactment of tuition tax credits in Iowa in 1987 demonstrates that the public education lobby is not always all-powerful. Nevertheless, policies that are supported—or at least not opposed—by important elements of the public education lobby are more likely to materialize than policies that face its united and adamant opposition. As we have seen, school boards and school administrators have good reason to support contracting out as a management option. Union opposition will certainly be a factor, but assuming that such opposition is insuperable is as unrealistic as ignoring it completely.

The basic advantage of contracting out is the fact that it does not require basic changes in the governance structure or the statutory framework of public education. To be sure, certain statutory changes would be very helpful, especially in states in which the statutory framework is not as conducive to the practice as it should be. Nevertheless, contracting out has enormous advantages over other forms of privatization, such as vouchers or tuition tax credits, which require new and highly controversial legislation.

If a reform requires a state law, it will be slower in coming than if school districts can implement it on their own. This is the case with contracting out. Its outcomes may be uncertain, but at least we may be able to find out what they are within a reasonable time.

In the not so long run, public school management may come to view contracting out instruction as a necessity instead of as an option. Those who favor increased public support for education are caught in a dilemma. Clearly, there has been a significant erosion of confidence in public institutions, including public schools, in recent years. This is the major reason why efforts to achieve more financial support for public schools are increasingly tied to "reforms" of one sort or another. As resistance grows to paying more for the same old services, educators show a corresponding tendency to treat cosmetic changes as basic reforms. Nevertheless, claims that public education is undergoing significant reform are becoming increasingly suspect, and public education may be closer to the brink than is commonly realized.[21]

What the public education establishment fears most are vouchers and tuition tax credits—that is, efforts to strengthen private schools. Contracting out instruction may constitute the only serious alternative to a quantum shift in this direction. As a matter of fact, Bendick makes precisely this argument with respect to spending for social welfare services. The American people appear to be willing to spend more for such services, but not through government delivery of them; the same argument may be applicable to education. Public school leaders may, therefore, be forced to reconsider their opposition or indifference to contracting out as a vehicle for educational improvement.

Even where contracting out instruction is legally possible, various restrictions on the practice may severely limit its implementation. The following suggestions are intended to eliminate or ease some of the most harmful restrictions.

1. Long-term contracts should be available, especially when contractors build educational facilities or would have to undergo heavy start-up costs.

2. Contracting out should not be a mandatory subject of bargaining. In negotiations at the local level, districts should seek a union waiver on the right to bargain on contracting out before any particular effort to contract out materializes. When it does, the district should have a plan to deal fairly with employees adversely affected.

3. Districts should be free to accept the best, not necessarily the lowest, competitive bids.

4. Districts should be allowed to dismiss employees on payment of a lump sum, based on their anticipated salary, years of service, and pension status. The lump-sum payments should come from savings generated by contracting out.

5. National and/or regional centers should be established as centers of research, training, and assistance to states and local districts interested in contracting out.

6. School finance should be restructured so that it shows the actual costs of public education and of the various components thereof.

While such suggestions do not cover all the important actions necessary to facilitate contracting out, they would be major steps in the right direction.

5

Educational Choice as a Means to Educational Improvement

In recent years the real or alleged deficiencies of public education have stimulated proposals that would enable parents to choose the school their children will attend. One type of proposal is educational tax credits, more commonly referred to as tuition tax credits. Such proposals call for income tax credits or tax deductions for the expenses of sending children to school. Another type of proposal is for government to provide parents with educational vouchers, redeemable for tuition and perhaps other expenses at a school chosen by the parents. Collectively, tuition tax credits and vouchers are widely known as family choice proposals. Their underlying assumption is that the best way to strengthen parental choice of schools is to strengthen parental ability to pay for education, whether in a public or a private school.[1]

Why should public policy seek to achieve this objective? We can identify at least five major arguments for doing so. I refer to them as the religious rationale, the educational improvement rationale, the civil rights rationale, the tax-payer rationale, and the political rationale. Theoretically, each rationale is or can be independent of the others. That is, acceptance of any one does not imply or require acceptance of any of the others; likewise, rejection of any does not necessarily imply or require rejection of the others. Each rationale can be implemented in some ways that are consistent with the other rationales and in other ways that are not.[2]

The following analysis attempts to explain these important points through an analysis of voucher proposals. One reason is that tuition tax credits and vouchers are based on essentially the same arguments. If an argument is valid for either tax credits or vouchers, it applies (or can be made to apply) to the other. Because each form of family choice can be modified to meet specific objections, the fundamental issue is whether the underlying rationale for either has merit. The focus on vouchers is also based on the fact that the most widely discussed family choice proposals, such as those made by noted economist Milton Friedman, favor vouchers over tuition tax credits.

Some analysts believe that voucher plans are likely to be administered by state education departments whereas tuition tax credits are more likely to be administered by state or federal agencies responsible for tax matters. For this reason they contend that tuition tax credits will require less government regulation of private schools than educational voucher plans. The issue is a debatable one but does not fundamentally affect the following analysis; in my opinion, the latter is as applicable to tuition tax credits as it is to vouchers.

The rest of this chapter and chapter 6 are devoted to the broad issue of vouchers and their potential for educational improvement. Chapter 7 surveys the noneducational arguments for vouchers. Chapter 8 then summarizes my view of the substantive issues and the political prospects for them.

The Educational Improvement
Rationale for Family Choice

The educational improvement rationale for educational vouchers asserts that vouchers are the way to improve education, public and private. This rationale is a relatively recent development. Most analysts agree that publications by Milton Friedman in 1956 and 1962 provided the intellectual basis for it. For this reason, a brief summary of his argument may be a helpful introduction to the issues.

Friedman's argument for educational vouchers was set forth in a chapter of his book *Capitalism and Freedom*.[3] His major argument is that a free enterprise economic system is essential to a democratic political system. As part of this general argument, Friedman contends that, insofar as practical, we should avoid providing goods and services through our political system. Instead he urges that services be provided through our economic system whenever it is feasible to do so.

Turning to education, Friedman first considers whether government should fund it all. He concludes that it should fund elementary and probably most of secondary education because of its "neighborhood effects." Some economists refer to such effects as "positive externalities" or "public goods." These are effects that cannot be provided to A without simultaneously providing a benefit to B. An example is national defense; it is impossible to protect A from invasion without also protecting B from it.

Although A and B both benefit from national defense, neither can be expected to purchase it individually. First, neither could afford it. Second, inasmuch as each benefits if national defense is paid for by others, each has an incentive to be a "free rider." For this reason, we rely on taxes raised through our political system to finance national defense. Similar reasoning led Friedman to accept government support for education albeit up to somewhat lower grade levels than is the practice today.

The view, however, that government should pay for a service does not lead automatically to the conclusion that government should *provide* the service. Government funds medical services through Medicare, but the services are provided mainly by physicians in private practice, not by those who are government employees. The government funds food for the indigent, but the food is made available through the use of food stamps at for-profit supermarkets. The government does not normally operate the grocery stores that redeem food stamps.

Analogously, Friedman outlines several reasons for educational vouchers. First, he regards public education as a huge, unresponsive bureaucracy. He views its lack of responsiveness as the inevitable outcome of its freedom from competition. To Friedman, most dissatisfied parents have only two options. They can enroll their children in private schools, in which case they have to bear the costs in addition to paying taxes to support public schools. Or they can resort to political action, an option Friedman regards as ineffective.

At this point, Friedman contrasts the delivery of educational services to the delivery of services in a market system. In the latter, dissatisfied customers can normally change service providers; for example, if you don't like your attorney, you can change to another. This consumer option forces attorneys to be more responsive to consumers' needs and preferences. Furthermore, in a market system, service providers are constantly under competitive pressures to improve their services. Such pressures do not exist in public education because it operates like a monopoly, although there is a small private sector. To end this monopoly, and to bring the benefits of a market system to education, Friedman proposes that government provide parents with educational vouchers that could be redeemed for cash by whatever school enrolled the children. Although he specifically proposes to make for-profit schools eligible to receive vouchers, Friedman does not elaborate on this issue. He suggests that the amount of the voucher be equivalent to the cost of educating pupils in the public schools and that parents should be free to add to the voucher if they so desired. Although he does not favor stricter government regulation of private schools, Friedman points out that such regulation is always an option if necessary to protect pupils and parents under a voucher system.

In discussing why the voucher idea did not emerge earlier, Friedman suggests two reasons. One is that the technology needed to implement a voucher system was not available in earlier periods. We did not have large-scale government transfer payments to individuals until well into the twentieth century. In his view, new technology, such as computers, created policy opportunities that were not feasible in an earlier era. Also, voucher plans did not emerge earlier because the American people were much more adverse to government assistance in earlier generations. Such assistance was widely perceived as a handout; those accepting it suffered somewhat in public esteem.

In a later publication, Friedman explicitly rejected the idea that education should be compulsory and government financed.[4] Recognizing the absence of public support for this view, he devoted most of his analysis to refuting criticisms of his voucher proposals. In his view, the way to get better education at a lower cost is to make it available through a market system.

Writing about vouchers in 1979, Friedman raised this question: "What reason is there to suppose that alternatives will really arise?" His answer lies at the heart of our discussion:

> The reason is that a market would develop where it does not exist today. Cities, states, and the federal government today spend close to $100 billion a year on elementary and secondary schools. That sum is a third larger than the total amount spent annually in restaurants and bars for food and liquor. The smaller sum surely provides an ample variety of restaurants and bars for people in every class and place. The larger sum, or even a fraction of it, would provide an ample variety of schools. . . .
>
> Many of the new schools would be established by nonprofit groups. Others would be established for profit. There is no way of predicting the ultimate composition of the school industry. That would be determined by competition. The one prediction that can be made is that only those schools that satisfy their customers will survive—just as only those restaurants and bars that satisfy their customers survive. Competition would see to that.[5]

Essentially, Friedman's argument is based on two assumptions. One is that a voucher plan would result in competition between schools for students. The other is that such competition would have positive effects on educational achievement. Our first task is to assess the validity of these assumptions. Such assessment must recognize that "competition" is a matter of degree, not a simple dichotomous alternative to "no competition." Economists have spelled out the conditions of competition, but there are few, if any, situations in which all the conditions exist without limitation or qualification; "pure competition" is the exception, not the rule, even in industries where competition has proved effective. Consequently, we will focus on the conditions required in order for competition to be effective. Then these conditions will be related to the situation likely to prevail in education under a voucher plan. The objective is to assess whether such a plan will result in the kind of competition envisaged by voucher supporters.

The Expansion of Supply and the Mobility of Resources

For competition to exist, it must be easy to expand supply in response to increased demand. Otherwise, increases in demand will be frustrated by supply shortages. Assuming that vouchers increase the demand for education in private schools, how will such schools expand promptly to meet the increased demand?

Regarding physical facilities, increases in the supply of private education could occur in two ways. One is by using any underutilized capacity; the other is by adding to capacity by building new schools.

There do not appear to be any systematic data on the capacity of existing private schools to absorb additional students. The following factors would limit this capacity.

1. Some private schools are already operating at capacity and have waiting lists. Furthermore, these are likely to be the most desirable private schools. Such schools

have shown little or no interest in expansion for decades at least.[6]

2. Most private schools are denominational and may not wish to enroll pupils outside of their own denomination. This is especially likely for those schools, such as Amish or Hebrew ones, that do not proselytize outside of their own faith. Often even Catholic schools accept non-Catholics only out of economic necessity. In brief, religious schools may not be willing to utilize excess capacity by enrolling students with a different religious orientation.

3. Undoubtedly, many private schools have some flexibility regarding enrollments—they may be able to increase class size to some degree. On the other hand, as they do so, they increase the risk of alienating their current clients. First, the latter may have been attracted by the small class size, or at least be willing to accept it, whereas they might withdraw if class size is increased. Furthermore, as enrollments increase, so does the likelihood of enrolling disruptive or difficult pupils who will detract from the educational attractiveness of the school.

4. As students are added to private school classes, the schools become less attractive to teachers. Private schools currently rely heavily on their ability to employ teachers willing to work for substantially lower salaries than public school teachers receive. Superior nonsalary conditions of employment are an important compensating factor in many cases. Increased enrollments weaken this tradeoff, so some private schools may opt for higher fees instead of increased enrollments under a voucher plan.

Thus the ability of private schools to increase enrollments with their existing facilities is highly problematic. What are the prospects for the construction of new private schools?

At best, they are not very promising. School construction is expensive. This is why most private schools are established by religious organizations. These organizations provide a great deal of the required financial support for new school construction. Raising the funds required for freestanding private schools is much more difficult.

Denominational schools are likely to gear capacity to their denominational needs, not to more general demands for better education. In any event, the construction of new nonprofit schools would face some formidable problems. First, funds for construction and possibly land acquisition have to be raised. Nonprofit schools have three sources: donations, retained earnings, or loans. All pose difficult problems of one kind or another.

Potential donors may exist, but the task of identifying and persuading them takes time. Significantly, donations have dwindled as a source of revenue for nonprofit hospitals; in fact, the latter rely overwhelmingly on retained earnings for revenue. Donations to religious organizations may also decline precipitously for a variety of reasons; significantly, a recent study documents a substantial long-term decline in donations to the Catholic church. From 1960 to 1984, contributions to Catholic churches declined from about 2.2 to 1.1 percent of parishioners' income. Although average Catholic income exceeded average Protestant income, the typical American Catholic church contribution was only $320 compared to $580 for the typical Protestant. Furthermore, the decline in Catholic contributions was greatest among the better educated, the more devout, and the more liberal Catholics. The decline is due at least in part to opposition among Catholics to church positions on abortion and premarital sex, but the implications are much broader.[7] As circumstances and social attitudes change, any denomination runs a risk that its doctrines will generate opposition from church members. Such potential opposition adds an element of uncertainty to religious organizations' ability to raise funds for capital construction.

Retained earnings are the excess of revenues over expenses; they would be "the profits" in for-profit enterprise. Efforts to raise funds for capital construction from retained earnings require several years. While increasing the spread between costs and fees might reduce the time required, such increases might also reduce enrollments. They would certainly be contrary to the goal of increasing choice.

The National Association of Independent Schools (NAIS) study provides some data on the issue. The study received financial data from 763 active member schools, 91.6 percent of all active membership schools. Because the coeducational day schools enrolling both elementary and secondary schools are the subgroup most similar to public schools, let me cite the 1984–85 data relating to such schools.

Table 5.1

INDEPENDENT SCHOOL INCOME AND EXPENSES, 1984–85

Total number of coeducational elementary/secondary schools	225
Income exceeded expenses by 5 percent or more	50
Income exceeded expenses by 0.25 to 5.0 percent	83
Income ± 0.25 percent of expenses	40
Expenses exceeded income by less than 5 percent	30
Expenses exceeded income by 5 percent or more	22

SOURCE: National Association of Independent Schools, *NAIS Statistics*, Spring, 1986, p. 7.

The results for 1983–84 were very similar. Thus overall, about 22 percent of the schools in this group showed fairly sizable net income; a much smaller number showed a net loss. Clearly, however, the data do not give much cause for optimism. The NAIS schools tend to be small and much more expensive than most private schools, especially the large number of denominational schools. If only 22 percent of the most affluent private schools show net earnings of 5 percent or more, there is little reason to believe that the vast majority of private schools can utilize net earnings to expand capacity.[8]

A recent study by NAIS raises the possibility that the main beneficiaries of vouchers would be private school teachers, not potential students. The study showed that the average teacher salary in NAIS schools in 1986–87 was $21,043, compared to $25,313 for public school teachers. The comparisons did not include all forms of teacher compensation, such as retirement benefits; had they done so, the compensation gap between public school and NAIS teachers would have been even larger. We should also note that teacher compensation in NAIS schools was substantially higher than in private schools generally. Even so, over 86 percent of the headmasters and trustees in the NAIS survey said they would raise teacher salaries if they "suddenly" had more money.[9] If vouchers are enacted, private school teachers are certain to insist on higher salaries, especially if their school raises fees and/or enrolls more students. For this reason alone, it is unrealistic to estimate transfers on the basis of prevoucher tuition and fees.

Efforts to finance school construction from retained earnings would have to overcome several other practical and ethical problems. Religious leaders might find it difficult to justify higher fees for current constituents in order to enroll later ones. Church members also might not be pleased by the prospect. Furthermore, the competitive position of religious schools could suffer if their fees covered future construction (as distinguished from depreciation). There would also be significant managerial problems. Not everyone is capable of managing the location, planning, financing, and construction of new schools. Note also that nonprofit schools would face difficulty negotiating loans for new construction. An empty school is not strong collateral. Location and zoning might inhibit other uses. Lending institutions would naturally demand a higher return than on a conventional loan for construction. Actually, because nonprofit organizations cannot use equity financing, they usually experience greater difficulty than for-profit

firms in borrowing for construction; if these difficulties are
compounded by reliance on a risky revenue stream, nonprofit schools are likely to pay interest rates above market
rates. If money is lent to construct an office building and
the borrower defaults, the lender presumably has adequate
collateral. If school buildings are not readily converted to
profitable use, the interest rate on the loan has to be higher
to cover the additional risk.[10]

The religious organizations that operate private schools
typically support other service activities: hospitals, senior
citizen programs, feeding the indigent, and so on. Consequently, decisions about the amount of resources to be devoted to education must take account of these other needs.
Suppose that a religious organization is operating an educational program at the break-even point. A voucher plan
might enable the organization to raise tuition and expand
the educational program. The increase in tuition might also
enable the organization to devote more resources to subsidize some of its other activities. In some cases, this latter
course of action will be chosen, at least to some degree.
Here the impact of the voucher plan primarily would be
increased assistance for other denominational activities.

Vouchers and the Number of Educational Suppliers

It can hardly come as a surprise to voucher proponents
that the number of suppliers is a critical factor; after all, the
educational improvement argument rests squarely on the
idea that the existence of only one supplier, or one overwhelmingly dominant supplier, is the basic cause of educational deterioration.

Effective competition requires a large number of suppliers who do not collude with each other in the market and
who are free to act as opportunities for expansion arise.
The number must be large enough so that no combination
of suppliers can affect the price of the service. Again, there
are strong reasons to doubt whether these conditions would
prevail widely under voucher plans.

All observers agree that vouchers are unlikely to facilitate choice in sparsely populated areas. Below a certain population base, per-pupil costs become prohibitive. As population density increases, the number of competing schools may increase also. Obviously, transportation, terrain, and weather will affect the competitive range of most schools. Nevertheless, given just the difficulties mentioned so far (more are forthcoming!), parents are not likely to find several new schools competing for students.

In my own research in recent years, I have encountered companies that had to abandon plans to operate for-profit schools because the cost of establishing new schools was prohibitive. Even purchase of existing schools was not feasible for the same reason. Granted, these decisions not to go into the school business were made in the absence of a voucher plan, but they point to a major obstacle to competition. Note also that as population density increases, so will the operating as well as the construction costs of new schools. Teachers in urban areas must be paid more than teachers in rural areas. Insurance, food, maintenance, and other costs will vary roughly with population density.

Effective competition also requires that buyers and sellers be free to act in response to market conditions; for example, sellers must be free to expand supply promptly in order to meet increased demand. This brings us to the role of state regulation of private schools. The extent of state requirements relating to private school construction is not clear, but both state and local requirements and codes could be major obstacles. Extensive building programs are not likely until legislation is enacted. Legal challenges could delay every aspect of school construction for years.

Where state approval is mandatory, extensive delays before construction can begin are a possibility, especially if the state department officials are not sympathetic to private schools. Note also that state approval is often required for other aspects of private school operations—teachers may have to be certified, school buses must meet state standards, and so on.

Needless to say, strong efforts will be made to tie increased state regulation to any voucher legislation. For this reason, existing regulation is more likely to be favorable to vouchers than postvoucher regulation. If increased regulation of private schools is the political price that must be paid to enact vouchers, some groups that would otherwise support voucher legislation may turn against it. If the legislation is enacted, they may refuse to enroll any voucher students. Voucher opponents will publicize incidents of private school abuse or deficiencies to terminate vouchers or intensify state regulation of private schools. As the possibility of increased regulation already deters some private school leaders from supporting vouchers, state regulation must be seen as a deterrent even where it has not been enacted into law.

In addition to problems emanating from state regulation, local zoning ordinances may also present difficult obstacles to overcome. Such obstacles may or may not be due to opposition to vouchers per se. Significantly, local school boards that have voted to close certain schools and lease the buildings have sometimes refused to lease them to private schools. Although such leases do happen, discontinued public schools are not likely to be widely available for expansion of private schools.

Considered in toto, the delays just discussed will undoubtedly deter some transfers in private schools. The evidence from other fields, such as automobiles, indicates that some consumers who have to wait for their preferred choice simply abandon this choice rather than wait.[11] This situation might happen more often in education than in the purchase of consumer durables. Car buyers waiting for an imported car do not lose a great deal by waiting. In contrast, parents who want to enroll their child in a first grade that has no openings may not be willing to countenance a delay. By the time an opening is available, the parents may be unable to change arrangements made or to complete the arrangements (such as transportation) that have to be made. The parents may have changed their views about the public school or believe that a transfer during the school year would not be in their child's best interests. Finding a convenient car pool during the school year, or in the following year, might not be as easy as it would have been initially. In short, delays in enrollment will probably lead to some losses that would not be made up by replacements.

Competition: Service Dimensions

Competition is most effective when it involves a standardized product or service. The educational implications of this point are so important that it is necessary to elaborate on it briefly.

Consider a consumer who wants to buy a car. The easiest situation to resolve is when two or more dealers offer the same car, equipment, and warranties, but at different prices. Outside of distance factors and dealer reputations for fulfilling warranty obligations, the decision as to which car to buy is easily resolved—the consumer buys the least expensive car.

Suppose, however, the consumer is considering two or more cars that differ in size, comfort, price, warranties, convenience of repair, mileage, and just about every other criterion. In this situation, there may still be some "competition," but it is highly attenuated and may not even be a factor in the final decision. Because of a disability, the consumer may decide to buy the car that is easiest to enter and operate, regardless of all other factors. True, we could say there was "competition" with respect to ease of entry and operation, but the decision to buy would not be based on any comprehensive assessment of value to most car buyers.

Let us now visualize how the principles involved would work in education. Suppose A is a public school and B is a denominational school with the same program, facilities, quality of teaching staff, and so on. Let us say the only two differences in the schools are that B provides religious instruction and that A does a slightly better job of teaching science.

Now let us suppose that parents with full knowledge of these differences use the voucher to send their children to B. This would be a perfectly plausible outcome. Could we say there was "competition" in this case? To do so would certainly create a dilemma for proponents of the educational improvement rationale. The educational improvement rationale does not assert that public schools can or should compete with denominational schools in indoctrinating religious beliefs. Thus there is a question as to whether competition really existed in this situation. If it did, the school that performed second best on secular education criteria won. This would be contrary to the educational improvement rationale for vouchers.

To avoid any confusion here, let me elaborate. Essentially, it is important to distinguish between the different arguments for vouchers. If you accept the religious or the political rationale, then transfers out of public schools for religious reasons are not a problem, regardless of the secular educational consequences. If, however, you support vouchers as a means of improving education on non-denominational criteria, transfers for religious reasons—at least those that result in lower educational achievement—are at least a potentially serious problem.

The basic problem here is that vouchers run a risk that services provided directly by government do not—vouchers may be used for purposes not envisaged or even antithetical to the objectives of the voucher plan. For instance, providing housing vouchers instead of public housing has generally been successful in terms of cost, efficiency, and housing quality. At the same time, it has not generally resulted in increased expenditures for housing; in fact, less than 20 percent of the increased purchasing power made available by housing vouchers actually is spent for housing. Most of the additional purchasing power goes for food, clothing, medical and dental care, and so on.[12] Similar examples can be cited from other types of voucher plans. In short, if the policy is to give the consumers control, it is more difficult to impose taxpayer preferences that the money be spent for a specific purpose, such as educational improvement on secular criteria. The important question is the extent to which parental decisions would weaken the educational improvement rationale. Unfortunately, it is often difficult to determine why parents enroll their children in private schools; frequently the motives are mixed, and even the parents may be hard pressed to assess their influence. In any case, if transfers to private schools are based on private benefits, such transfers will not necessarily be a means to educational improvement. Furthermore, religious motivations will not be the only basis for transfers that are irrelevant to, or even inconsistent with, the educational improvement rationale. Suppose a private school is not as good as the public school, but the former offers day-care services after the regular school day. Because of this service, parents may enroll their child in the private school; this could be a rational course of action, even though it is contrary to the educational improvement rationale. Again, vouchers would not necessarily be used as the policymakers had envisaged.

Competition: Parents as Consumers

Vouchers have sometimes been characterized as the way to restore "consumer sovereignty," that is, as the way to enable educational consumers instead of producers to control the kind and quality of services. Our concern here is whether the conditions under which competition is effective would apply to parents as consumers. Ideally, these conditions include adequate information about the service, knowledge of market conditions (what others are paying and charging for the service), convenience in changing to a better service, and minimal costs of getting the necessary information and making the change. As we shall see, none of these assumptions can be taken for granted.

Private schools, especially at the secondary level, frequently do not offer certain curricula that may be important to parents who would like to transfer their children from a public school. For example, private secondary schools often do not offer vocational-technical programs.[13] Whether a voucher plan would induce private schools to offer such programs is problematical; the outcome will depend on the specifics of the plan, such as the amount of the voucher.

Educational choice has also been criticized on the grounds that individuals often sacrifice long-range interests for short-range benefits; for example, smokers and gamblers often choose the pleasure of immediate gratification to the detriment of their long-range interest in good health. Inasmuch as most of the benefits of education are long-range ones, family choice proposals allegedly place the long-range benefits of education at unacceptably high levels of risk. Indeed, to be realistic, some voucher proposals treat the ideal parents as average ones. Reading their idealized versions of parents, one would never realize that millions of children are the offspring of parents who were not living together at the time of conception or that millions of fathers contribute nothing to the support of their children.

It is also contended that parents cannot evaluate the quality of educational services until after the services are purchased. Choosing a school is more like choosing a career than like choosing a necktie. In the former, some of the most important information about the wisdom of the choice is not available until years after the choice is made. Although the same problem may arise with respect to products, it can usually be resolved by warranties. For example, in buying a car, maintenance costs are an aspect of quality but are not known when a car is purchased. Even so, buyers can factor in the cost of a warranty, so the uncertainty factor is not so critical. Such protection is thought to be impractical in education because we cannot readily fix responsibility for the outcomes. The diagnosis of why a car doesn't run usually clarifies whether the seller or the buyer should bear responsibility for poor performance; the diagnosis of why a student hasn't learned is more likely to be inconclusive. For this reason, parents may lack reliable bases for comparison and choice, thus undermining the market rationale for vouchers. As will be explained in chapter 11, I disagree with this conclusion, but its widespread acceptance is undeniable.

A related argument is that parents may not know or

care about the side effects of their individual decision. For instance, parents may choose private schools on the basis of their exclusivity; the wider social effects of this exclusivity may be undesirable. Market models do not necessarily take into account such side effects—they are not based on all the relevant information concerning choice of school.

Public opinion polls reveal some interesting data relevant to "the parents can't choose" objection to vouchers. As table 5.2 shows, public support for vouchers appears to have increased in recent years; in a 1983 Gallup poll,

Table 5.2

GALLUP POLL ON VOUCHERS, 1970–83

In some nations, the government allots a certain amount of money for each child for his education. The parents can then send the child to any public, parochial, or private school they choose. This is called the "voucher system." Would you like to see such an idea adopted in this country?

	1970	1971	1981	1983
	%	%	%	%
Favor	43	38	43	51
Oppose	46	44	41	38
Don't know	11	18	16	11

SOURCE: Reprinted, by permission of the publisher, from Stanley M. Elam, ed., *The Phi Delta Kappa Gallup Polls of Attitudes Toward Education 1969–1984 A Topical Summary* (Bloomington, IN: Phi Delta Kappa, 1984), p. 30.

51 percent of those polled supported the voucher concept, with 38 percent opposed and 11 percent expressing no preference. The increase in voucher support suggests that "the parents can't choose wisely" objection is losing ground, since it would not be sensible to support vouchers if the objection were deemed valid.

The objection that parents will not be able to choose

schools wisely is sometimes thought to be especially applicable to disadvantaged urban minorities, especially blacks and Hispanics. Table 5.3 provides an interesting bit of evidence on the issue. As the table shows, the proportion of urban school teachers who send their own children to private schools is much higher than for the population as a whole.

Table 5.3

PERCENTAGE OF PUBLIC SCHOOL TEACHERS WHO SEND CHILDREN TO PRIVATE SCHOOLS

	% of Public School Teachers Who Send Children to Private Schools	*Overall % Students in Private Schools*
Albuquerque	30%	14%
Denver-Boulder	22	13
Atlanta	25	14
Memphis	36	21
Nashville	30	16
Austin	25	13
Los Angeles-Long Beach	29	17
San Francisco	28	19
Seattle	23	14

SOURCE: *Education Update*, vol. 9 (Fall, 1986), p. 7. It was not possible to determine the separate responses of black and Hispanic teachers, but Gallup poll data suggest that their responses would probably be even more favorable to private schools than the averages. In any event, the notion that parents can't choose schools wisely is not very popular among the minority parents who supposedly most need protection from their own choices. In fact, a 1988 Gallup poll on the issue showed that the "partisan poor" supported vouchers by a 62 to 17 percent margin, the highest ratio of support among any of the major voting groups in either party.[14]

Table 5.3 also weakens the argument that parents will sacrifice children's long-range interests for short-range benefits. When public school teachers send their own children to private schools, are the teachers sacrificing the long-range interests of their own children for short-range benefits? In view of the moderate economic status of teachers, this is very unlikely. On the contrary, they are undergoing immediate sacrifices for what they perceive to be long-range interests of their children.

The "parents can't choose wisely" argument is also based on the concept of "transaction costs." In this context, they are the costs of acquiring the necessary information about schools. Schools may have to be visited. Conferences with school officials, other parents, and students who have attended the schools being considered might be advisable. Publications by and about the schools, such as fee schedules and conditions of acceptance and expulsion, may have to be reviewed carefully. Even if parental time were the only cost of acquiring the information, it could be a significant deterrent to informal choice.

Yet whether information costs would frequently preclude informed choice is doubtful for several reasons. First of all, it seems unlikely that there would be a large number of choices, desirable as this might be from the standpoint of competition. Needless to say, it is much easier to choose between two or three options than among a much larger number.

Furthermore, school choice is likely to be a better informed one than choice of other professional services. We employ most professional workers for a very limited number of service occasions. The student who goes to school 180 days a year sees a doctor or dentist only a few times annually, perhaps fewer; most children do not break a leg or have teeth extracted frequently. Thus in these services there is relatively little opportunity for parents or students to know the provider before the services are rendered. With schools and teachers, however, the opportunities are more frequent. As Burton A. Weisbrod, a leading authority on the nonprofit sector, points out:

The informational advantage of the seller often disappears rapidly after purchase. This has an important implication for choosing an institutional structure: the private, for-profit market can work quite satisfactorily—rewarding producers effectively—even when sellers have the advantage at first, provided that buyers eventually close the information gap. Buyers can, under these conditions, reward the desired performance.[15]

The notion that parents will not choose schools wisely is also based on the anticipated role of advertising under voucher plans. Opponents assert that vouchers will lead to false and exaggerated advertising about what schools can do for students. The harmful consequences would be much greater than result from false advertising for toothpaste or detergents or gasoline.

In assessing this criticism, it is essential to avoid a double standard of judgment. We must avoid the assumption that parents are adequately informed about the educational performance of their children or the public schools they attend. For instance, public school leaders often complain about comparisons that overlook the selective nature of private schools. They are largely silent, however, about the fact that public schools often manipulate test data in order to present school performance in a favorable way. For example, school districts have raised average test scores by deliberately failing to require low achievers to take the tests. In some cases where state funds are based on average test scores, the practice has been used to secure additional funds.[16] Indeed, it can plausibly be argued that public school officials have misled the public more on this issue than private schools have ever done. The latter are more the beneficiaries than the makers of public attitudes on the issue.

Test data manipulation is hardly the only case of deceptive practice by public schools. In one highly publicized case in the 1970s, parents sued a public school district that had promoted their illiterate child for years.[17] Although the lawsuit was unique, the situation giving rise to it was not;

large urban school districts are about as forthright about their student deficiencies as used car dealers are about "lemons."

Furthermore, public school districts and organizations sponsor an endless stream of news releases and press conferences. These efforts to influence public opinion, usually in the context of larger appropriations for public education, are as biased as advertisements. Whether or not we label these efforts "public relations," "advertising," or "lobbying" is not so important. What is important is the recognition that statements made to generate political and financial support for public schools are not necessarily more accurate than commercial advertising. Indeed, since commercial advertising is or can be regulated in ways that political statements cannot be, the commercial approach might result in greater public sophistication about educational issues. I do not assert this would be the case, but I see no reason to rule it out either.

We must also consider the probability that educational advisory services would emerge if choice of school emerges as a widespread practical issue. Thousands of companies sell advice on investments, plant location, travel, family relationships, legal problems, and so on. A large number of publications are also devoted to giving advice, including advice on choosing a college. Such firms and publications do not flourish in education below the college level because there is a very limited market for them. With vouchers, a much larger market would probably emerge. As a matter of fact, college counseling for high school students is already a small but growing private industry.[18] Some private sector counselors are former high school guidance counselors seeking to capitalize on parent dissatisfaction with public school counseling services.

Furthermore, although some parents would choose schools without any investment of time or effort, their actions might have little or no practical effect on school quality. To appreciate this, consider that many car buyers are indifferent to safety features. The automobile manufacturers, however, have responded to the demands of the activist minority of car buyers concerned about safety. As a result, the car buyers indifferent to safety also enjoy the safety features; buyer indifference to safety does not result in manufacturers' neglect of it. By the same token, the schools are likely to respond to the wishes of activist parents, not the indifferent ones. For instance, suppose some parents prefer a dress code but others are indifferent. Schools can cater simultaneously to both groups of parents only by instituting a dress code. Consequently, even parents indifferent to dress codes may end up enrolling their children in schools that adopt them. In other words, because the more demanding parents are the most likely to transfer if their demands are not met, schools are more likely to meet these demands. As a result, the demanding parents will often achieve benefits in school markets for the indifferent ones.[19]

At the present time, most advertising in education occurs at the level of higher education. At various times throughout the year, both public and private institutions place advertisements in newspapers and in radio/television commercials. One may question why colleges should use taxpayer funds to recruit students, but the practice seems to be well established. Of course, proprietary schools typically advertise, as do other businesses of one kind or another.

At all levels of education, however, advertising tends to be rather genteel. Especially below the college level, denominational schools are under some pressure to avoid criticizing public schools. First, most denominations have members who teach in public schools. Strong criticism of the latter would raise intradenominational problems. Second, most nonprofit schools are the junior partners in an uneasy relationship. Frequently they utilize services provided by public schools: remedial, transportation, diagnostic, and so on. Although vouchers would supposedly foster competition, the rhetoric of public/nonprofit school relationships is a rhetoric of partnership, not of competition. Public school officials are also severely constrained, since any criticism of nonprofit schools, especially denominational ones, would risk severe political retaliation.

Consequently, both public and nonprofit schools are content to treat the private school option largely as a matter of religious preference. To do otherwise poses high risks for each sector.

Suppose, however, for-profit schools enter the picture. For the most part, their appeal has to be based on superior educational performance. "Your children will read better if they attend our school"—that is the type of claim for-profit schools will have to make, and make good on. In other words, the competition will have to be on secular educational grounds. Presumably this is precisely the outcome sought by the educational improvement rationale. Needless to say, "secular" includes not only academic achievement but student attitudes and conduct as well.

Whatever the merits, the argument that parents can't choose wisely appears to be a loser politically. Obviously, private schools would object vigorously to any such conclusion; regardless, telling parents that they cannot distinguish good schools from bad ones is not an attractive political position.

Parent Ability to Choose Schools: A Perspective

For the most part, objections to vouchers relating to parental competence to choose are information issues. In brief, the objections are that vouchers are based upon *caveat emptor*. The concept may be appropriate for products or services that can be evaluated and compared adequately by sight, but it is not deemed appropriate for services rendered long after they are purchased, that are difficult to identify and evaluate, and that affect third parties who are not directly involved in the transactions.

Realistically, however, we do not avoid *caveat emptor* issues by having government provide a service. Instead, the issues simply arise in a different format under different circumstances. True, educational services cannot be evaluated as easily as most products or services. Nevertheless, on this issue, voucher critics are characterized by a double standard of judgment and by failure to recognize the informational improvements likely to emerge under parental choice of school. The double standard is the unstated assumption that parents are well informed about public school performance, or can rely upon school districts to monitor it. This double standard leads to the assumption that government delivery of services is the solution to the informational problems parents would face under voucher plans. Knowing whether we have chosen the right job often depends on information not available when the choice is made. Nevertheless, we do not allow public officials to choose our work because some people choose poorly.

Indisputably, some parents would not choose schools wisely. Just as indisputably, some government decision makers do not choose wisely either, even when their decisions affect large numbers of people. The basic issues are what information is needed for this purpose, and who should generate, disseminate, store, and pay for it. Focus on these issues would be more productive than simplistic arguments over whether or not parents can choose schools wisely.[20]

To say the least, antivoucher groups present inconsistent, not to say suspicious, conclusions on information issues. Parents who can evaluate public schools as voters supposedly cannot evaluate private schools as customers. Advertising in the economic order is characterized by misinformation and bias, whereas advertising in the political order by education lobbies is not. And so on. Realistically, our economic as well as our political system require reliable information to function effectively, but both are often deficient in this regard. In education, the way to overcome these deficiencies may be to provide market incentives for implementing public policy. Such incentives may generate the information that is sadly lacking under public provision of educational services.[21]

Parental inability to choose sometimes may be less of a problem than parental *unwillingness* to choose the better school. Such unwillingness may occur among students or parents who do not regard educational achievement as their highest priority. For example, students, especially at the secondary level, may be reluctant to leave their friends in a public school. If a student is on the football team or is an elected class officer, or is deeply involved in social affairs, his or her opposition to transfer may outweigh parental hopes for educational improvement; as private schools typically provide fewer extracurricular activities than public schools, this may often happen, especially at the secondary level.

Although real enough, the problems of parents as educational consumers do not seem more formidable than they are in other services where parental choice is taken for granted. Every parent will not be a fully informed consumer, determined to maximize educational achievement, but overall, parental choice will probably meet the conditions required for effective competition. Significantly, no individual parent is likely to affect price of private education; furthermore, turnover among parents and the costs to them (especially the time required) of attempting to act in concert on school costs will preclude parental collusion to restrict competition on the demand side.

VOUCHERS AS THE "EXIT" OR "VOICE" ISSUE IN EDUCATION

The voucher issue is only one dimension of a much broader political and intellectual controversy over whether certain services should be provided through our political or our economic system. The controversy is often characterized as a choice between systems providing "exit" or systems providing "voice." Albert O. Hirschman, an internationally renowned economist, who first suggested this terminology in 1970, subsequently stated the distinction as follows:

> . . . social actors who experience developing disorder have available to them two activist reactions and perhaps remedies: exit, or withdrawal from a relationship that

one has built up as a buyer of merchandise or as a member of an organization such as a firm, a family, a political party, or a state; and voice, or the attempt at repairing and perhaps improving the relationship through an effort at communicating one's complaints, grievances, and proposals for improvement. The voice reaction belongs in good part to the political domain, since it has to do with the articulation and channeling of opinion, criticism, and protest. Much of the exit reaction involves the economic realm, as it is precisely the function of the markets for goods, services, and jobs to offer alternatives to consumers, buyers, and employees who are for various reasons dissatisfied with their current transaction partners.[22]

The exit or voice distinction is applicable to a wide range of decisions and situations. Emigration, divorce, changing political parties or religious affiliations, quitting one's job—are all examples of exit. A letter of support (or of opposition) to a government official would be an example of voice, as would be complaining to public authorities about their policies or practices.

Although his publications frequently refer to public education, Hirschman does not categorically oppose vouchers. Nevertheless, he has expressed several reservations about Friedman's strong support for the exit option in education. According to Hirschman:

In the first place, Friedman considers withdrawal or exit as the "direct" way of expressing one's unfavorable view of an organization. A person less well trained in economics might naively suggest that the direct way of expressing views is to express them! Secondly, the decision to voice one's views and efforts to make them prevail are contemptuously referred to by Friedman as a resort to "cumbrous political channels." But what else is the political, and indeed the democratic, process than the digging, the use and hopefully the slow improvement of these very channels?[23]

In education, the issue is whether we could expect schools to be more responsive if a voucher plan was enacted. Hirschman's comment that the political system is inherently not very expeditious hardly conveys the problems of "voice" in school situations. Suppose, for example, that your child is being taught by a tenured teacher who appears to be incompetent. To whom do you voice your objection?

1. The principal, who may respond by saying she did not want the teacher assigned to her school but her hands were tied?
2. The assistant superintendent for personnel who has not insisted on rigorous teacher evaluation because (a) the principals are afraid of the union's reactions and (b) the chances are against being able to fire a teacher unless the written evaluations are clear and specific about his or her deficiencies?
3. The superintendent, just hired by the board?
4. The college at which the teacher received her B.A. degree? Her M.A.?
5. The members of the school board responsible for employing and keeping administrators who did not do their jobs properly? If so, how do you find out which board members were responsible, and what do you do if they have left the board or are not up for reelection for three years?
6. The state board of education that established low standards of teacher certification?
7. The legislature that enacted the tenure law which renders it extremely difficult to fire incompetent teachers? Or if the law was enacted twenty years ago, to whom in the existing legislature, no member of which has introduced legislation to change the tenure law?
8. The governor, perhaps elected with the strong support of teacher unions?

Not surprisingly, just ascertaining who (if anyone) is responsible for a policy or an action can be a difficult, time-consuming task.

It is sometimes thought that parents should express their concerns at school board meetings. For the moment, let us put aside such issues as how often board meetings are held, whether they are held at convenient times and places, and whether sandwiching one's concerns into a school board agenda is an effective way to articulate one's concerns. Since the early 1960s, there has been a massive increase in collective bargaining by teachers. Recent estimates indicate that about three of every four teachers in the United States are employed pursuant to a contract between a board of education and a teacher union.

In many districts teacher unions have tried to negotiate contract language bearing on parental complaints. For example, the following contractual article was proposed by scores of teacher unions in New Jersey:

ARTICLE XVI

COMPLAINT PROCEDURE

A. *Procedural Requirement*

Any complaints regarding a teacher made to any member of the administration by any parent, student, or other person which does or may influence evaluation of a teacher shall be processed according to the procedure outlined below.

B. *Meeting with Principal or Immediate Superior*

The principal or immediate superior shall meet with the teacher to apprise the teacher of the full nature of the complaint and they shall attempt to resolve the matter informally.

C. *Right to Representation*

The teacher shall have the right to be represented by the Association at any meetings or conferences regarding such complaint.

D. *Procedure*
   Step 1.

In the event a complaint is unresolved to the satisfaction of all parties, the teacher may request a conference with the complainant to attempt to resolve the complaint. If the complaint is unresolved as a result of such conference or if no mutually acceptable conference can be agreed on, the complaint shall move to Step 2.

   Step 2.

Any complaint unresolved under Step 1 at the request of the teacher or the complainant shall be reviewed by the building principal or counterpart supervisor in an attempt to resolve the matter to the satisfaction of all parties concerned.

   Step 3.

Any complaint unresolved at Step 2 may be submitted in writing by the complainant or the teacher to the building principal or counterpart supervisor who shall forthwith forward a copy to the superintendent or his designee and the complainant.

   Step 4.

Upon receipt of the written complaint the superintendent or his designee shall confer with all parties. The teacher shall have the right to be present at all meetings of the superintendent or his designee and the complainant.

   Step 5.

If the superintendent or his designee is unable to resolve a complaint to the satisfaction of all parties concerned, at the request of the complainant or the teacher he shall forward the results of his investigation along with his recommendation, in writing, to the Board and a copy to all parties concerned.

   Step 6.

After receipt of the findings and recommendations of the superintendent or his designee, and before action thereon, the Board shall afford the parties the opportunity to meet with the Board and

show cause why the recommendations of the superintendent or his designee should not be followed. Cop-
ies of the action taken by the Board shall be
forwarded to all parties.
Step 7.

Any complaint unresolved under Step 6 may be
submitted by the teacher to the grievance procedure
as set forth in ARTICLE III of this Agreement and
shall commence at Level 3.[24]

Before discussing the proposal, let me explain its gene-
sis. After New Jersey enacted a teacher bargaining law in
1974, the New Jersey Education Association (NJEA) disseminated a model contract to its local affiliates. The clause
just quoted was included in this contract. In other words,
the clause reflects model language prepared by a large state
union for its local affiliates. Having served as a school
board negotiator in six states, I can assure readers that the
proposed clause is by no means the worst from the parents'
point of view.

Obviously, the NJEA proposal would have a devastating impact on parental complaints. First, a requirement
that complaints be put in writing would virtually insure that
no complaints would be received from illiterate parents or
from parents who are ill at ease in using bureaucratic channels or institutional means of redress. In New Jersey, the
numbers of such parents are substantial.

The requirement that the teacher be present at all meetings on the complaint, after it was put in writing, would
probably discourage any further expression of parental concern. One need only contrast the proposed procedure with
the complaint procedures in virtually any large retail store.
I know of none that requires complainants to put their
complaint in writing and present it in the presence of the
employee. On the contrary, retail stores typically try to
make it easier, not more difficult, for patrons to express
their concerns. Furthermore, the fact that the consumer
can exit—take his or her business elsewhere—usually plays
a significant role in retail complaint procedures. Company

reputation is an important asset that often underlies company policy toward customer complaints. Thus on returned merchandise, company policy may be to avoid challenging the customer; the company does not want to antagonize a $1,500-a-year customer over a $100 purchase.

Although the problems associated with voice may be formidable, so may be the problems associated with exit. Supporters of family choice rely on the efficacy of choice (exit) in simple commercial transactions. In practice, however, exit applies to a broad continuum in which the difficulties vary considerably. Emigrating from one's country is a form of exit that is much more daunting than changing one's dry cleaner. Even exit in certain commercial relationships, such as renting a different residence or place of business, can be a very complex and very costly way to solve a problem. We must, therefore, avoid conclusions that ignore the problems associated with either option.

Insofar as exit involves changing schools, there may be significant costs involved. Here I am referring to the costs of actually transferring from school A to school B. There may be schedule or transportation problems. A student may have friends or teachers who are difficult to leave. Membership on an athletic team may be a strong inducement to stay. Although I shall not outline in detail the costs of exit, clearly they can be formidable despite the fact that voucher proponents neglect them.

We must also be careful to avoid confusing the problems of individual parents with those of policymakers on the issue. Because the costs and outcomes of both exit and voice can vary so much, parents have to compare their advantages and disadvantages in a specific context. Nevertheless, for policymakers, the issue is whether a significant number of parents would find the exit option helpful, regardless of whether they exercise it.

Educators rarely compare the responsiveness of local school districts to the responsiveness of companies in a market system. Typically, it is impossible to say whether the absence of complaints in schools is due to parent satisfaction or the absence of expeditious complaint procedures.

After all, most people do not like to complain. They do not want to devote time and energy to the process. The rhetoric of education assumes that parents want "participation" and will avail themselves of Parent-Teachers Association and school board meetings and elections to make their wishes known. The reality is very different, to say the least. Most people do not want participation. They want their institutions to work so that participation is unnecessary. Democratic ideology notwithstanding, political action appeals only to political types, who make up a small minority of the population. When school board elections are held independently of other elections, typically an extremely low percentage of the electorate votes. In larger school districts, the teachers tend to be well organized and dominate the process. Parents outnumber teachers, but it is impractical for the former to act effectively as a group; it is not impractical for teachers to do so.

In the school situation, exit frequently has two critical advantages over voice. First, insofar as voice is directed to a policy, it often cannot be effective without the collaboration of others. With exit, a dissatisfied parent need not rely on such collaboration and can resolve the problem more or less independently. The parent who can exit enjoys a tremendous advantage over one who must organize a community or state campaign to change a policy. Such campaigns themselves may require a new organization that gives rise to various complaints by its members, and the exit/voice issue must be confronted all over again.

Legal actions constitute an interesting variation of the voice option. Parents who sue a school district are not trying to exit but to change its policies. Although some litigation is not over educational policy (for example, suits for breach of contract or tort actions), a great deal is essentially an effort to change district policies by legal instead of political action. Such litigation has increased dramatically in recent years and must be regarded as a challenge to the efficacy of other forms of voice in public education.[25]

Voice is much more effective when an exit option is also

available. For most parents, voice is especially crucial because there is no exit option; paradoxically, however, although the absence of exit renders voice more important, it also lessens the attention school officials pay to voice. The parent who needs expeditious channels of communication to teachers and school officials because there is no exit option faces school officials who may ignore parental concerns for precisely the same reason. This problem has been intensified in recent years as higher and higher proportions of school revenues have been provided by state instead of local governments.

6

Competition Under Voucher Plans

The educational improvement rationale assumes that voucher systems would create markets and that, as a result of competition, the better schools would achieve a growing share of these markets. The inferior schools would have to improve or lose their clientele.

There are two kinds of objections to this rationale. One is that the effects of competition under voucher plans will be bad for children and for our society. Another is that the competition will not happen, and thus its beneficent effects will not happen either. This chapter is devoted to both objections. It should be emphasized, however, that all the arguments for and against vouchers will not be discussed. Chapter 7 discusses various noneducational arguments for vouchers, along with the specific objections they raise. Here our focus is on objections raised by the presence or absence of competition under voucher plans.

Because most objections to vouchers are based on the assumption that competition between schools will in fact

occur, we begin with these objections. Studies have demonstrated that private schools enroll a disproportionate
number of students from the more affluent groups in our
society. Although the numbers vary from place to place,
time to time, and school to school, the generalization is
valid. Voucher critics base several objections on this fact.
One is that a voucher plan will mainly benefit parents who
are economically favored. Another is that low-income parents will not be able to afford private schools even with a
voucher. If vouchers are instituted, private schools will undoubtedly raise their tuition, thus reducing or eliminating
the voucher's usefulness. In addition, the lack of private
schools, especially in inner city areas, the time and expense
of transportation to and from them, and related school
costs will also serve to undermine the utility of vouchers for
less affluent parents.

Voucher opponents also assert that private schools
would avoid low achievers to bolster school reputation. Inasmuch as disadvantaged minorities include a disproportionate number of low achievers, private schools would
tend to avoid both groups. Such an outcome would tend to
stigmatize public schools, with negative consequences for
the morale and incentives for their students, parents, and
teachers. A great deal of this concern is based on opposition to "tracking"—the practice of grouping students according to aptitude or achievement. Sometimes the term is
also applied to grouping students by their educational objectives, such as "the vocational track" or "the college pre-
paratory track." There is concern that vouchers would
encourage tracking, with undesirable effects on the tracks
that imply less aptitude, lower achievement, or less ambitious
educational objectives. Furthermore, diversity within a
school supposedly has positive educational consequences.
That is, while there is nothing wrong in having your tooth
extracted by an all-white or all-black dental team, a good
education arguably requires some interaction with students
from other ethnic and socioeconomic groups.

One other potential negative should be noted. All students, even of the same age and grade level, are not

equally expensive to educate. For example, it usually costs more to educate disabled students than those who are not disabled. Thus even if vouchers are related to parental income, private schools will seek those students who are the least expensive to educate; the others will be ignored or relegated to inferior schools.

In short, the objection to vouchers is that if education is bought and sold on free market principles, we can expect a highly segregated and stratified educational system. Just as the wealthy purchase the more expensive (and presumably better) houses, and segregate themselves accordingly, they will enroll and segregate their children in the more expensive schools. At the other end of the economic spectrum, the poor will be left to struggle with a voucher insufficient to pay for a good private school while being relegated to public schools gravely weakened by the financial, educational, and leadership losses that would result from a voucher system.

Voucher supporters have responded to these objections in various ways. One is to frame voucher proposals in ways intended to alleviate the objections. For example, the amount of the voucher could be related to parental income, thereby providing low-income parents with higher vouchers than middle- or high-income parents. One problem with this type of solution is that it erodes the political support for vouchers from middle- and upper-class parents. A few leading academic supporters of vouchers have proposed that parents be prohibited from adding to the vouchers. Such prohibitions, however, are not likely to be enacted. For one thing, the voucher amounts would have to be very substantial if parents could not add to them. This would probably make the voucher legislation prohibitively expensive and also lead to increased state regulation of voucher schools. Prohibitions against add-ons would also lead to a situation in which parents could spend their income for liquor, cigarettes, casino gambling, whatever—but not to improve their children's education. As prohibitions against add-ons are likely to destroy support from several otherwise supportive constituencies, they are not likely to be included in any voucher legislation that has a realistic chance of enactment. Another legislative approach is to require voucher schools to enroll a certain proportion of children from low-income families and to avoid increased segregation.

In some instances, voucher supporters rely on a different factual or policy analysis to counter these objections. For instance, schools seeking to establish reputations for high achievement will not ordinarily try to enroll low achievers. It does not follow, however, that there will be no competition to enroll the latter and improve their educational achievement. Gourmet restaurants do not compete with McDonalds, but there is plenty of competition at both ends of the restaurant business. Similarly, private schools that specialize in educating low achievers will compete for them, just as other schools compete for high achievers. As a matter of fact, as a result of federal legislation prohibiting discrimination against disabled children, large numbers are enrolled in proprietary schools; the latter compete to enroll them, often across state lines. Thus, while voucher opponents charge that private schools will avoid the difficult-to-educate students, private schools are already educating large numbers of them.[1] Inasmuch as they are doing so with the knowledge, cooperation, and financial support of public school systems, the dumping ground argument appears inconsistent, even hypocritical; the antivoucher forces are not objecting to dumping grounds as long as they are in private schools.

Similarly, voucher proponents assert that vouchers would facilitate, not foster, racial integration. At this time there is no feasible way for inner city black parents who want to spend more for a better education to do so. They cannot afford private schools; enrolling their children in a better public school would require moving to a more affluent neighborhood, which most would find prohibitive. Yet by supplementing the voucher from personal income, these parents could improve their children's education. In other words, vouchers would break the connection between residence and school, making it possible for schools to enroll a more racially diverse student body than if their students are drawn only from the surrounding neighborhood.

The pro-voucher position receives some support from the concern sometimes expressed that vouchers will be used by high-achieving minority students. The concern is that the students who are most needed as role models in inner city schools would be the ones most likely to transfer out of them. Presumably, this would have negative effects on the remaining students.

First, we might ask why this "creaming" objection is not applied to public housing. After all, it could be argued that with housing vouchers, the model tenants would be the first to leave for better housing in safe neighborhoods, thereby leaving other tenants without desirable models to emulate. It would be surprising if any such argument could be used effectively to block housing vouchers; it calls for immediate concrete restrictions on freedom to improve one's situation in exchange for amorphous long-range benefits to others. I see no reason why the restriction should be more persuasive in education.

In fact, comparisons of housing and education policy are instructive. Public housing must rate near the top of anyone's list of dumping grounds. Precisely for this reason some public agencies are turning to housing vouchers as a way to eliminate these dumping grounds, or to prevent the emergence of new ones. That is, instead of providing housing in public facilities, the disadvantaged receive vouchers that enable them to rent private housing. Although housing vouchers have not proved to be an unqualified success, they are perceived to be useful under certain circumstances. Certainly they have not evoked the kind of opposition that is galvanized when educational vouchers are the issue. Why are vouchers viewed as part of the solution to the dumping-ground problem in housing, but a potential cause of the problem in education? In my opinion, political not substantive differences explain the different receptions accorded the policy. A much smaller and thus less influential number of public employees are adversely affected by housing than by education vouchers.

Both supporters and opponents of vouchers appeal to "diversity" in education and pledge to strengthen it. Not surprisingly, "diversity" means different things to these two groups. To private school leaders, "diversity" refers to the importance of schools organized on a religious, cultural, or philosophical basis. Although leaders in both groups praise diversity, they are really applying the same term to different concepts—in fact, contradictory ones. The school diversity envisaged by private school leaders is unlikely to result in the kind of student diversity within classrooms sought in the public schools.

In all likelihood, voucher plans would be more supportive of the private school interpretation of diversity. Objections to vouchers based on a melting-pot concept do not seem strongly persuasive. Middle-class students in public schools usually are not enrolled in the same ones as the disadvantaged minorities. Nor is it likely that they will be as long as public school enrollments are based on residence. In any case, some homogeneity is required to facilitate education. While this is not a popular idea in public education, it is unassailable if not pushed to extremes. If students, parents, and teachers do not share some skills, values, and attitudes, it becomes virtually impossible to operate a school effectively.[2] In fact, the Coleman studies (to be discussed in chapter 7) strongly suggest that the community of values and attitudes in Catholic schools is a major reason for their effectiveness. This community minimizes the resources that must be devoted to conflict resolution and makes it possible to establish educational programs that are not compromised by opposing interest groups.

One additional consideration weakens the objection that vouchers would encourage racial segregation. As Nathan Glazer has pointed out, the availability of private schools has been a critical factor in maintaining residential integration in Manhattan.[3] Families that would have moved out of the city if there was no alternative to its public schools have remained because of the private schools. These schools are racially integrated but less subject to the academic, drug, and discipline problems that characterize many inner city public schools. A great deal of "white flight" might have been obviated if acceptable private schools had been available. In short, vouchers may contribute to residential integration, even while they lead to segregative effects in the schools. Failure to consider, let alone rebut, this argument seriously weakens racial segregation objection to vouchers.

Several additional objections to vouchers, based on the consequences of competition, remain to be considered. Because these objections are intimately related to the role of schools for profit, they will be discussed together. At this point, however, let me conclude by pointing out that voucher supporters see only the good effects of competition; opponents see only their negative effects. The actual outcome will undoubtedly lie between these extremes—but precisely where will depend on the specifics of the voucher plans adopted. The objections should be viewed as matters to be considered and perhaps monitored; they should not be regarded as insuperable, regardless of the specifics of a plan and the circumstances of its application.

NONPROFIT STATUS AND COMPETITION UNDER VOUCHER PLANS

We turn next to concerns about voucher plans based on the possible absence of competition instead of on its possible consequences. The educational improvement rationale is obviously based on an analogy to for-profit enterprise in competitive markets. What the analogy consistently overlooks, however, is that private schools are predominantly denominational and overwhelmingly nonprofit; nonprofit schools probably enroll more than 98 percent of total enrollments in private schools.[4]

The nonprofit status of most private schools raises a number of basic questions:

1. To what extent, if any, will the benefits of competition in the for-profit sector emerge from a voucher system in which nonprofit schools are overwhelmingly dominant? Indeed, in some voucher legislation, only nonprofit schools are eligible to accept voucher students.
2. What policy justification for nonprofit status is applicable to private schools that compete effectively in education markets? To phrase the question somewhat differently, if nonprofit schools can compete successfully, why should they need or have nonprofit status?
3. If competition in education markets is desirable, as is assumed by the educational improvement rationale for vouchers, is there any reason to exclude for-profit schools from the competition, for example, by rendering them ineligible to accept voucher students?
4. How can competition between nonprofit and for-profit schools avoid the unfair competition that results from tax exemptions and subsidies going to the former?
5. What public policies, if any, are needed to ensure fair competition between nonprofit and for-profit schools?

Obviously, these questions are interrelated.

Paradoxically, the first one has not been raised by either supporters or opponents of vouchers. I say "paradoxically" because it seems counterintuitive to rely on nonprofit organizations to act like for-profit ones, at least without any questions or reservations. Furthermore, nonprofit schools are governed by their nonprofit status as well as their status as educational institutions. To focus exclusively on their educational role would overlook several critical factors that will affect their future, including their role under voucher plans.

The Role of Nonprofit Organizations

A nonprofit organization is defined as one that is legally prohibited from distributing any net earnings to individuals who exercise control over the organization. That is, nonprofits are differentiated from for-profit organizations by the "nondistribution constraint."[5] If the revenues of non-profit organizations exceed their expenses, they can expand their services or lower their prices, but they cannot legally distribute such earnings to officers, directors, or other individuals who control the organization. Later we shall have occasion to consider various efforts to avoid the non-distribution constraint.

In recent years the increased size of the nonprofit sector has led policymakers, business groups, and scholars to devote more attention to it.[6] It turns out that the number of organizations deemed tax exempt by the Internal Revenue Service (IRS) increased from 309,000 in 1967 to almost 900,000 by 1984. The number of tax-deductible "charitable" nonprofits increased from 138,000 in 1969 to 366,000 in 1985. (These are nonprofit organizations that receive a variety of subsidies and privileges, including the deductability of contributions to them.)

The total revenues of nonprofit organizations increased from $115 billion in 1975 to $314 billion in 1983. The IRS annually approved about 5,000 requests for tax-exempt status through 1963; by 1984 over 44,000 such requests were approved annually. The assets of nonprofit organizations (land, reproducible consumer goods, semidurables, and financial assets) are almost 50 percent of the assets of the federal government and almost 15 percent of all governmental assets in the United States.

Although estimates vary widely, it appears that the nonprofit sector included about 9 million full-time employees in 1976. In addition, nonprofit organizations utilize an enormous amount of volunteer labor, adding perhaps as much as 6 percent of the employed labor force.

The size of the nonprofit sector is likely to have important repercussions for educational policy. Currently, law and policy lack a unified, coherent view of the role to be played by the nonprofit sector. Because of its growth and size, however, this omission is not likely to continue. Questions about what nonprofits do, what they should do, their sources of support, how they should be regulated, and what reporting requirements should be imposed on them are increasingly coming to the fore in legislative and academic forums. Nonprofit organizations are largely in service industries, and education is the second largest component in the nonprofit economy. As our nation resolves the issues relating to the nonprofit sector, it is virtually certain that private schools will be greatly affected. While educators are apt to think of regulation in terms of educational issues, such as curriculum, class size, or teacher qualifications, regulation resulting from nonprofit status may also impact private schools in several important ways.

It is not feasible here to examine in detail the structure of the nonprofit economy. Instead, I shall summarize briefly the major categories of nonprofit organizations. Inasmuch as each category includes some private schools, the categories will be discussed in the school context.

Nonprofit Schools as a Response to Unsatisfied Demand for Educational Services

In the colonial period, schools were usually established first by private citizens. This meant that the family had to bear the costs of providing educational services. When citizens who supported formal education were able to persuade a legislative majority to finance public education, it was logical for them to shift the cost of education from their private resources to public funds. Needless to say, any such change had to be characterized in more idealistic terms, and so it was. Education was deemed to benefit everyone, so it deserved public support. Such support solves the "free rider" problem; that is, the fact that some of the beneficiaries of education are not paying for it.

Public support also makes possible a higher level of support, since the costs are shared by a much larger group—including, of course, the otherwise unwilling taxpayer.[7] Nevertheless, the level of public support is not geared to the most avid supporter but rather to the preferences of a hypothetical "median voter." If support were lower, political leaders would lose out to advocates of higher spending for education. If it were higher, they would lose out to advocates of less spending. For this reason, the actual level of support is the level that satisfies the wishes of the median voter.[8]

Obviously, this level does not meet the demands of parents who want a higher level of public provision. Insofar as they can, these dissatisfied parents will meet their needs through private schools, which provide the public good but also maximize the private benefits (such as religious indoctrination). Inasmuch as the dissatisfied citizen/consumers are paying for the school themselves, they can exercise more control over the service and can pay less attention to the benefits going to those who do not pay.

Some additional points should be noted. Resort to the private sector will be affected primarily by the demand heterogeneity of the population in a given governmental unit and the income levels of consumers/taxpayers. Although heterogeneity in the population with respect to income, religion, location, lifestyle, occupation, and so on cannot be equated with heterogeneity of demand for public goods, there is certainly a strong correlation between the two. Thus there is less dissatisfaction with public schools over religious issues and less resort to private schools in Japan, where the population is relatively homogeneous from a religious point of view, than in the United States, where religious heterogeneity is common.

Level of income is a critical variable. As income levels increase, dissatisfied consumer/taxpayers are better able to support nongovernmental provision of the service. Indeed, voucher proponents emphasize the alleged superiority of vouchers over tuition tax credits as a means of providing less affluent parents a way to exercise effective choice.

These observations may help to explain resort to the private sector; they do not, however, explain why the alternative to public provision should be nonprofit schools. One reason is the nature of consumer/taxpayer dissatisfaction. If based, for example, on religious reasons, it would be difficult to use for-profit organizations to provide the service.

Until the 1970s, most private schools were Catholic schools that relied heavily on the contributed services of teachers in religious orders. Such teachers would not have been available to for-profit schools, so the latter would not have been able to survive except for parents at a very high income level.

Nonprofit Schools as Trustworthy Producers: The Contract Failure Argument

Another view of nonprofit organizations is that they are a response to "contract failure"—that is, the inability of donors or purchasers to monitor the goods or services they have paid for. Ordinarily, purchasers are also the recipients of whatever they purchase: groceries, dry cleaning, automobiles, haircuts, and so on. Suppose, however, you want to help survivors of the earthquakes in Armenia. If you donate money or goods, you have no practical way to make sure your gift actually helped anyone; going there would be too expensive. Theoretically, a profit-making organization could sell assistance for a certain price, but the risk that funds would be siphoned off to increase profits would discourage prospective purchasers of such assistance. In contrast, nonprofit organizations have no incentive—or less incentive—to cheat, since the distribution constraint supposedly precludes profiteering. For this reason nonprofit organizations sometimes emerge as the solution to contract failure.

Distance is not the only factor that may weaken the ability of donors or purchasers to monitor performance. Whenever the person who pays is not the direct recipient of the services, there is a possibility of contract failure. Obviously, this is the normal situation in education, so it is not surprising that parents' ability to monitor the educational services received by their children is a basic issue in the controversy over vouchers.

Interestingly enough, some applications of the contract failure argument have been criticized for their allegedly weak empirical foundation. For example, it is often doubtful whether purchasers know which organizations are for profit and which are not. (I have met college students who did not know whether their secondary school was for profit or nonprofit.) Perhaps the most important issue is whether consumers really care. Monopolies aside, consumers are likely to be more interested in price and quality, not how much profit management is making.

Most important, nonprofit status does not solve the most basic problems of contract failure. Nonprofit management may be scrupulously honest but also incompetent. I believe that incompetence is a much more pervasive problem than dishonesty. Whether it is or not, nonprofit status cannot be viewed as tantamount to quality control.

Nonprofit Organizations as the Result of "Backward Integration"

Citizens dissatisfied with a public service may decide to purchase the service in the private sector. Under some circumstances, however, they may unite to provide the service themselves. Inasmuch as their interest lies in the service, not in making a profit, the nondistribution constraint presents no problem. If income exceeds revenues, the fees charged can be lowered or the quality increased.

Private clubs often fit this pattern. For example, a group of tennis players may be dissatisfied with the public courts. By starting their own club, the players can control location, membership, amenities, and availability; were they to purchase time on courts operated for profit, they would have less control over these matters.

This process has been referred to as backward integration because it reflects integration from the consumer back to the process of production. Although some private schools were established this way, ordinarily they do not continue in this mode for long. Changing conditions and parent turnover lead to a loss of control by parents, especially since the parental time required for school governance is often prohibitive. The parents who follow the founders often do not have the interest and the drive that led their predecessors to establish the school.

Nonprofit Status in Theory and Practice

In considering the implications of private schools' nonprofit status, we must recognize that the differences between for-profit and nonprofit organizations are often not as sharp in practice as my discussion might suggest. In many fields, the distinction has been diminishing in importance. Because the reasons are also applicable to private schools, let us review them briefly.

1. The revenues of certain kinds of nonprofit organizations, such as schools and hospitals, have come increasingly from fees for services. Consequently, these nonprofit organizations raise most of their capital through retained earnings and by borrowing. This is an important change from an earlier time when they raised most of their capital from donations and government grants.

2. Nonprofit organizations, including schools, are subject to economic pressures even if they are not required to show profits.

3. Although nonprofit organizations do not accumulate profits in a legal sense, they do so in an accounting sense. To survive even without expansion, nonprofit organizations must have revenues to cover the costs of renovation and capital equipment. For this reason, nonprofit organizations try to accumulate surpluses that are used for some of the same purposes as for-profit organizations, such as expansion or renovation of capital facilities.

4. Organizational structure is not a guide to individual motivation and conduct. "For profit" and "nonprofit" are legal terms not necessarily indicative of anyone's attitude toward charitable service or making money. A teacher in a Catholic school is not necessarily motivated by Christian charity; the job may be the best one available. Although efforts have been made to identify group differences in values, personality, and behavior among graduate students

who enter for-profit and not-for-profit sectors, the evidence of actual differences is rather weak. Aside from the fact that the group differences were not always more flattering to those entering the nonprofit sector, it is doubtful whether they would emerge or be as pronounced in education. Even if there were some group differences, conclusions about individuals based solely on their sector of affiliation would not be justified.

5. Along with a tendency to overemphasize the service motivations of employees in not-for-profit firms, there is a tendency to overstate the profit motivations among employees of for-profit firms. For-profit companies give money, products, and services to universities, to charities, to civic, religious, and cultural institutions, and otherwise conduct their affairs without trying to squeeze the last penny from every transaction. Such activities often characterize the personal as well as the corporate activities of individuals employed by such firms. Actually, the extent to which for-profit companies should allocate resources to activities that are not clearly intended to enhance the long-range profitability of the company is a matter of dispute. Ironically, while some observers assume that corporate managers care only about maximizing profits, these same managers are often criticized for not doing just that.

6. Both for-profit and nonprofit firms contract and interact with each other in ways that blur the distinction. For-profit organizations often set up nonprofit foundations that receive a substantial income from corporate revenues. In other cases, corporations contract with nonprofit organizations for services. Similarly, nonprofit organizations, such as universities, hospitals, and schools, frequently contract with for-profit firms for goods or services.

7. The legal limitations on nonprofit companies vary widely from state to state. In some states a tax exemption is the only criterion that distinguishes them from for-profit organizations.

8. Nonprofit organizations use a variety of techniques and legal mechanisms to evade the legal restrictions against the distribution of "profits" to management. Pension plans

can build a huge management equity. Managerial residences, travel, club expenses, and other perquisites can be paid as organizational expenses. In some ways it is easier to pay managers more in the nonprofit sector; they do not have to be concerned about shareholders perusing the annual report to find out why the return on their investment is so low. The revelations in 1987 of the salaries and benefits paid in some television ministries provide a case in point.

9. In some instances for-profit firms build and operate municipal facilities under long-term agreements. The facilities are bought by the municipality (thereby becoming tax free) and then leased back to the firm, which manages them for profit. This approach to capital construction has not been used often in education, but as noted in chapter 3, it may be in the future.

On some issues, the lack of data constitutes a major obstacle to sectoral comparisons and analysis. To illustrate, consider the important question of whether a voucher system will lead to an increase or to a decrease in private support for education. Theoretically, either outcome is possible. The reason it might foster an increase is that under the present system, it is usually not feasible for parents to devote an increase in disposable income to education. If a parent receives a salary increase (e.g., $100 a month), the parent can spend it for better food, better clothing, a better automobile, a better vacation, or for many other amenities. It would, however, be impractical to try to buy a better education with the salary increase.

Under a voucher plan, however, buying a better education would arguably be a practical outcome. Parents who could afford $2,500 a year to send their children to private school could do so by adding to a voucher from personal funds. There could be a range of schools, catering to the range of parents willing to supplement vouchers from personal funds. Thus, despite the concerns of voucher opponents, vouchers might lead to increases in total spending for education—an outcome voucher opponents presumably support.

It is also possible that vouchers could result in less personal and total spending for education. In some fields, such as the arts, government spending sometimes has the effect of "crowding out" private spending for the same purposes. Obviously, if a voucher merely replaced parental funds, the dollar spent by government would not add to educational spending but would simply rearrange the sources of it. Nonprofit schools might simply replace parental funds with educational vouchers. As this happens, schools might become more oriented to government regulators than to parents. There is some evidence that this is what happened after the enactment of a voucher plan in British Columbia.[9]

Another factor complicating sectoral analysis is that the functions of nonprofit organizations often change over time. This is especially obvious in the case of higher education. Many private institutions were founded to train leaders of a particular religion. Over time some of these institutions, such as Harvard, became nonsectarian, emphasizing different objectives than those motivating their founders. Similarly, the objectives of nonprofit schools below the college level can and do change from time to time.

Even apart from the foregoing complexities of analysis, it is open to question whether a voucher system utilizing only nonprofit schools, or an overwhelming preponderance of them, can achieve the benefits of competition in the for-profit sector. Granted, the ideal conditions for competition seldom exist, even in the for-profit sector; the issue is one of degree, not whether competition would exist at all under a voucher plan dominated by nonprofit schools. Nevertheless, the persistent neglect of the issue is cause for concern. To cite just one reason, some voucher proposals exclude schools for profit from eligibility to participate in voucher programs. Inasmuch as schools for profit are a minuscule lobby, especially compared to denominational nonprofit schools, the exclusion of for-profit schools from voucher programs does not encounter significant political opposition. Nonetheless, the exclusion is certain to weaken the possibility that vouchers would result in competition leading to educational improvement. If one supports vouchers for other reasons, neglect of this sectoral issue may not seem important, but it is critical if educational improvement is the objective.

Service Differentiation

In education, one often encounters the view that it is important "to meet the needs and interests of pupils." However this is interpreted, implementing the concept requires differentiated services. Both evidence and theory support the conclusion that for-profit schools would provide such differentiation more effectively than nonprofit schools. For-profit companies are constantly searching for markets that can be used as profit centers. Studies of three-sector industries show rather conclusively that the services provided by public and nonprofit organizations tend to be very similar, whereas those provided by the for-profit sector tend to be much more varied. Book publishing, hospitals, and employment agencies illustrate this point.[10]

The greater service differentiation in the for-profit sector has important implications for vouchers. Nonprofit schools do not exist to educate anyone who comes down the pike; they tend to enroll a certain constituency. Although each for-profit school may also have a distinctive constituency, schools to serve specialized groups are more likely to be established in the for-profit sector. The substantial increase in for-profit organizations serving the disabled is a case in point.

Implications of the Labor-intensive Nature of Education

The conventional efforts to improve education focus on such means as reducing class size, adding resources, training teachers differently, providing student incentives, or rearranging human resources in one way or another. Unfortunately, the record of increased productivity in other fields strongly suggests that such approaches are very limited in what they can do to improve productivity. Outside of education, productivity improvements rely heavily on improving technology: agricultural machinery, medical instruments, new drugs, computers, word processors, jet airplanes, and so on. As the amount of capital equipment per worker increases, workers become more productive. Industries with a low ratio of capital equipment per worker tend to be less efficient. Because they are less efficient, they tend to require more workers to maintain a given level of services; the more workers needed, the more difficult it is to provide them with a high level of compensation.

What conditions encourage the development and introduction of better technology, and how can these conditions be introduced into education? The evidence is overwhelming that for-profit enterprise is quicker to develop and/or use technology than either the public or the nonprofit sector. As critical as the issue is, however, educational policymakers pay virtually no attention to it. When they do, the results are usually much worse than if the issue had been ignored. Let me cite just one example.

As we have seen, California law provides that at least 55 percent of the operating budget of unified school districts must be devoted to teacher salaries.[11] In other words, no matter how much the district could improve education by allocating more resources to technology or paraprofessionals or whatever, teachers must receive at least 55 percent of the expenditures. Needless to say, it would be ridiculous for a business firm to restrict itself this way. If a firm can reduce its labor costs by introducing technology, it does so. That is how companies increase their productivity. It would not make sense for a company or a hospital or law firm to impose a minimum budget allocation to any factor or production. As a matter of fact, if there is to be legislation on the issue, it would be more sensible to impose a *limit* on labor costs—that teacher salaries cannot *exceed* 55 percent of the district budget. This might force districts to be more receptive to improved technology than to inefficiencies in its expenditures.

For several years, educational and political leaders have embraced the idea that the teaching profession should be "restructured." In practice, such restructuring turns out to be giving teachers opportunities to observe other teachers, making paraprofessionals available to teachers, providing teachers with offices, or authorizing teachers to purchase instructional materials. These efforts assume that restructuring can be achieved by legislation or certification procedures or collective bargaining. Such approaches are consistently unproductive because they overlook the role of technological change as a condition precedent to changes in personnel structure. In medicine, there are physicians, nurses, therapists, X-ray technicians, dietitians, pharmacists, and a host of other specializations. Without the technology, however, we would still be using the Hippocratic personnel structure.

I do not assert that personnel restructuring apart from technological change is always futile. Such restructuring at best, however, is not likely to achieve major gains in educational productivity. The basic issue is not how to restructure education. It is how can we foster the development of an educational technology which will lead to a more efficient personnel structure? On this issue at least, for-profit schools unquestionably offer much more promise than public or nonprofit ones. The tendency of public school managers to overspend on immediate benefits for public employees, and to underinvest in capital equipment as well as research and development, is beyond dispute; I see no reason to expect any change in the matter. For several reasons, especially the nondistribution constraint and lack of access to equity capital, nonprofit organizations are also less likely than for-profit ones to invest in new technology.

If this analysis is correct, and I believe it is supported by a wealth of evidence, the overwhelming predominance of nonprofit schools raises serious doubts about the likelihood that a voucher system will lead to educational improvement. Granted, this observation does not invalidate the other rationales for voucher systems, but it poses a critical issue for the educational improvement rationale. The predominance of nonprofit schools would not be a major problem if voucher legislation allowed schools for profit to participate in voucher programs. Actually, the exclusion of schools for profit is more prevalent than their inclusion in proposed voucher programs. Such exclusion clearly weakens the possibility that educational vouchers would foster changes in educational technology and a restructuring of the teaching profession.

Lessons from the Health Care Industry

Recent developments in health care support the view that for-profit organizations should be allowed to participate in educational voucher plans. While developments in other fields may not be directly applicable to education, they should be considered. Health care is our largest industry in which public, nonprofit, and for-profit organizations have achieved a significant market share. Ignoring this evidence would be as undesirable as uncritical application of it to education.

In 1982 for-profit hospital chains owned 10 percent of the hospitals in the United States and managed another 4 percent. In addition, another 5 percent of American hospitals were independent proprietary hospitals (not owned by a company owning three or more hospitals). From 1976 to 1982 the number of for-profit hospitals owned or managed by hospital chains increased from 533 to 1,040, despite the fact that the total number of hospitals in the United States declined slightly in this period. Thus by 1982 approximately 19 percent of American hospitals were for profit. This increase is remarkable in view of the fact that some of the largest for-profit hospital chains did not even exist until the 1970s.[12]

The hospital chains have expanded rapidly mainly by acquisitions from all sectors: government, nonprofit, and for profit. In addition to the problems of financing the acquisitions, the hospital chains have had to overcome several obstacles that are similar to those that would be present in school situations. One is the attitude that there is something reprehensible about making money off the sick. Another is the fear that hospital chains would serve only the affluent, leaving the poor worse off than before, or that the drive for profits would result in inferior levels of health care. Over time these fears and attitudes have diminished, partly as a result of specific agreements that address the problems; in fact, in recent years the initiatives for acquisition have often come from government or nonprofit hospitals rather than the for-profit chains.

Actually, for-profit enterprise plays a prominent if not a dominant role in virtually every service associated with health care. In addition to the fee-for-service orientation of physicians, the percentage of hospitals (15) that are for profit is higher than the percentage of schools (10) that are nonprofit. Ambulatory service centers, nursing homes, and dialysis centers are predominately for profit, as are primary care or urgent care centers. In addition, for-profit companies play an important and increasing role in cardiac rehabilitation, physical rehabilitation, radiology, hospice care, birthing centers, and diagnostic imaging, to mention just a few areas.[13]

This brief overview suggests several points of major interest to education. One is that negative attitudes toward education for profit are not necessarily immutable. If providers of health care can overcome opposition to "making money off the sick," educational providers should be able to overcome opposition to "making money off children."

Medical care experience also highlights an important difference in the potential benefits of service for profit. For-profit companies often operate at lower cost without any service implications. For example, if a for-profit operator can hire equally qualified employees at lower salaries, it can achieve savings without any quality reduction. On the other hand, some potential benefits have direct implications for the quality of service; for example, because they operate on a larger scale, for-profit hospitals can purchase and use expensive equipment not available in small public or nonprofit hospitals.

Of course, large public or nonprofit hospitals might also be able to buy and use the equipment efficiently. The point is, however, that hospitals operated for profit are more likely to be organized and operated in a way that enables them to take advantage of efficiencies of scale. Hospitals that are owned nationally are more likely to provide services that require expensive equipment and that must serve larger than local markets to be viable than are locally based public or nonprofit hospitals. Also note that equipment that cannot be used efficiently is not likely to be invented. In other words, the larger scale of for-profit hospitals fosters technological improvements that would be impractical in a cottage industry.

In health services, nonprofit providers have been the main challengers to the emergence of for-profit enterprise. For-profit hospitals are not ordinarily viewed as a "threat" to government hospitals. In specific situations, the establishment or expansion of a for-profit hospital may adversely affect the economic viability of either a public or nonprofit hospital, but public hospitals do not constitute a united lobby in opposition to for-profit ones. One reason is that for-profit hospitals often offer physicians financial and professional incentives that are not available in government or nonprofit hospitals. Another is that public officials as well as the trustees of nonprofit hospitals are concerned about the costs of medical care and are inclined to consider alternatives to the existing system.

The health care experience also highlights the importance of the motivations underlying objections to service delivery by for-profit organizations. For instance, when access to health care was a genuine concern in a proposed acquisition by a hospital chain, contractual arrangements that allayed the concern usually could be worked out. This would not have been possible if the concern had been merely an excuse for the opposition. Whether access to education is a genuine concern or merely another excuse for opposition remains to be seen. If the former, solutions can often be negotiated; if the latter, they cannot be.

The Exploitation of Children for Profit

The discussion thus far has raised some concerns about the anticipated benefits of competition between nonprofit schools. It has also suggested that if voucher plans are enacted to facilitate educational improvement, schools for profit should be allowed to participate in the plans. Some might object that for-profit schools would take advantage of students to maximize profits. This objection has not been widely raised because of the tacit assumption that for-profit schools would not be eligible to participate in voucher plans; if medical experience is relevant, however, the assumption would not hold and the objection would be inevitable. Indeed, its relevance is heightened but not necessarily dependent on a large-scale increase in schools for profit.

To some extent, the objection ignores business realities. Successful businesses are alert to opportunities to cut costs, but they do not systematically take advantage of customers at every short-range opportunity. Indeed, most successful companies are very much concerned about retaining customers. To this end, they absorb a variety of costs that actually should be borne by customers; for example, policies on returned items are not based upon *caveat emptor* but on the importance of a satisfied customer over a long period of time.

This is not to deny that in some instances, for-profit schools will try to use unethical means to maximize profits. On this issue, however, it is vitally important to heed my initial warning about a double standard of judgment. As I pointed out elsewhere, public school teachers on strike have frequently:

- Made pupil records inaccessible so substitutes cannot teach effectively.
- Told pupils not to attend school if their teachers were on strike. This, of course, is encouraging pupils to violate the compulsory attendance laws in order to increase the effectiveness of the strike.
- Refused to give credit for student work performed during the strike in some districts, and threatened to do so in others.
- Utilized children on picket lines with picket signs supporting teachers, in order to generate public support.

- Used the children of teachers and others to enter schools during a strike to lead student walkouts and student efforts to disrupt and discredit school operations during the strikes.
- Discussed actual or threatened strikes in classes, where it was not relevant to the curriculum, in ways calculated to gain student and parental support.
- Created fears among students that their opposition to a teacher strike, or even their refusal to support it, could lead to reprisals against the students.[14]

These actions are simply the most visible ways that public school teachers exploit pupils for their own welfare. The most harmful ways are to be found in the legislation, such as the excessive duration of compulsory education, which is ostensibly designed to protect young people but in fact benefits the service providers at the children's expense. In fact, all three sectors (public, private nonprofit, and private for profit) have exploitation problems; in my opinion, none has solved them more effectively than the others. The basic issue is how the form of organization influences conduct. Would the same hospital administrator be more likely to take advantage of a patient in a for-profit than a nonprofit hospital? Would the teacher or principal who emphasizes student welfare in a public school or a nonprofit school subordinate such welfare in a for-profit school? These are rather broad questions, which are answered in more detail in chapter 11. At this point, however, let me comment briefly on relationships between sectoral status and ethical conduct.

First of all, there is an existing for-profit sector in education. It is much larger than is generally realized because our procedures for estimating educational expenditures substantially understate its size.[15] Because this point is relevant to several issues in this book, let me explain it briefly.

Data on expenditures for education are generated by local school districts according to accounting procedures established by state governments. The data are then sent on by the state departments of education to the Center for Statistics, an agency of the U.S. Department of Education.

Consider a high school student taking Spanish. The students are counted, as are the teachers. Our expenditures for education include the salaries for these teachers. Let us suppose, however, that instead of being enrolled in Spanish courses in public schools, the same students were paying private tutors for Spanish lessons. In the latter case, students, teachers, and expenditures would not show up in federal statistics on the costs of education.

In other words, if we consider the subject instead of the source of payment, total spending by school districts, states, and federal agencies understates total educational spending for elementary and secondary school pupils. This is true even if the estimate is restricted to subjects that would be counted if offered in an elementary or secondary school. For example, computer education is counted if taken in high school, but it is not counted if taken at a summer camp. Music is counted if studied in school, but music lessons outside of school are not counted. And so on.

Obviously, our nation is spending a great deal more for education than is suggested by U.S. Department of Education statistics on the issue. The point to be emphasized here, however, is different. It makes little sense to debate how educators for profit would act while ignoring how they do act. After all, we are not talking about minuscule expenditures. Minimally, the for-profit education sector runs into billions already. Nevertheless, there is no public outcry over its ethical or professional standards; the issue seems to be dormant. This is not to say that instances of unethical conduct in this sector are unknown; they do arise, and no doubt will in the future. The issue, however, is whether this sector reveals such persistent patterns of undesirable conduct that it should be prohibited. The answer seems to be clearly in the negative; trade schools aside, increased regulation of education for profit does not seem to be an active issue in any state.

As is widely recognized, the issue of whether doctor profits will take precedence over patient welfare has emerged in health care. If anything, this question is more urgent there than it is in education; at least, most people would agree that consumer protection is more urgent in life or death than in educational decisions. Nevertheless, there is no persuasive evidence that patient interests are being systematically sacrificed in for-profit hospitals. As one recent study summarized the evidence:

> A major issue in physician/hospital decision making is the extent to which control of costs or improved efficiency can be achieved only at the expense of the quality of care. Most of the studies to date, however, suggest that efforts at containing costs are positively associated with quality. For example, a study of Chicago-area hospitals found that the more efficient hospitals, as measured by lower costs and lower manhours per standardized unit of output, also provided higher-quality care, as evaluated by outside experts and as indicated by accreditation and severity-adjusted death rates. A study of hospitals in Massachusetts revealed that higher cost per case was associated with higher medical/surgical death rates, even when differences in case mix were taken into account. Other studies have generally found similar results . . . existing evidence offers little support for the argument or expectation that efficiency or cost containment goals are inherently incompatible with effectiveness or quality of care.[16]

One of the critical issues here is whether the nonprofit mode actually compensates for a lack of consumer sophistication about service providers. On this issue at least the data from health care show no superiority of nonprofit over for-profit providers. For example, studies designed to assess the extent of fraud, unnecessary surgery, and unnecessary hospital care do not show that nonprofit hospitals are more protective of consumer interests than for-profit ones. That is, if the nonprofit mode is supposed to serve as a consumer protection in health care, there is little if any direct evidence that it does so more effectively than hospitals for profit.

As Harvard law professor Robert C. Clark summarizes,

"the most reasonable conclusion on the evidence is simply that organizational form appears to play little role in solving or worsening information problems and other causes of market failure." Furthermore, "At the very least, one can conclude that the case for believing that nonprofit hospitals are organized as fiduciaries and are therefore socially superior has not been established."[17]

As a matter of fact, the most significant development in the medical field is not the substantial growth of the for-profit sector. It is the growing challenge to the policy rationale underlying the nonprofit sector.[18] At least some elements of this challenge (for example, the tax-exempt status of nonprofit hospitals) are applicable to nonprofit schools. In addition, the legislative and lobbying activities of nonprofit schools, like such activities in the nonprofit sector generally, will probably be more restricted legally in the future than they have been.[19]

For educational policymakers, perhaps the main lesson to be learned from the health care industry is the importance of avoiding stereotypes about the for-profit sector. Earning a profit may not be as antithetical to high-quality education as many educators assume. Parents who have entrusted their health and even their lives to for-profit hospitals are not so likely to be concerned about for-profit schools. If sector neutrality continues to gain acceptance in medical care, the educational community may have to face the issue in the near future, quite apart from any voucher plans.

The case of medical care suggests two additional outcomes that are widely ignored in the debate over educational vouchers. Most hospitals were established by denominational groups and were intended to serve the needs of their constituents. In this respect, these hospitals were similar to schools established by denominational groups. Over time the denominational character of hospitals has declined, especially as they have become more dependent on government support and payments by health insurance companies.

Insurance companies are not a major source of revenues

for private schools. It is not likely that they will be, at least for many years to come. The hospital experience suggests, however, that educational vouchers may not be as efficacious in maintaining denominational unity as is commonly assumed. Given a way to implement their choices, some parents who now choose denominational over public schools may choose nondenominational over denominational private schools.

Finally, our experience with health care suggests that the major private school concerns about voucher plans may not materialize. As we have seen, some private school leaders oppose vouchers because they fear increased regulation will result. Interestingly, the American Medical Association (AMA) initially opposed Medicare on the grounds that it would lead to increased government regulation of medical care. When it became clear that a federally financed plan would be enacted, the AMA redirected its efforts to protect doctor interests. Unquestionably, the AMA was very successful in this effort. This fact suggests that government regulation of voucher plans is not necessarily a threat to the service providers; the issues can be resolved in their interests. I am not advocating such an outcome, but increased regulation of private schools under voucher plans is not a foregone conclusion.[20]

Transfers Under Voucher Plans

If the educational improvement argument for vouchers is valid, poor schools, whether public or private, must either improve or go out of business. Thus the ultimate test of the educational improvement rationale is not how many students transfer. It is what happens to the levels of teaching and learning in schools generally. Although widely overlooked, this point is absolutely critical.

First of all, the mere fact that students transfer under a voucher plan would not be evidence per se that the educational improvement rationale is valid. Students enroll in private schools for a variety of reasons, many of which have nothing to do with educational improvement. Some may even transfer for educationally negative reasons. As a matter of fact, even transfers based on such goals as learning to read and write better would not sustain the educational improvement rationale. Unless educational achievement actually improves as a result of transfers or potential transfers, the educational improvement rationale will have failed.

Some implications of this conclusion are worth noting. One is that the rationale poses some difficult assessment problems. Even if educational improvement takes place, it may be impossible to say what was responsible for it in a given school. And what if educational achievement declines, as it inevitably will in some schools for reasons beyond the influence of any educational program; for example, what if demographic changes result in lower achievement levels? Can the improvement rationale survive such situations?

Notice also that other arguments for vouchers will have other criteria for their success or failure. If vouchers are proposed for religious reasons, the test of their success will be whether public schools are more hospitable to religious beliefs and/or whether there are more transfers for religious reasons. Either of these outcomes could happen without any educational improvement. Similarly, other rationales for vouchers have other criteria for evaluating the success or failure of voucher plans.

The economic level of transferees is another matter of considerable uncertainty. Voucher opponents assert that students transferring to private schools would be overwhelmingly from affluent families because poor families could not afford private schools, even with vouchers. The fact that the voucher amounts (or tax credits) usually proposed are rather modest ($250 to $750) lends some support to this conclusion. On the other hand, a strong argument has been made that the students who transfer as the result of a voucher plan are more likely to be from lower-income families.[21] The reason is that the small amount of the vouchers is not likely to have deterred affluent parents. In contrast, relatively modest amounts would have been much more important to low-income parents who prefer private schools. Of course, if few students transfer as a result of vouchers, voucher funds would largely benefit the parents whose children would have attended private schools anyway. At any rate, it is doubtful whether vouchers would result in a large-scale exodus of middle- and upper-class students from public schools. This might happen where such students attend schools characterized by racial conflicts, but its occurrence elsewhere is doubtful.

The low-income parents who wish to transfer their children to private schools may encounter some noneconomic hurdles to doing so. School effectiveness is related in significant ways to student characteristics. Speaking generally, and recognizing that exceptions are numerous, students from upper–middle-class families will have a more positive effect than lower-class students on the educational achievement of fellow students. For this reason, private schools emphasizing academic achievement may be more reluctant to accept low-income students, especially if some students must be turned away.[22]

COMPETITION IN EDUCATION:
SOME OBSERVATIONS

In 1953 I was appointed assistant professor of education at the University of Oklahoma. As a bright-eyed and bushy-tailed professor, I participated in several faculty meetings devoted to this question: How many semester credits of academic work earned at other institutions should receive credit for an M.A. degree at the University of Oklahoma?

The records of these interminable discussions may not show it, but after all the educational arguments, pro and con, the question was resolved by one simple fact: If we did not allow at least eight semester hours of transfer credit, we would lose graduate students to our archrival, Oklahoma State University. Ergo, we allowed eight semester hours of transfer credit.

Since that time I have been employed in a variety of

institutions all over the United States. Competition issues have arisen frequently. In all the cases that I can recall, however, the issues were resolved in ways that were good for the professors and students seeking the least educationally demanding solution, but bad for everyone else.

My experience here is relevant to voucher issues. A high school student may be more interested in a piece of paper (a diploma) than in the quality of educational achievement or service supposedly reflected in a diploma. When this happens, competition is not a matter of providing better service in the sense assumed by voucher supporters. On the contrary, it is a matter of getting the requisite piece of paper in the least expensive way. If a student needs a diploma to get a driver's license, or a job, the student's interest is in the diploma, not the educational achievement it presumably stands for. In such cases, competition can have disastrous consequences.

Let me cite another example that plays an extremely important role in education below the college level. The overwhelming majority of teachers below that level are paid on the basis of their academic credits and years of experience. Teachers with a master's degree are paid more than teachers with only a bachelor's degree. Teachers with thirty hours of credit beyond the M.A. are paid more than teachers with only an M.A. And so on.

In most school districts, there is no quality control over the process of accumulating credit for salary purposes. It matters not whether additional academic work is relevant to the teacher's assignment, whether the teacher received A's or D's in the courses, or whether the institutions offering the courses had high or low standards, or even any, for granting credit.

Under these circumstances, competition has turned out to be competition to offer credit in the least expensive and least educationally demanding ways. The teachers who respond by taking the least demanding and least expensive courses are acting in a rational manner. Competition is working; teachers are getting the desired credit in the least expensive way. Similarly, in the absence of any external standards for evaluating student performance, we can expect a great deal of school competition to be antieducational in effect. That is the reality; one need usually look no further than the nearest institution of higher education to see a concrete manifestation of it. Opposition to vouchers among public school officials and organizations is often ascribed to monopolistic and/or self-seeking motives. Such motives do play a significant role in this opposition. Realistically, however, similar motives underlie some support as well as some opposition to vouchers. The rhetoric of competition serves some private school interests; at bottom, these interests are just as eager to avoid competition as their public school counterparts.

This is not a matter of conjecture. In 1969 Marjorie Webster Junior College, a two-year proprietary institution in Washington, D.C., filed an antitrust action against the Middle States Association of Colleges and Secondary Schools (MSA). MSA was one of six regional accrediting associations in the United States. It accredited institutions of higher education and secondary schools in New York, New Jersey, Pennsylvania, Delaware, Maryland, District of Columbia, Puerto Rico, Canal Zone, and Virgin Islands. At the time of the lawsuit, MSA's membership included 346 nonprofit institutions of higher education, including 106 public ones. Proprietary institutions were not eligible for accreditation or membership in the association.

The legal basis for the suit was the fact that although the lack of accreditation was damaging to the college, it was not eligible for accreditation because of its proprietary status. Testimony at the trial brought out the fact that all regional accrediting associations excluded proprietary institutions. In any case, the plaintiff college alleged that MSA had acquired monopoly power over regional accrediting in its area and that it was exercising this power in such a way as to prevent competition from proprietary institutions. The relief sought was a decree declaring the exclusion of proprietary institutions to be illegal and an order that the plaintiff's application for accreditation be accepted and that the institution be accredited if it were otherwise qualified. The case was heard by a judge without a jury in the District of Columbia. The trial court upheld the claim of Marjorie Webster College virtually *in toto*. On appeal to the federal circuit court of appeals, the decision was reversed, and the U.S. Supreme Court declined to review the appellate court decision in December 1970.[23]

The trial record takes up fourteen volumes, and any summary of it necessarily oversimplifies the issues. Nevertheless, the major issues were of the utmost importance to our analysis. Marjorie Webster College introduced a wealth of testimony to prove that nonprofit colleges competed for students, faculty, donations, and research contracts. The MSA just as vigorously asserted that its members did not compete with each other. Indeed, in its defense it went to great lengths to show that the notion of competition in the business sense was utterly foreign to the field of higher education. And in taking this position, it clearly had the support of the other regional accrediting associations, which represented most of the institutions of higher education and secondary schools, public and private, in the United States.

One of the reasons the case was so important was that it was viewed as a test case of the exclusion of for-profit institutions. Public and nonprofit institutions were categorically opposed to allowing for-profit institutions to be evaluated on the same standards. If an institution was for profit, it was not to be accredited, no matter what. Its students, faculty, financial standing, program—all might be outstanding, yet the institution could not hope to be considered for accreditation. And this was true even though accreditation conferred certain legal rights on institutions, such as eligibility for federal aid of various kinds. Literally, the national leadership of both public and nonprofit institutions and secondary schools asserted that competition did not, should not, and would not prevail in education if they had anything to say about it. According to the MSA brief on its appeal to the federal appellate court:

> In industry, free competition for a commercial market, motivated by desire for profit, is deemed to be the

soundest method for assuring maximum production. The forces which tend to produce the highest quality in education are entirely different from the forces which tend to produce the best automobiles or television sets. In education, the highest achievements have been obtained by the cooperative search for improvements and mutual assistance between institutions . . . (". . . the policy unequivocally laid down by the [Sherman] Act is competition") . . . Given this goal of competition between contending economic units sought to be attained by the antitrust laws, it is clear that the entire regulatory scheme is wholly foreign to higher education. This is so because the relationships among colleges is cooperative, not competitive . . . Thus to apply the Sherman Act in the instant case is to impose alien concepts on higher education . . . The Sherman Act's purpose is to *preserve* the competitive relationship between business entities. The Act is not intended to *impose* competition as the fundamental relationship among institutions which never have before economically competed with each other.[24]

There is widespread agreement that competition between institutions of higher education is much more prevalent than between institutions below the college level. If colleges do not and should not compete, as the MSA contended, how could educational leaders view competition as appropriate below the college level? Most emphatically, I do not agree with the argument or the legal result in the Marjorie Webster case. My point in discussing it is to show that nonprofit as well as public school leaders are eager to avoid competition. Of course, this attitude is not unusual, even in the competitive business sector. Most businesses look at competition as they do taxes; they prefer to avoid it if they can. If they cannot, they try to shape it to their advantage as much as possible.

Businesspeople welcome competition among their suppliers. When it comes to the sale of their own products, they would prefer to be a monopoly. Propriety requires that this preference not be expressed openly, so we are subjected to an immense amount of rhetoric praising competition from business leaders who work diligently at avoiding it if they can. Thus educators who praise competition while trying to avoid it are no more and no less hypocritical than their counterparts in the business world.

Public school opponents of vouchers are opposed to vouchers for several reasons, including their desire to avoid competition. Rightly or wrongly, however, the voucher opponents have assumed that competition would ensue under a voucher plan. They could hardly object to voucher proposals both on grounds that competition is bad and that it would not exist. Objecting to vouchers on the grounds that they would not generate competition implies that support would be forthcoming if vouchers did generate competition. Of course, public school voucher opponents have no such thought. Thus neither proponents nor opponents of vouchers have had any compelling reason to raise competition issues. Ironically, interscholastic athletic competition is sacrosanct in most school districts. A school board that suggested eliminating it would be quickly out of office. At the same time, academic competition is not widely encouraged (in some districts it is fair to say it is discouraged). Analysis of these different attitudes toward competition would take us too far afield, but I believe they suggest that teacher attitudes toward competition are shaped largely by their own interests.

Teachers tend to be hostile to economic competition for several reasons. First, the politics and culture of education are dominated by the redistribution of wealth, not the creation of it. Of course, teachers assert (and believe) that larger appropriations for education are a productive social investment; this conclusion, however, merely illustrates Italian sociologist Vilfredo Pareto's observation that men find it easy to convert their interests into principles. In the meantime, teacher organizations focus on a larger piece of the pie in legislatures and at bargaining tables. To be sure, an emphasis on the redistribution of wealth is a widespread tendency in our society; some observers believe it is a pervasive characteristic of advanced industrial nations generally.[25] Still, outside of public employees, most groups that focus on improving their economic status by redistributive measures cannot avoid some exposure to economic competition as participants.

Second, a substantial number of teachers have never competed economically. Of course, when someone applies for a teaching position, he or she can be said to be "competing" with others seeking the position. Likewise, when teachers applied for college admission, they were "competing" with others.

Nevertheless, most teachers have not been competitive in market situations. That is, they have not achieved a larger share of a market by producing a better product or better service, or by producing products or services more efficiently. As I am commenting on a group of several million, there are many exceptions and qualifications, but I believe that my basic contention is valid. The kind of competition familiar to most teachers is the kind that exists everywhere. Even in socialist economies there is competition to be admitted to college or to get a job one wishes.

As previously noted, reluctance to confront competition issues characterizes private as well as public school leaders. Unquestionably, however, some private nonprofit schools, including denominational ones, do compete for students. Nonprofit schools are beginning to conduct market research, to advertise, and to conduct a variety of promotional efforts to recruit students.[26] We can expect these efforts to intensify, especially if the market for private education declines in the 1990s. Regardless of whether voucher plans are enacted, however, it will be essential to clarify the rationale for the nonprofit status of private schools. It may turn out that nonprofit status will depend on the nature of the clientele served or willingness to provide a certain amount of unpaid service; for example, I see no reason why schools catering to affluent parents, who are the first to assert their ability to choose schools wisely, should continue to enjoy nonprofit status. Be that as it may, the notion that public school teachers should enjoy monopoly status for what they sell but the benefits of competition for what they buy will become increasingly difficult to sustain.

The Effects of Vouchers on
Nonpublic Schools

Controversies over vouchers typically focus on their educational consequences. In addition, their effects on religious freedom, neighborhoods, parents, tax rates, political parties, and racial harmony are widely debated. Insofar as attention is paid to the effects of vouchers on private schools, it is usually thought that vouchers would help them financially. In addition, private school leaders are deeply concerned by the possibility that vouchers would lead to increased regulation of private schools. The possibility that vouchers could affect the educational role of nonprofit schools is seldom considered, but deserves some attention.

Hospital experience illustrates the problem. Some hospitals were founded to serve the indigent or a particular religious or ethnic group; such hospitals were often funded mainly by donations. With the advent of Medicare, Medicaid, and health insurance, many of these hospitals came to depend more upon these sources of funding, less upon donations and payments by patients. As this happened, the operation of nonprofit hospitals, including denominational ones, became increasingly dominated by a fee for service orientation, indistinguishable from commercial operations. Such transformations are not unusual when nonprofits compete in competitive markets; their original purpose may become secondary or even disappear altogether.[27]

Many institutions of higher education have followed this pattern. Initially, they were established to train religious leaders. Over time, financial exigencies led them to recruit other students and rely upon nondenominational sources of revenue. Many became nonsectarian or were eventually incorporated into public systems of higher education. The changes were not necessarily undesirable, but they underscore the possibility that a competitive milieu would lead to changes in the educational mission of nonprofit schools. Clearly, if denominational schools compete for students on secular criteria, the latter may eventually take precedence over the denominational ones. The structure and management of an organization devoted to denominational objectives differ from those engaged in competitive economic enterprise. It is wishful thinking to assume that the two kinds of objectives can be reconciled in the same organization.

7

Noneducational
Arguments
for Vouchers

We turn next to arguments for vouchers based on non-educational objectives. Even in these cases, however, the educational consequences are very important. Although the primary objectives of a voucher plan may lie outside the field of education, its educational effects are unavoidably an important consideration. If, for example, voucher plans could increase religious freedom but only by reducing educational achievement, policymakers would face a dilemma. Obviously the dilemma would not exist if educational achievement was as high or higher under voucher plans as under conventional arrangements. The following discussion, therefore, is not limited to the noneducational objectives of voucher proposals. It also seeks to assess their educational impact. This impact may or may not be similar to the educational impact of voucher plans consciously formulated to raise levels of educational achievement.

The Religious Rationale for Vouchers

Perhaps the most important noneducational argument for vouchers is that they are essential to protect religious freedom. The argument is based on the fact that education is compulsory in every state. Because they cannot afford private schooling, many parents are forced to send their children to schools that violate their religious convictions. A voucher system could avoid this outcome by making it possible for parents to enroll their children in schools of their choice.

The factual premises of the religious rationale are indisputable. Historically, denominational schools have always existed in the United States; typically, they preceded public schools. Prior to 1850 state and local assistance to denominational schools was commonplace.[1] The influx of Catholic immigrants in the latter half of the nineteenth century created a policy dilemma for political leaders, who were overwhelmingly Protestant. State aid to religious schools now required aid to Catholic as well as Protestant schools. Rather than accept this alternative, the dilemma was resolved by compulsory education laws. By simultaneously denying aid to Catholic schools, it was anticipated that most Catholic children would be enrolled in public schools. The latter were not viewed as "nonreligious"; on the contrary, they were permeated with a strong Protestant bias characterized publicly if inaptly as a "nonsectarian" approach to religion.[2]

This bias was most clearly reflected in the Bible-reading statutes. During the nineteenth century Massachusetts was the only state that required Bible reading. In the twentieth century, however, thirty-six states enacted statutes requiring or allowing public school teachers to read passages from the Bible at certain times.[3] These statutes typically prohibited teachers from discussing the passages that were read. For example, Pennsylvania law required that "At least ten verses from the Holy Bible shall be read, without comment, at the opening of each public school on each school day. Any child shall be excused from such Bible reading, or attending such Bible reading upon the written request of his parent or guardian."

In many states Catholic parents objected to Bible reading, and not simply because a Protestant instead of a Catholic edition of the Bible was used. The statutes were consistent with Protestant theology that regards people as capable of interpreting the Bible correctly without intermediaries. They were not consistent with Catholic theology, which holds that the Catholic Church is necessary to reveal and interpret the Word of God.

Feeble defenses aside, there was no question about the Protestant bias in the Bible-reading statutes. Nevertheless, out of a total of twenty-five cases on the issue from 1854 to 1924, the protestors, most often Catholic, lost about three out of four cases.[4] This type of bias was reflected in other ways too numerous to be recounted here. What were the aggrieved parents to do? They could—and sometimes did—establish private schools, but such schools had to operate without public financial help. Needless to say, for opponents of Bible reading to appeal for financial help to the very same legislatures that enacted the Bible-reading statutes was not a very promising way out of their predicament.

The Bible-reading statutes were held to be unconstitutional in 1963.[5] Today some of the Protestant denominations that were instrumental in enacting the statutes are expanding their denominational schools as a response to the religious restrictions on public schools. Bible reading is only one of several factors in this situation, but it illustrates two important points. First, whatever public schools do about religious issues, some group is likely to cite the action as a reason to establish private schools. Second, although couched in constitutional terms, the religious rationale is based primarily on the alleged unfairness of compulsory education without financial support for those who object to public education on religious grounds.

Although the religious argument per se has not changed much over the years, several facts pertinent to it have changed. Programs of sex education and restrictions on Bible reading, school prayer, and the teaching of "creation science" have led some Protestant fundamentalists to conclude that public schools are hostile, not merely neutral, to their religious beliefs. This attitude is frequently expressed in charges that public schools are promoting "secular humanism"; the latter is said to be a nontheistic religion that emphasizes human instead of divine sources of moral authority. In addition, many parents who think this way believe that public schools are too permissive in matters of drugs, alcohol, dress, language, and manners. The result is that the number of Protestant fundamentalist schools increased rapidly during the 1970s and 1980s; their rate of increase outstripped every other denominational category. Paradoxically, Christian fundamentalist school officials tend to be more hostile to government regulation than Catholic school leaders, who are more likely to recognize the legitimacy of state regulation of private schools.[6]

The upsurge in Christian fundamentalist schools has occurred at a time when Catholic schools faced a number of difficult problems. A sharp decline in the number of Catholics entering religious orders has been a major problem. As the number of nuns and priests available to teach in Catholic schools has declined, the schools have been forced to employ a higher proportion of lay teachers. This has led to greater financial strains on Catholic school budgets and increased interest in government assistance.

For our purposes, the important considerations are these: First, there has been and still is some religious bias in public schools. I make no effort to quantify the bias but simply accept the fact that from time to time and place to place, public school policies and practices violate good-faith religious convictions.

At the same time, it is equally clear that some critics of public schools will not be satisfied with genuine neutrality, whether it takes the form of objective pedagogical treatment or of avoidance of denominational issues entirely. In other words, I see no immediate end of either justified or unjustified criticism of public schools on religious grounds. Whatever the merits, conflicts over religious objections to public education are likely to continue into the foreseeable future. We can, therefore, expect a religious base of support for family choice no matter what public schools do.

Family Choice and the Separation of Church and State

As most private schools are denominational, there has been opposition to most government efforts to aid them. Such assistance would allegedly violate the First Amendment and several state constitutions that incorporate it. The relevant portion of the amendment states that "Congress shall make no law respecting an establishment of religion or prohibiting the free exercise thereof. . . . On its face, the language applies only to Congress; in 1940, however, the U.S. Supreme Court held that the First Amendment applies to the states as well as the federal government.[7] Although this was a momentous limitation on state action, it is not the crux of current controversy on First Amendment issues. Such controversy emerges from conflicts between the establishment clause and the free exercise one. This conflict is especially acute under compulsory education. If parents who regard the public schools as antireligious cannot afford private education, compulsory education is an interference with the free exercise of religion. If government provides vouchers which make such attendance possible, the vouchers may be deemed contrary to the establishment clause. This dilemma lies at the heart of religious conflict over education vouchers.

In 1983, in the *Mueller* v. *Allen* case, the United States Supreme Court upheld a Minnesota law that provided tax deductions for educational expenses.[8] Legally, the deductions were available to parents of both public and private school children; as a practical matter, they were used overwhelmingly by denominational school parents. Although the Supreme Court decision to uphold the law was by a five to four vote, it seems likely that educational vouchers available to all parents would also be upheld. As was the case with the tax deduction, the benefits would (or could) be made available to parents; the assistance to denominational schools would be secondary.

Undoubtedly, church/state issues will continue to play an important role in voucher controversies. In my view, however, the issues are fundamentally political ones, to be resolved in the political arena. Of course, voucher legislation will have to run the gamut of legal challenge; judges will have to decide whether voucher legislation is or is not constitutional. Nevertheless, the judges themselves will be designated through our political processes; the ultimate legal fate of voucher legislation thus depends primarily on the outcome of our political processes.

Since the *Lemon* v. *Kurtzman* decision in 1971, the Supreme Court has adopted a threefold test for deciding the constitutionality of legislation that allegedly violates freedom of religion, establishes a religion, or does both. The legislation must: (1) have a valid secular purpose; (2) not have the primary effect of advancing religion or interfering with the free exercise thereof; and (3) avoid excessive entanglement of religion and government.[9]

Any one of the rationales for vouchers previously mentioned would satisfy the first criterion. In view of the *Mueller* v. *Allen* decision, it is unlikely that voucher legislation would be held unconstitutional on the second criterion. Indeed, if vouchers were successful in introducing competition among schools, some parents would transfer their children from denominational to nondenominational schools. Obviously, if this happens, it would be more difficult to argue that the legislation had the primary effect of promoting religion.

The entanglement issue presents difficult legal as well as political problems for voucher legislation. There is very little regulation of private schools now because most are denominational; most legislators are eager to avoid the political problems inherent in increased regulation of religious organizations. If, however, voucher opponents cannot block vouchers directly, they will try to do so indirectly by demanding increased private school regulation. The argument will be that even though the vouchers are made available to parents, they are actually a subsidy to the schools that redeem them. Allegedly it will be necessary to regulate the schools that redeem vouchers in order to avoid huge expenditures of public funds without accountability for the results.

In short, voucher legislation must avoid interfering in religious affairs but also provide sufficient accountability for expenditures of public funds. The question is whether the voucher legislation that eventually emerges from the political process will be able to emerge unscathed from the judicial process—and whether what is required to survive the judicial process can be negotiated through the political process. Inasmuch as we do not have the legislation at hand or know the composition of the Supreme Court that will resolve the issue, the constitutional outcome is uncertain.

The second major legal issue likely to affect the future of educational vouchers is the constitutional definition of "religion." The First Amendment prohibits government from establishing a religion or interfering with its free exercise. What, however, is a "religion" or a "religious belief" from a constitutional point of view? The Supreme Court has already held that a "religious" belief need not be based on belief in a Supreme Being or on belief in a supernatural realm; Confucianism illustrates the kind of nontheistic belief system that can neither be established nor prohibited by the First Amendment.[10] The difficulty lies in distinguishing which nontheistic views are religious and which ones are not.

If the Supreme Court adopts an expansive definition of "religion," the public school curricula will be correspondingly restricted; more of what public schools do will violate someone's religious beliefs or constitute establishment of religion. An expansive definition will, therefore, lead to a more restricted public school curriculum and to more defections over the restrictions. Ironically, a restrictive definition of religion could have the same result, albeit in a different way. If "religion" is defined narrowly, the public schools will have greater legal freedom to teach subject matter that is contrary to the beliefs of some parents. The latter may then defect, as some already have, to private schools. In other words, no matter how "religion" is defined constitutionally, the definition is likely to lead to some defections from the public schools.

Overall, however, it is clear that both legal and popular opinion are becoming more receptive to public support for denominational schools. First of all, it is indisputable that the First Amendment was not intended to proscribe non-sectarian aid to Christian, especially Protestant, religious organizations. On the contrary, and disconcerting as it may be to strict separationists, a major purpose of the amendment was to prevent the federal government from interfering with state legislation that provided nonpreferential aid for religious activities. The evidence for this is too overwhelming to be in serious question.[11]

Proponents of such aid will also rely on the argument that any aid to private schools that excludes denominational schools constitutes unconstitutional discrimination against such schools. It is impossible to predict the weight that will be accorded this argument, but it does command some support from constitutional scholars.

More important, the restrictions on aid to denominational schools are the exception, not the rule, in church/state relations generally in the United States. As pointed out by Thomas Vitullo-Martin and Bruce Cooper:

> The Court has permitted direct government contracts and grants to churches in the areas of higher education; medical institutions; care of the elderly, the poor, young children, orphans, the hungry, the homeless, the sick, addicts, the mentally imparied; food stations; prison release programs; job training programs; youth shelters; and even burial. It has permitted the state to build churches (on government reservations); to donate to churches the land for their buildings (the land for St. Patrick's Cathedral in New York City); and to pay the salaries of priests, pastors, rabbis, and other religious officials who serve as chaplains. In short, the Court has approved state support of churches in virtually every as-

pect of their self-defined mission, except in their operation of elementary and secondary schools. Even in the area of schooling, churches can receive public funds to operate preschool programs, after-school youth programs, post-secondary schools, and adult training programs. In addition, the Court has approved the government's giving churches tax exemptions, which in effect means providing churches with free municipal and state services (by eliminating property taxes), and reducing the cost of supplies (by removing sales taxes). Most Americans agree with these policies, which apply evenhandedly to all churches. The Court-appointed policies in these areas could not pass the tests the Court has developed for school aid, and the Court itself has struggled to limit to schools alone the constitutional principles it has developed in the elementary school cases.[12]

These inconsistencies might well be resolved by a more tolerant legal posture toward aid to denominational schools, especially if such aid results from direct assistance to parents or children. Later in this chapter I shall try to show that there are strong public policy reasons for providing such assistance.

Educational Achievement in Public and Private Schools

Attitudes toward vouchers are often dominated by perceptions about private schools. Typically, voucher supporters believe that private schools are educationally more effective than public schools. Thus vouchers are seen as a way to enable more students to take advantage of the superior education provided by private schools.

Needless to say, voucher opponents challenge the view that private schools are educationally superior. Logically, the issue may be irrelevant since a voucher plan might affect either the advantages or the deficiencies of private schools—or both. Logic notwithstanding, perceptions of private school effectiveness play an extremely important political role in voucher controversies. Apart from this, comparisons of public and private school effectiveness may contribute to our understanding of several voucher issues. For these reasons, a brief consideration of school effectiveness is essential.

First we must recognize the problems inherent in such comparisons. One is whether the services offered in public and private schools are close substitutes for each other, or whether they are essentially different services.

To illustrate the problem, consider a public school mathematics class of twenty-five students and a private school class of ten in the same subject. Is the public school teacher providing the same service as his private school counterpart? The private school may enroll students precisely because its classes are smaller and provide much greater teacher-pupil interaction. In other words, parents may view the situation as one in which they are buying different services from what they would get in public schools. Similarly, if denominational instruction is important to parents, the latter are likely to view denominational schools as providing a different service instead of a close substitute. There is no simple way to resolve the issue, and inconsistent treatments of it are commonplace. The fact that the problem is not confined to education does not render it less important or easy to resolve.[13]

Another pervasive problem results from the fact that it is prohibitively expensive to evaluate certain outcomes of schooling. For example, consideration for the rights of others may be an important objective of both public and private schools, yet the cost of assessing performance on this criterion may be prohibitive. Consequently, schools tend to be evaluated on the basis of criteria that ignore important but difficult-to-evaluate instructional objectives. Student outcomes are a mix of what is or can be measured and what is not or cannot be. Focus on only the measurable outcomes may lead to erroneous conclusions about school performance. More important, it may also lead to undesirable allocations of school resources. If, for example, schools are evaluated solely on the basis of academic achievement, school resources are less likely to be used for other important objectives. Again, the problem is not confined to education; it arises in many fields.[14]

Even when there is agreement on the dimensions to be evaluated, it can be extremely difficult to compare school performance with respect to them. Perhaps the most difficult problem is how to distinguish the school effects from the nonschool factors that affect educational outcomes. Obviously, if private schools enroll brighter students, or students who are more motivated to learn, or students who receive more parental support for learning, the students could show a higher level of achievement even though the private schools per se were not more effective than the public schools. Unfortunately, several factors affect school achievement, and reasonable people can and do disagree on the weight to be accorded them. In addition, there are difficult technical problems in assessing the factors.

We must also be aware of the dangers inherent in comparing vastly dissimilar private schools with vastly dissimilar public schools. If we lump together a Catholic parish school, a nondenominational independent school, and a boarding school, our "averages," whether of educational achievement, student characteristics, teacher salaries, or anything else, may be very unrealistic. Furthermore, the school categories often include subcategories that raise the same issue. For example, a boarding school may be simply a custodial institution for the children of parents who don't want to be bothered by child-raising problems. In another case, the parents may be required to travel frequently, but they and the school may have the highest ideals and standards. Thus even conclusions about private residential schools or parents or students in them may aggregate data that is very misleading when reduced to "averages." Needless to say, public school averages often raise the same problem.

To begin with, some studies do not support the conclusion that private schools are more effective educationally than public schools. For example, one major comparison of public/private school effects was conducted under the auspices of the National Assessment of Educational Progress (NAEP). The NAEP study involved 104,000 children ages nine, thirteen, and seventeen, in 1,377 schools. The study concluded that "when the data are adjusted to compensate for socio-economic differences in the composition of private and public school student populations, national differences cease to be statistically significant."[15]

Conclusions more favorable to Catholic schools have been reached by James S. Coleman, a sociologist who is widely acknowledged to be the leading scholar on the effects of schooling. In recent years Coleman has been the principal investigator in several studies that compare public to private school achievement. These studies were characterized by extensive efforts to isolate the school effects from other factors that affect student achievement. Coleman's major study relied on a sample of sophomores and seniors among 58,728 U.S. high school students enrolled in 893 public schools, 84 Catholic schools, and 11 non-Catholic private schools. Because of the small number of the latter and the wide variation among them, the study focused on the comparisons between public and Catholic schools. The study itself was based on the results of standardized tests in reading comprehension, vocabulary, mathematics, science, civics, and writing.

High school sophomores were tested in all six areas; seniors were tested in the first three using some items identical to those in the sophomore tests. Coleman first published his analysis in 1982; after considerable controversy over the research methods and reassessment of the data, in 1987 he asserted:

> At this point, it is sufficient to say that most critics have come to agree . . . that there is a positive Catholic sector effect on achievement in the areas of reading comprehension, vocabulary, mathematics, and writing, but not in science or civics. The remaining disagreement about the Catholic sector effect appears largely to focus on the size of the effect. With respect to the effect of other private schools, we agree with the critics' point . . . that no

strong inferences could be made about achievement effects of this sector.[16]

Although comparisons of public to Catholic schools necessarily omit several important issues, they are useful for at least three reasons. In the first place, Catholic schools enroll almost 60 percent of all students enrolled in private schools. Second, they enroll pupils from all socioeconomic classes; in this respect, their student population is more comparable to the public school population than to that of any other category of private schools. Finally, insofar as the denominational aspect of Catholic schools is a relevant variable, most conclusions about them are likely to apply to other denominational schools as well.

In view of the political, economic, and educational stakes involved, it is not surprising that several major controversies have arisen over public/private school comparisons. For example, Coleman concluded that students attending Catholic high schools averaged about one grade higher in reading and mathematics achievement than comparable students in public schools. Critics have disputed this conclusion. A recent critique emphasizes that most research on the effects of schooling deal with short-term effects that shrink or disappear completely in a longer time frame. In reanalyzing the Coleman data, the critique asserts that no Catholic school superiority is shown in reading achievement and there is a small but distinct Catholic school inferiority in mathematics achievement.[17] After reviewing Coleman's studies, another analyst concluded that "the advantage of Catholic secondary schools in promoting cognitive development, if it exists at all, is so small as to be practically unimportant. Certainly there is no convincing evidence that Catholic schools have an important advantage over public ones in this regard."[18]

Richard J. Murnane, a professor at Harvard's Graduate School of Education, has formulated a similar conclusion, although he is not so categorical in rejecting "the Catholic advantage."

While there is considerable disagreement about whether Catholic schools and other private schools are more effective on average than public schools, there is agreement that even the largest estimates of a private school advantage are small relative to the variation in quality among different public schools, among different Catholic schools, and among different non-Catholic private schools. Consequently, in predicting the quality of a student's education, it is less important to know whether the student attended a public school or a private school than it is to know which school within a particular sector the student attended.[19]

In other words, the critical issue is not necessarily whether there is "a Catholic advantage." It is whether any such advantage is large enough to justify public policies strengthening Catholic (and other denominational) schools on educational grounds. The answer to this question depends partly on the reasons for "the Catholic advantage" and whether or how these reasons might be affected by policies that strengthen family choice. Let us consider these issues briefly.

The "Social Capital" Hypothesis

To some extent, the resolution of policy issues may depend on the resolution of difficult technical issues. For example, if the reasons for "the Catholic advantage" are such policies as insistence on homework on a regular basis, the policy implication might be to insist on homework in the public schools, not encourage transfers to private schools. Actually, this underscores the inherent difficulty of isolating the school effects from the other factors affecting student achievement. Requiring students to do homework may be due more to parent pressure on the school—it may not be a school effect as much as a parent effect. Also, the reason that public schools may not require homework may be the lack of parental support for it, or that more of their students have outside employment. Thus regardless of whether there is a Catholic school advantage, or whether homework is a factor in it, it might be unrealistic to assume "competition" would improve matters in this regard.

Coleman's explanation of the Catholic advantage is worth noting.[20] In his view, a number of basic social changes have eroded the influence of parents over their children. In fact, intergenerational relationships, especially close personal ones, are declining generally in our society. In previous generations, especially when the extended family was much more common, young people were more likely to interact with adults in the home, at the marketplace, and in the neighborhood and community activities. Today, however, government is replacing the family as the provider of basic welfare services, such as education and safety net services. As this happens, close personal relationships, especially intergenerational ones that fostered school achievement, have diminished. School achievement depends on the interaction of school and nonschool factors, such as family and community support for what schools are trying to achieve. It appears that the family and community factors that are essential for high levels of school achievement have been weakened by the shift to government instead of family support for welfare services.

Coleman's point can be illustrated by the fact that about 80 percent of over 5 million single-parent households headed by females receive no financial support from the fathers; of those that do, a relatively small proportion receive a significant amount of support. In fact, about one in eight children in single-parent households were conceived by women who were not living with the father at the time of conception. In these cases, the fathers rarely contribute to child support. Needless to say, such absentee fathers also do not help to reinforce positive attitudes toward school and work habits among their children. Nevertheless, the declining role of families in raising children is by no means limited to any particular economic level or ethinic group. In some ways the displacement of family functions by government programs is even more pervasive among middle- than among lower-income groups. For example, government funding for higher education is increasing more rapidly than support from family sources.

In Coleman's view, therefore, our society is undergoing a major decline in "social capital"—the family, neighborhood, and community relationships that formerly helped to develop positive attitudes, habits, and conceptions of self among youth. Herein lies his explanation of the reasons for "the Catholic advantage." Religious institutions are the major nongovernmental institutions that foster constructive intergenerational relationships at the person-to-person level. In Coleman's terms, they are a major source of the social capital that is essential to foster constructive attitudes and effective study and work habits. Thus in his view students of comparable ability tend to learn more in Catholic schools because such schools (and their neighborhoods) are more likely to provide the social capital missing from the environment of many public school students. This explanation seems especially persuasive in view of the fact that the Catholic advantage is most evident in inner city areas characterized by the most severe deficiencies in social capital.

Dropout data also provide strong evidence that a decline in social capital is a major cause of educational deficiencies. As the Coleman studies show, the dropout rates among Catholic students in Catholic schools are much lower than the dropout rates for Catholic students of comparable scholastic ability and socioeconomic status in public schools. Furthermore, the dropout rate among students in other denominational schools is much closer to the rate in Catholic than in public schools; this is what would be expected if denominational schools provide more social capital than public schools. Significantly, the dropout rates in private independent schools that do not draw their clientele from clearly defined communities or religious groups are much closer to the rates for comparable students in public than in denominational schools.[21]

Obviously, it is difficult to isolate school from nonschool factors regarding the concept of social capital. As Coleman would be the first to agree, it is extremely important to avoid selectivity bias in assessing school effects. For example, we would not want to credit Catholic schools for a lower dropout rate resulting from the fact that its students were more likely to stay in school to begin with. I shall not here review Coleman's procedures for avoiding such selectivity bias, but to me they appear adequate.

SIMILARITIES BETWEEN PUBLIC AND CATHOLIC SCHOOLS

The similarities as well as the differences between Catholic and public schools have important implications for voucher plans. As far back as the early 1960s, the U.S. Office of Education studies showed substantial similarities in the curricula of public and denominational schools.[22] For several reasons, these similarities continue to exist. Some states mandate that certain subjects be taught in both public and private schools. State and regional accrediting associations to which both public and private schools belong also exert pressure toward similar curricula.

Another major factor is the tremendous mobility of the American people and its educational implications. Approximately 17 percent of the American people move every year. Inevitably, this leads to substantial interchange between public and private schools. Inasmuch as the public schools enroll 90 percent of the students, they are not especially concerned about the articulation of public and private school curricula. Private schools, however, must be. Their concern is not primarily because children move in and out of their attendance areas but because the overwhelming majority of private schools do not teach grades 1 through 12. Many are just high schools. Consequently, there will often be transfers to and from public schools even among students who do not move. The inevitability of such transfers exerts considerable pressure on private schools to adjust their curriculum to that of the public school.

The Coleman studies tried to estimate school differences in curricula. For example, an effort was made to compare the semester hours of coursework taken by comparable students in public and private high schools. Coleman concluded that even when nonschool factors were taken into account, students in Catholic schools completed more semesters of academic coursework in mathematics, English/literature, foreign languages, history/social studies, and science. Nevertheless, as table 7.1 shows, the differences were not very large except in foreign languages.

Table 7.1

AVERAGE SEMESTERS OF COURSEWORK COMPLETED, 10TH TO 12TH GRADES, STUDENTS IN ACADEMIC PROGRAMS

Subject Area	Public	Catholic
Mathematics	5.01	5.38
English/Literature	6.01	6.12
Foreign Language	2.85	3.84
History and Social Studies	4.75	4.82
Science	4.38	4.52

SOURCE: Reprinted, by permission of the publisher, from James S. Coleman and Thomas Hoffer, *Public and Private High Schools: The Impact of Communities* (New York: Basic Books, 1985), p. 48.

The table applies only to students in academic programs; the differences in academic coursework taken among students in general and vocational programs were larger than those shown. Regardless, a variety of factors suggests that public and Catholic school curricula are substantially similar. Textbooks play an extremely important role in what students learn. In many situations, the textbooks *are* the curriculum, despite pedagogical advice to avoid such a limitation. In many fields, however, the public school textbooks are modified only slightly or not at all for use in private schools. College admission requirements also encourage common curricula. Students seeking admission are often required to have taken a certain number of units in specified courses, such as mathematics or English. Practically speaking, such requirements force all schools to devote the same minimum amount of time to the subjects required for college admission.

Actually, the time devoted to religion was the major difference in public/private school curricula in the 1960–62 Office of Education study. Because public high schools do not offer courses in religion, the Coleman study did not discuss how much time students in Catholic schools devote to such courses. Voucher critics emphasize that the time devoted to courses in religion is time devoted to a private, not a public, good. Although even some voucher supporters accept this point, it is a weak objection to vouchers. In most denominational schools, only a small proportion of school time is devoted to religious training per se; rather regular subjects are taught in a religious atmosphere. For instance, the reading materials may be devoted to religious themes, or the room decor may evidence a religious orientation. Such policies fulfill the school's religious mission while also approximating the public school allocation of instructional time. Voucher opponents, however, have cited these practices to defeat government assistance to denominational schools. Ironically, and despite their philosophical position, denominational schools have often minimized religious elements in order to be eligible for various forms of state support. For example, where denominational schools use textbooks provided by the state, the textbooks do not include religious content.

Actually, courses devoted to religion often include subject matter acceptable to, or even taught in, public schools. Nevertheless, even if this subject matter is not appropriate in a public school, it is hardly a persuasive reason to oppose denominational school participation in voucher plans. Religion courses are as helpful as any others in fostering good work habits, respect for others, punctuality, patriotism, and a host of other objectives that public schools claim to foster. The philosophical importance of a religious environment or religious content should not obscure the tremendous overlap between public and denominational schools on secular content and objectives.

Interestingly enough, the Coleman study indicates that among students enrolled in Catholic schools, the more religious students perform better on secular subjects than those not as religiously oriented.[23] This finding appears to support the social capital hypothesis; minimally, it suggests that school-based religious activities are not an obstacle to improvement on secular outcomes. Paradoxically, it also suggests that the Catholic school advantage would decline as those schools enroll more non-Catholics or more Catholics not so committed to their religion.

Extracurricular activities often play an important role in fostering school climate and student attitudes toward school. Significantly, the Coleman study indicated that the percentage of public and Catholic school students participating in extracurricular activities was substantially similar; in Coleman's words: "The comparability of the public and Catholic school participation rates suggest that these two types of school rely to a similar extent on the extracurriculum to integrate students."[24]

Finally, it should be noted that school operations, especially where public and Catholic schools are in the same states and attendance areas, are also likely to foster similar curricula. The closer they are geographically, the more public and private schools tend to operate with similar school calendars and teacher/student work days. School bus schedules are similar, often even identical. Family work and vacation schedules may also require similar school calendars to accommodate families with children in both public and private schools.

Similarities in Staff

Although not subject to precise quantification, there are important similarities between teachers in public and non-profit schools. The training of teachers in both sectors differs more in quantity than in quality. In some states teacher certification laws apply to teachers in both sectors. Even where private school teachers are not legally required to be certified, private schools often insist on, or prefer, certified teachers because of accreditation or public relations reasons. In 1981, 98 percent of public and 84 percent of private school teachers were certified to teach their major assignment by the state in which they were teaching.[25] Furthermore, many teachers in both public and private schools are trained in the same institutions; even when the institutions tend to be different, the same textbooks are often used in all courses.

In addition, there is considerable overlap in the professional activities of teachers in both sectors. They are active in the specialized organizations of teachers, such as the International Reading Association, National Science Teachers Association, National Council of Teachers of Mathematics, and so on. Obviously, such common membership implies considerable overlap in professional publications read, conferences attended, and leadership in professional activities.

Finally, a substantial number of teachers in private schools eventually accept positions in public schools. Although the number may not be very large in terms of the total public school complement, the transferees probably include a higher proportion of younger career-oriented teachers. Private school teachers whose salaries are the second income probably do not place as much emphasis on the higher salaries in public schools. There is also a smaller flow of teachers from public to private schools. It would be helpful to know the teacher characteristics associated with these transfer patterns, but systematic data on the subject are not available.

Policy Implications of the Similarity and Social Capital Hypotheses

The suggestion that public and private schools may not be very different seems counterintuitive. Why would parents pay if there are no significant differences? Surely they are not all being misled by private schools.

They are not being misled, but this does not negate the

point being made about the similarities between public and private schools. First of all, to the extent that private schools are maintained for religious reasons, their performance on secular criteria becomes secondary if not irrelevant. This does not mean that schools maintained under denominational auspices fail to achieve better educational results. It means only that the latter outcome is fortuitous *in terms of the operative rationale*. Paradoxically, "denominational auspices" may be regarded as a proxy for several secular factors that contribute to educational achievement. Thus even if parents enroll their children in denominational schools for religious reasons, the school environment may be more conducive to secular educational achievement than the environment of public schools.

Even parents who send their children to private schools for secular educational reasons are not necessarily being misled if private schools offer no educational superiority. Parents faced with a choice between an extremely poor public school or a much better private school may reasonably choose the latter option. Such parents may be the first to agree that private schools in general are no better than most public schools. In terms of our analysis, therefore, parents who send their children to private schools for secular reasons may be acting in a way that is completely consistent with the similarity hypothesis.

Whether or not nonprofit schools are more efficient than public schools, two important points must be emphasized. One is that any private school superiority does not rest on any greater expertise or technical superiority over public schools. The second is that nonprofit schools would lose some of their efficiency advantage under a voucher system. Let me comment on these points, since they are critical in many ways.

As previously noted, even if per-pupil costs are much lower in private schools when all costs in both sectors are fully accounted for, that fact does not necessarily constitute a valid efficiency argument for vouchers. If private school teachers were to receive higher salaries as a result of vouchers, as is virtually certain, the major efficiency advantage of their schools would be reduced correspondingly. Of course, there would be efficiency gains as well as losses; for example, by paying higher salaries, private schools might be able to increase class size without impairing educational output. In the short run, however, vouchers would probably result in decreased efficiency in private schools.[26]

The similarities between public and private schools pose several difficult questions for the educational improvement rationale for vouchers. According to this rationale, competition between public and private schools will lead to rapid and widespread adoption of better practices. Will this interactive process actually happen? The question inevitably raises another: Has this process taken place in the past? The answer seems to be a rather sweeping negative; at least I have not been able to identify any such improvements.

One can argue that the reason this has not happened is that public schools are, in effect, a monopoly and are under no pressure to adopt better practices. Yet even if we ask only what innovations would be incorporated into public schools if they were not monopolies, the answer seems to be "none." One can hardly argue that insistence on regular homework or better discipline are private school "innovations." Furthermore, after generations in which private schools have educated tens of millions of pupils, it ought to be possible to identify some improvements that originated there and were incorporated into public education. The absence of examples along this line weakens the argument that competition from nonprofit schools under a voucher plan will lead to educational improvement.

The similarities between public and Catholic schools support two somewhat conflicting conclusions. On the one hand, the similarities add credibility to the conclusion that the outcomes of public and Catholic schools are not very different, especially when the students being compared have adequate social capital. Minimally, the similarities are consistent with the conclusion that the choice of public or Catholic school has little effect on the educational achievement of large groups of students.

In this connection, it is surprising how little attention is paid to the fact that private schools appear to achieve comparable results while paying their teachers substantially less than public school teachers. This fact surely raises some questions about conventional approaches to school improvement. For instance, why is there such an urgent need to raise all teacher salaries if private school teachers with lower salaries seem to be achieving comparable results? Clearly, the Catholic advantage is not due to better teachers (at least insofar as higher salaries are a proxy for them). And insofar as we can exclude other factors such as "better teachers" as the explanation for the Catholic advantage, we strengthen the case for greater social capital as the explanation.

Perhaps the most fundamental policy implication of the social capital concept is that the separation of church and state in the United States has been a disservice to education, especially of disadvantaged children. Such separation has forced our society to avoid utilizing religious institutions to educate our youth. Inasmuch as disadvantaged children are the ones who are most handicapped by the absence of social capital, government inability to provide education through denominational schools has been especially harmful to them.[27]

Whether anything can or should be done in this regard are matters to be discussed; obviously, separation issues involve several matters that have not been considered thus far. At this point, however, let me say only that the issue is not whether to abandon the concept of separation of church and state. It is whether the concept should be interpreted to allow more extensive use of denominational schools to carry out secular governmental objectives in education. Inasmuch as government already utilizes religious organizations to deliver various noneducational services that are publicly funded, it is questionable whether any changes in the concept of separation are needed.

Unquestionably, there are strong political forces opposed to increased utilization of denominational schools to deliver publicly funded educational services. Any changes along this line face an uphill struggle. Although I regard such changes as both desirable and constitutional, their limitations should be recognized. Increased utilization of denominational schools may help a significant number of students who lack social capital, but it cannot help most of them. Furthermore, although improving the educational achievement of students from the underclass is very important, so is improving educational achievement among the vast majority of the student population. In other fields, for-profit enterprise has been our major source of increased productivity. For this reason, both denominational schools and schools for profit should be allowed to participate in voucher plans.

THE POLITICAL RATIONALE FOR FAMILY CHOICE

In *Capitalism and Freedom,* Milton Friedman argues that education vouchers are desirable as a means of reducing social conflict. As he points out, education, like public policy generally in the United States, is often characterized by intense political, religious, economic, and cultural conflict. Conflict over sex education, prayer in schools, and abortion rights illustrate such conflict.

When government provides a service like education, it tends to provide the same service for everyone. Consequently, the only way *A* can get the kind of education *A* wants is to force *B* to have it also; unfortunately, *B* may be strongly opposed and prefer a kind of education to which *A* is strongly opposed. Family choice is therefore viewed as a means of reducing social conflict. If parents could afford the kind of education they want for their children, there would be much less incentive for them to impose their educational views on others. Such imposition is unavoidable when government monopolizes educational services. For this reason, it is better to have their disagreements resolved through the marketplace instead of the political process.

The political rationale is clearly an independent argument for vouchers. One might reject all other arguments but still conclude that vouchers are needed to reduce political conflict over education. Furthermore, the political rationale need not be based solely or even primarily on religious conflict. Its existence might be an important element of the political rationale, but the latter is not necessarily dependent on any particular kind or source of educational conflict. As a matter of fact, many citizens who are indifferent to religious issues have strong convictions about political, economic, or social issues that arise in schools. Parents who have strong convictions about economic issues may not care one way or the other whether public schools have a moment of silent meditation or conduct Christmas pageants with Christian orientation or include "creation science" in the curriculum.

The political argument for vouchers is also based on a concept of equity. All citizens are taxed to support education. Arguably, it is unfair to subject parents to "double taxation" because they choose one type of school over another for reasons of conscience. The alleged inequity gives rise to political conflict as those excluded from the benefits seek redress. Presumably, a voucher system would eliminate this inequity and therefore this source of political conflict. Of course, whether the remedy would lead to even more conflict is another matter.

The strongest arguments for the political rationale are: (1) the existing system creates too much dissatisfaction and requires excessive allocation of resources to conflict management; and (2) it is frequently impossible to provide program integrity when educational programs are subject to the political process. Let us see why these arguments do indeed have considerable merit.

The educational program of public schools represents a compromise among citizens with different points of view. These compromises, although inevitable politically, may be indefensible educationally because they often apply to educational or technical issues that cannot be compromised without undermining all of the different positions on it. Sex education can be cited as an example. Some citizens don't want it in the schools. Some want it under various restrictions and limitations. Some want schools to advocate abstinence. Some want schools to present virtually any sexual code as a student choice to make. And so on.

Now, it may be that a program that vigorously and consistently emphasizes abstinence would be effective. It may also be that a clinical program with explicit instruction in the use of contraceptives would be effective. And it may also be that programs that are a compromise between the two are a waste of time and resources. If, however, the issue is to be resolved politically, the third alternative is most likely to happen.

Problems of this kind emerge in every field. A doctor may have to decide whether to operate immediately or delay the operation a few weeks in order to strengthen the patient. A compromise, such as delaying the operation for only a few days, may lose the value of both alternatives. In brief, interests are subject to compromise; technical solutions may or may not be. The issue is whether a compromise destroys the technical integrity of a proposed policy or program.

This issue arose frequently in my experience as a labor negotiator for school boards. One way or another, school boards and teacher unions agree eventually in the overwhelming majority of cases. Any consistent approach will usually achieve an agreement. What was most likely to fail, however, were compromises that eliminated the integrity of any approach. Boards would adopt a "hard line" but take action that was inconsistent with it. The result was that the board was not perceived as either "tough" or "liberal" but as a body that could not be trusted from one day to the next.

In any event, providing educational services through market instead of political processes would probably reduce social conflict over education. A personal example may help to illustrate this important point. In 1985 I visited a proprietary school in California. Students were required to wear uniforms. If parents refused, they had to enroll their children elsewhere.

My point is not that uniforms are better than no uniforms. It is that the structure of control enabled the school to adopt and implement a consistent policy. Contrast this private school with a public school board trying to formulate a dress code. Because the code is the result of a political process, it may lack any coherent rationale or consistent objective.

The OEO experiments discussed in chapter 4 also illustrate this point. OEO might have conducted an experiment to see if contracting out could improve basic skills. It might have conducted an experiment to see if the basic skills could be taught as effectively at a lower cost. It might have tested the value of teacher or student incentives to achieve certain goals. Due to political factors, however, it was forced to compromise among these objectives. As a result, what it did shed no light on any of them. The technical integrity of the experiment was destroyed by the compromises reached.

For-profit schools are more likely than nonprofit schools to avoid such outcomes, because nonprofit schools are often subjected to political or quasi-political pressures similar to those in the public schools. The principal of a denominational school is unlikely to enjoy the same degree of managerial discretion as the owners of for-profit schools. Of course, compromises are made in the marketplace as well as in government; one difference is that parents would have more freedom to reject marketplace compromises.

Antidemocratic Schools

Potentially at least, there is a political downside to vouchers that should not be ignored. I refer here to the possibility (opponents would say "probability") that vouchers would be used to fund extremist schools that foster antidemocratic views. As the objection runs, it is bad enough that parents can establish such schools using their own money; to allow public funds to be spent for them would be simply intolerable.

Clearly, there are extremist groups in our society: the Ku Klux Klan and neo-Nazi groups are examples. Still, we are dealing with a system issue, and it is essential to avoid a double standard in comparing system outcomes. It is, therefore, pertinent to ask whether the members of these groups received their education in public or private schools. I have no data on the issue but seriously doubt whether a disproportionate number were educated in private schools.

Significantly, most extremist groups do not survive for long. The notion that they could build schools, employ teachers, and transport their children to their schools implies a population base, a cohesiveness, and a durability that is doubtful, to say the least. Even antidemocratic parents are presumably interested in their children's welfare; the belief that such parents will act solely out of ideology for long periods of time seems doubtful.

Efforts to establish extremist schools can be anticipated, and antivoucher groups will publicize these efforts. In this connection efforts to use voucher systems to avoid racial integration are sometimes cited to show that vouchers will be used to achieve antidemocratic objectives. Such efforts were made, but the outcome does not necessarily support an antivoucher position. First and foremost, the efforts failed, which suggests that regulatory and judicial remedies can deal effectively with them. Second, some public as well as private schools try to evade their constitutional obligations; the files of federal civil rights agencies and the U.S. Department of Education include thousands of cases of school district failure to respect their constitutional obligations. (In fact, I served as an expert witness for the NAACP Legal Defense and Education Fund in such cases in six states.) As previously noted, private schools in the South were often racially integrated long before the public schools in their vicinity.

Most emphatically, I am not contending that antidemocratic schools would never be a problem under a voucher system. Instead, my point is that the problems will be manageable; the frequency and scale of their emergence is not likely to justify an antivoucher position. On the other hand, schools conducted largely in a foreign language, especially Spanish, may become a serious problem. Such schools may handicap students from full participation in our society. Most ethnic/language groups are too small to avoid familiarity with English, but the Hispanic population is not. States cannot prohibit private schools in which English is not the language of instruction, but they can decline to support them.

The Taxpayer Rationale

Family choice is sometimes supported as a means of minimizing our tax burdens. To illustrate, suppose that it requires $4,800 per child in tax revenues to educate students in public school. Suppose also that a voucher worth $1,000 would induce large numbers of parents to transfer their children to private schools. The taxpayer savings would be $3,800 per child, less the amounts paid to parents who enroll their children in private schools even without vouchers.

The example ignores several critical issues, including some factors that might reduce the savings, but it is intended only to illustrate how vouchers might minimize taxes. Obviously, the argument does not depend on any assumptions about religious freedom or social conflict or educational improvement. Instead, it asserts only that government contributions to a private service provider may be ultimately less expensive (to government) than not contributing. In the context of vouchers, efficiency issues are often confused with taxpayer ones. The taxpayer interest is not: Which schools are more efficient? It is: Which schools will cost taxpayers the least? Again, it must be emphasized that the questions are asked on the assumption that other things, such as the quality of service, are equal or do not favor the more expensive provider. Significantly, the National Taxpayers Union (NTU), a national organization seeking to reduce the costs of government, has actively supported family choice in education.[28] This support illustrates the point that the taxpayer rationale constitutes an independent argument for family choice.

Contrary to popular belief, the taxpayer rationale does

not necessarily assume that private provision of education is more efficient than public education. Conceptually at least, private schools might be less efficient than public schools, but if the inefficiencies are subsidized from private instead of public funds, the taxpayer rationale would still be valid. Nevertheless, efficiency and taxpayer issues are closely related. The more efficient private schools are, the more likely it is that a voucher system would lead to taxpayer savings. The less efficient the private schools are, the more they would need high tuition fees or donations to generate any taxpayer savings. Thus we should not ignore efficiency comparisons even though they do not necessarily tell us whether a voucher system would result in taxpayer savings.

Not surprisingly, comparisons of public to private school efficiency are characterized by intense controversy over the facts and their policy implications. The literature supporting vouchers sometimes asserts that per pupil costs in private schools are only about half the costs in public schools.[29] This assertion is probably not true, even though the full costs of public education are systematically understated and not factored into the comparisons.

In education, efficiency is the relationship between resources used (inputs) and educational outcomes produced (outputs). The common assumption is that private schools use fewer resources to produce the same or better outcomes than the public schools. This is probably true, but cost statements for nonprofit schools frequently omit certain costs, such as for utilities that are paid from church funds. Factoring in these costs might not affect the amounts saved by taxpayers under a voucher plan, but it would reduce the efficiency level of the nonprofit school.

This point is fundamental but widely overlooked. Many school expenses paid separately from tuition by parents or by religious organizations in private schools are paid from public funds in public schools. Consequently, the expenses do not show up on private school budgets. When these budgets are compared to public school budgets, it can seem that private schools are more efficient than public ones.

Donated labor is another example of a resource that must be included to develop an adequate view of the efficiency of nonprofit schools. It is virtually certain that such schools receive much more uncompensated labor than public schools.[30] Such donations, which benefit taxpayers as well as the nonprofit schools, cannot be ignored in estimates of private school efficiency. If individuals worked for wages that were donated to nonprofit schools, their contributions would be regarded as school revenues; likewise, so should contributions of time.

Furthermore, as mentioned, private schools enroll a much lower proportion of students who are difficult to educate and require higher than average per pupil costs. These categories include disabled, retarded, and disruptive pupils as well as certain types of vocationally oriented pupils. To this extent, lower per pupil costs in private schools cannot be attributed to their greater efficiency. As shown by table 7.2, private schools receive some publicly funded educational services.

Table 7.2

PERCENT OF PRIVATE SCHOOL STUDENTS WHO RECEIVED PUBLICLY FUNDED SERVICES, BY TYPE OF SERVICE AND RELIGIOUS AFFILIATION OF SCHOOL, 1983–84 SCHOOL YEAR

| Type of Service | School Affiliation | | |
	Catholic (%)	Other Affiliated (%)	Not Affiliated (%)
Transportation	76	12	12
Library	80	12	8
School lunch, milk	77	15	8
Health services	82	11	6
Remedial education	79	5	15

Bilingual education	47	13	40
Handicapped	12	4	84
Vocational education	41	7	52
Guidance	80	4	16
Speech therapy	67	11	22
Other services	68	10	21

NOTE: Because percentages are calculated on unrounded numbers, details may not add to totals.

SOURCE: Reprinted, by permission, from *Publicly Funded Services to Private Elementary and Secondary Schools and Students, 1983-84,* Center for Education Statistics, Office of Educational Research and Improvement, U.S. Department of Education (November 1986), p. 3. The data in this table were collected prior to the U.S. Supreme Court decision in *Aguilar* v. *Felton* (1985), which severely limited the provision of publicly funded services in denominational schools.

The Department of Education estimates that in fiscal year 1981, $608 million in federal funds were spent for kindergarten through grade 12 private schools; in that year federal expenditures per pupil were $277 in public schools and $121 in private schools.[31] Because these expenditures are not always reflected in the financial statements of private schools, their efficiency is correspondingly overestimated. As a matter of fact, Dennis J. Encarnation of the Harvard Business School estimated that just over 26 percent of private school income is received from public funds.[32] Whatever the correct percentage, it is ignored in the voucher controversy. Supporters do not want to weaken the impression that private school parents pay the full cost of private education while sharing the costs of public education. Voucher opponents do not want to reconcile their objections to vouchers with the acceptance of public funds for other costs of private schools.

Encarnation's estimate of private school income includes the value of "taxpayer expenditures." Such expenditures, which were approximately equal to the value of direct assistance, include property tax exemptions, tax deductability for donations, exemptions from corporate and sales taxes, lower postal rates, exemption from minimum wage, bankruptcy and antitrust laws, and other forms of indirect assistance to nonprofit schools.

Whether "taxpayer expenditures" should be considered a government subsidy to nonprofit schools, and whether they should be viewed as reducing any taxpayer savings resulting from the existence of nonprofit schools, are highly controversial issues. If taxpayer expenditures are factored into the costs of private schools, how does such inclusion affect the argument that nonprofit schools result in savings to taxpayers? One study of this issue has led to some interesting conclusions. A study by economist Marc Bendick, Jr., indicated that when taxpayer expenditures are taken into account, the differences between per pupil costs in the public and the nonprofit sectors decrease dramatically.[33] Although this study necessarily relied on data that was far from precise, clearly the taxpayer rationale for nonprofit schools is much more complicated than its proponents assume.

Thus far, I have discussed the ways that financial and recordkeeping procedures may lead to erroneous comparisons of public to private school efficiency. Let me turn next to some factors affecting their actual efficiency, not the accuracy or completeness of our data on the issue. First, if we focus on the resources actually used, the efficiency advantage of private schools may be substantially reduced. Their main advantage clearly lies in the fact that their teacher salaries and benefits average about one-third less than in public schools. It is unlikely that the resources used but not counted by private schools offset the savings from their lower levels of compensation. Bendick's study of the issue concluded that "the more comprehensive the accounting of revenues, the more similar are the patterns of financial support among the sectors."[34] As a matter of fact, although his analysis indicated that denominational schools had lower costs per-pupil than public schools, the per-pupil costs in nondenominational private schools (where class size is lower than in public schools) were much higher than in public schools.

A main reason why nonprofit schools are less efficient

than public schools is their lack of either economic or political accountability. That is, nonprofit schools, like most nonprofit organizations, are less subject than for-profit organizations to the discipline of the market. At the same time, nonprofit organizations are not subject to whatever discipline is imposed through our political system. To the extent that they operate without market or political accountability, nonprofit schools may be able to operate inefficiently without corrective action.

Merely to suggest that many private schools may be less efficient than public schools may seem absurd, especially to those associated with the former. It does not, however, seem absurd to those who have studied efficiency in the nonprofit sector. On the contrary, several researchers have concluded that nonprofit organizations are usually less efficient than either government or for-profit service providers.[35]

Generally speaking, private schools do not rely upon donations for most of their income. Although some denominational schools are heavily subsidized by their denominational sponsors, tuition fees are the largest source of income for denominational as well as independent private schools. Insofar as nonprofit schools rely on tuition and fees instead of donations, they are more likely to be efficient, but there are also countervailing factors. Most private schools are denominational schools and are not concerned about competition in the area of denominational instruction. To the extent that parents rely on denominational criteria for choosing schools, the denominational rather than the public schools constitute the monopoly. Thus the undesirable effects of monopoly can characterize nonprofit as well as public schools. Furthermore since management of nonprofit schools is legally constrained from receiving profits, it may have less incentive to identify inefficiencies but more incentive to tolerate management perquisites. These countervailing factors should not be dismissed, regardless of whether they characterize existing nonprofit schools.

The efficiency advantages of private schools are primarily their lower costs for faculty and support staff, their ability to use resources more effectively because their student bodies tend to be more homogeneous, and their freedom from regulatory costs. The largest savings are the lower teacher costs in private schools; as a rough estimate, teacher salaries and fringe benefits in private schools probably average about 25 percent less than such costs in public schools. This estimate is somewhat lower than most, but takes into account the fact that about one in four private school teachers receives some in-kind income. Housing, meals, and tuition allowances for family members are the major components, which probably total over $3,000 a year for teachers receiving them. A much smaller proportion of public school teachers, located mainly in isolated areas, receives a significant amount of in-kind income.

Aside from neglect of in-kind income, the salary differentials typically overlook certain facts which reduce the significance if not the differentials themselves. In 1985–86, private school teachers averaged four years less teaching experience than public school teachers. In addition, private school teachers had less training and were less likely to have received advanced degrees (master's or doctoral degree).[36] In other words, even if the private school teachers were placed on public school salary schedules, they would be earning less on the average than the current complement of public school teachers. To put it another way, the group comparisons overstate the differences between what a given teacher would earn in public as compared to private school employment.

Actually, school efficiency comparisons are characterized by several unanswered questions that raise serious doubts about the validity or usefulness of the results. For example, religious instruction is not one of the services provided by public schools. The latter, however, often provide services not often available in private schools: counseling, vocational, and special education services. Thus the extent to which differences in costs reflect differences in the services or in efficiency, or both, must be considered.

To cite just one additional example, locational issues

are subject to different interpretations. Because of its location, a private school may pay very little for security services. A public school in an inner city ghetto may have to pay a great deal for such services. Does the latter payment reflect a difference in efficiency? After all, if the public and private schools reversed their locations, their expenditure patterns for security might also be reversed.

Dozens of issues like these render valid comparisons very difficult to make. Nevertheless, such comparisons are often cited to justify policies relating to private schools. Because so many subjective judgments are involved, Daniel J. Sullivan, a leading analyst on the subject, has concluded that the comparisons merely spread confusion about an issue that cannot be resolved objectively.[37] Sullivan goes on to suggest that more attention be devoted to delineating the unique roles of each sector, rather than to the futile task of comparing their efficiency. Whatever the merits of the suggestion, it raises a question about competition between the sectors. If each sector performs a unique role, are they truly competitive?

Whatever the answer, the taxpayer rationale may overlook two factors that would reduce anticipated tax savings from vouchers. First, if vouchers are enacted, parents will have to pay more than they do now to enroll their children in private schools. If private school costs to parents are raised by all or most of the amount of the voucher, there would be little or no savings to parents and few if any voucher-generated transfers to private schools. Instead, there would only be a taxpayer loss resulting from the subsidies to children already enrolled in private schools—or who will enroll in the future, regardless of voucher availability.

The second neglected point relates to the political dynamics of appropriations for education. In the absence of vouchers, parents of children in private schools lack strong economic incentives to support spending for education. These parents are not merely a cross-section of parents generally; they include a disproportionate number of politically active citizens. A voucher system would provide these parents with economic incentives to support instead of oppose increased spending for education. In short, if the private school lobby were to join forces with their public school counterparts, the taxpayer rationale might well sink in a sea of red ink. Indeed, these groups might embrace each other as allies in the near future even in the absence of a voucher plan.

The Civil Liberties Rationale for Vouchers

Vouchers are also justified as a protection of civil rights. Although this rationale overlaps with the religious one, they differ in significant ways. Clint Bolick, an attorney active in civil rights litigation, has recently stated the civil liberties rationale as follows:

> . . . In modern society, the pursuit of education is critically important in exercising fundamental rights. Thus, any arbitrary interference with the pursuit of education constitutes a deprivation of civil rights. Moreover, as the Supreme Court observed in *Brown* v. *Board of Education,* the principle of equality under the law requires that education, "where the state has undertaken to provide it, . . . must be available to all on equal terms."
> The denial of educational liberty stands as one of the most flagrant and crippling violations of civil rights today. The principal source of this deprivation is the monopoly public school system, which limits opportunities for alternative types of education on the one hand while allocating benefits unequally on the other.[38]

In Bolick's view, "civil rights" means essentially three things: fundamental rights, individualism, and equal opportunity under the law. Fundamental rights include freedom to pursue economic opportunities not hindered by unjustifiable government obstacles. In some cases, however, government actions have weakened instead of strengthened equality of opportunity, especially in the economic realm.

Licensing laws illustrate this point. Although racially neutral on their face, they often have highly disparate effects on minorities and the disadvantaged.

An example cited by Bolick illustrates this point. In 1982 licensing requirements to drive a taxi in the District of Columbia were minimal. As a result, Washington had twelve cabs per one thousand people, and almost two thousand blacks owned taxis. In Philadelphia, where the licensing requirements were much more expensive, there were only three cabs per thousand people, and only fourteen owners were black.

Bolick concedes that education is not a fundamental right, like freedom of speech. Nevertheless, because of its importance to the economic welfare of individuals, arbitrary interference with the right to freely choose an education should be viewed as a violation of an individual's civil rights. His contention is that a voucher system would not have this result, so vouchers should be considered a civil rights issue.

Because this rationale for vouchers has been articulated only recently, it has not as yet been subjected to widespread analysis and criticism. It appears, however, that the rationale faces several empirical and constitutional problems. For example, plaintiffs alleging that our system of public education violated their civil rights would have to show they are damaged by the public school monopoly. It would be extremely difficult to show that the plaintiffs would be better off if they could attend a private school. The argument would be that although government need not support education at all, its support must be made available in ways that do not unreasonably limit parental choice in education. This is a minority position in legal circles at this time. In the short run at least, the civil rights rationale is unlikely to have any legal impact on voucher controversies. It does have some political appeal, but it is not clear whether the appeal will lead to policy changes.

8

The Politics
of Choice

Voucher controversies constitute an unprecedented philosophical turnabout on equality issues. By and large, vouchers are supported most strongly by "conservatives." The opposition to vouchers is centered largely among "liberals": the teacher unions, the American Civil Liberties Union, the liberal religious denominations such as reform Judaism and Unitarians, and various public interest groups typically supporting liberal positions, such as People for the American Way.

This widespread conservative-liberal split is a reversal of the roles these groups usually play on equality issues. For decades liberals and conservatives have clashed over a wide variety of government programs. In general, the liberal position has been that A and B are "equal" when both have the same power to do something. Thus A and B are equal with respect to educational opportunity if both can afford to attend the same college. They are equal with respect to health care if both have the funds to get the medical services they need. And so on. On the other hand, conservatives have been more apt to define equality in terms of legal rights. In the typical conservative outlook, the government's role is to ensure legal but not economic equality.

The liberal emphasis on the "power to do" has led inevitably to support for government programs that provide that power. In education, for example, the more government provides, the less individual students and parents must provide from their own resources. If government expands facilities for higher education and absorbs most of the operating costs xrom general revenues, it can keep student charges to a minimum. This is thought to be more conducive to equality of educational opportunity than charging students higher fees for their higher education.

In the voucher controversy, however, it is the conservatives who have adopted the idea that equality must be viewed as equal power, not merely as an equal legal right, to take an action. Conservative support for vouchers has repeatedly emphasized the goal of providing the poor with the effective choice now available only to the more affluent. Meanwhile, the liberals have ignored their traditional approach to equality as the equal power to do something.

This role reversal does not tell us anything about the merits of the controversy. No matter what the service, there are practical limits to how far government can and should go to equalize access to it. Each step toward equality as the power to do requires additional resources; additional resources require additional taxes, and at some point, the additional tax burdens are questionable substantively and/or politically disadvantageous.

The liberal/conservative role reversal on vouchers illustrates how interests dominate the discussion of voucher issues. The contention that vouchers would result in the destruction of public education also illustrates this point. It is contended that public schools have been an important means of fostering social and racial integration, and of economic and social mobility, especially for the disadvantaged. Essentially, this idea is based on the assumption that under a voucher system, public schools would end up with the disadvantaged minorities, disabled, disruptive, and/or otherwise difficult or expensive-to-educate students. Thus public education would lose its middle-class support, while private schools would be the beneficiaries of it; public schools would become the "dumping ground" of our educational system. Public schools would continue to exist, but their role as a means of upward mobility and social and racial integration would disappear.

The destruction of public education argument is, to put it mildly, not very persuasive. Essentially, it implies that the means are more important than the ends. If by any chance the dire prediction came true, the destruction would probably be deserved or self-inflicted or both. That would seem to be a reasonable conclusion in view of our tremendous exposure to public education as students, parents, and taxpayers, its enormous public revenues, and its interest group support.

The apocalyptic assessment of vouchers is based on the validity of several dubious assumptions. For instance, it assumes that public education will be helpless to do anything about the reasons why parents enroll their children in private schools. It assumes that parents in affluent suburbs with prestigious public schools will have as much incentive to transfer as beleaguered inner city parents. It assumes that private schools will maintain their real or alleged advantages even if and when such schools enroll many more students than they do now. It assumes that private schools will expeditiously solve the host of financial, legal, personnel, management, and regulatory problems that are likely to emerge from voucher legislation. Minimally, all of these assumptions are doubtful. Reliance on them illustrates the fact that both voucher supporters and opponents find it advantageous to exaggerate the effects of voucher plans. The difference is that proponents exaggerate to generate support while opponents do so to generate opposition to vouchers.

The Changing Patterns of Consumption

Education is a service industry; as such, it is not immune to changes affecting consumption patterns in our economy as a whole. Some of these changes are virtually certain to strengthen the voucher movement. Let us see why this is so.

Generally speaking, our economy is moving toward increased differentiation of products and services. The automobile industry illustrates this point for products. It is very unlikely that a single automobile will dominate the market, as the Model T did generations ago. The same trend is evident in services; for example, travel services were formerly a simple matter of how to assist X to travel from A to B. Today travel services include hotel reservations, car rentals, medical data, dining guides, special events, sightseeing information, travelers' checks, mail forwarding, and specialized insurance protections. The changes include both new services and the coordination of existing services.

Increasing differentiation and proliferation of services is directly tied to changes in income levels. As income levels rise, consumer decisions are more oriented to specialized and what might be called lifestyle activities. That is, consumption shifts from basic needs for food and shelter to goods and services that fulfill more personal needs.

If average incomes are low and meeting basic needs dominates the economy, there is relatively little demand for services geared to individual needs and tastes. The U.S. economy has passed through this stage of development; now its economy is oriented largely to products and services designed to fulfill personal needs and lifestyles. The emergence of two income households, with or without school-age children, has accelerated this development.

This change in the pattern of consumer demand does not occur at the same pace in every industry. It is safe to say that it lags somewhat in education, even taking into account the huge for-profit educational sector that caters to school-age children. We can reasonably assume, however, that the increasing demands for specialized educational services outside of regular school will eventually be reflected in consumer attitudes toward schools per se. If this occurs, it will herald a strong shift to voucher plans; it is very unlikely that public schools can respond as effectively as private schools to this shift in patterns of consumption. In view of the expansion of choice in religion, politics, marriage, higher education, occupation, spouse, residence, and lifestyle, in addition to the enormous increase in choice of products and services, the absence of educational choice below the college level may be simply an anachronism.

CHOICE WITHIN PUBLIC SCHOOLS

Feminists regard themselves as "pro-choice." Opponents of abortion characterize their position as "anti-abortion"—significantly, not "anti-choice." Similarly, parental choice in education is politically difficult to oppose. In fact, the public education lobby does not oppose it; instead it supports choice, on the condition that it be exercised within the public school system. Choice within public schools is also receiving widespread political support; for example, President Bush, the National Governors Association, and the President's Commission on Privatization have characterized it as a promising reform initiative. As of June 1988, choice legislation had been enacted or introduced in thirteen states, and the number has undoubtedly increased since then.[1]

Minnesota has enacted the most extensive legislation on choice within the public schools. Under a statute enacted in 1988, students in public schools will have the right to transfer to another district in the 1990–91 school year.[2] The district of residence cannot prohibit the transfers; the district of choice can refuse to accept students only if they exceed class, grade level, or building capacity. Districts are prohibited from rejecting students on grounds of previous academic record, handicapping conditions, lack of English proficiency, previous disciplinary record, or for athletic or extra-curricular reasons.

The state school board and school administrator organizations as well as the state teacher unions opposed the legislation. Reasons given include the fact that students could transfer every year; if a substantial number do so, districts would be unable to operate effectively. Also, no educational reason is required; if students want to transfer for social reasons, they can do so. It will be interesting to see what happens when the plan is implemented.

The supporters of choice within the public school system emphasize that "choice" need not be viewed as choice of district or of school. On the contrary, there can be choice of program, course, activity, schedule, and/or teacher. It is, therefore, quite common for public school leaders to assert that choice already exists or can be provided in public schools.

Unquestionably, this position has often been adopted in order to forestall family choice legislation. Regardless of motivation, however, the substantive issue remains: Can choices within the public schools achieve the benefits and avoid the drawbacks of a system that allows parents to choose private schools? In some respects at least, they clearly cannot. One reason is that the restriction to public schools necessarily excludes some choices that would be uppermost in parents' minds. For example, no matter what choices are available in public schools, they cannot include religious instruction, yet that might be why parents want a choice of school.

"Choice within public schools" encompasses a variety of widely disparate policies. Conceptually and practically, some students may choose to attend schools offering little or no choice of program. Others may not be able to choose their school, but may have a wide range of choices within the schools they are required to attend. To treat these and other versions of choice within public schools as examples of the same policy can (and does) lead to widespread confusion. For example, choice of school district has significant financial implications that do not arise in choice of program within the same school; the latter does not affect state aid to the school district. Students' willingness to exercise choice is another illustration. Choosing a different school or school district may involve differences in travel time and costs that are not present in choices within schools. As is the case with voucher proposals, there is a danger of identifying the concept with specific arrangements that can be drastically modified.

Unquestionably, there is a great deal of choice within public schools, especially in comprehensive secondary schools. Students typically can choose from a wide range of programs, subjects, and activities; often they can choose their teachers, at least within the limits of class size and room capacity. It appears doubtful, however, that such choices play a significant role in improving educational achievement. On the contrary, there is significant evidence that many students choose the least demanding and ultimately the least helpful subjects simply to get through school with as little hassle as possible. For these students, "choice" is a way to avoid the personal requirements of effective schooling.[3]

In short, "choice" per se is hardly more than a slogan. To understand its actual consequences, we must consider what the choices are, who can choose, the conditions and limitations of choice, and the effects of choice on other parties, including the nonchoosers. Viewed from such a broad perspective, choice within public schools offers at best only marginal opportunities for increasing educational achievement. This is not to argue for no choice within public schools or to question the wisdom of expanding choices in specific schools. Instead it is simply to say that expanding choice within public schools does not appear to be a promising route to educational reform.

To understand the reasons for this negative assessment, it is essential to recognize that choice within public schools means choices set by the producers, not the consumers. It is as if you could buy any automobile you wished—as long as it was sold by the state-operated automobile manufacturer. To say the least, bureaucratic decisions are a less accurate guide than market decisions to consumer preferences. Moreover, choice of public schools inherently involves constraints that limit its usefulness to parents. If parents prefer public school A over public school B, there is no necessary implication that B's teachers are incompetent; the choice may be based on programmatic or other reasons unrelated to teacher competence.

Thus a question arises: What to do with the teachers in school B? These teachers cannot be fired for incompetence merely because all the parents prefer the teachers in school A. For this reason, the choices within public schools will necessarily be severely limited to what is possible using existing staff. (New hires made possible by attrition are not likely to ease this limitation significantly.)

School capacity raises the same issue. Suppose schools A and B are excellent buildings operating at capacity, but all students in both schools prefer A to B. The school district is not likely to build an addition to A, or run double sessions at A, while school B is empty. Instead, choices will be limited by the capacity of existing buildings; in a voucher system, the expansion of preferred schools would not be limited by the need to utilize the less preferred schools.

As imposing as they are, the foregoing limitations on parental choice within public schools are probably not the most restrictive factors. About 80 percent of the nation's teachers are employed pursuant to collective bargaining contracts. Typically, these contracts limit school district flexibility in teacher transfers, hours of employment, assignments, and/or class size; the larger the district, the more likely this will be the case. If the contract says that teachers may not be assigned more than thirty pupils, it indirectly but effectively limits parental choice of teachers. As a matter of fact, many contracts require school districts to equalize class size or at least make a good faith effort to do so. Class size provisions are only one way that teacher union contracts would limit choice within a public school system; in most cases several contractual provisions would limit choice of school or teacher. Furthermore, it would be highly unrealistic to anticipate contract changes that would allow greater parental choice of schools or teachers. Such changes would require years of intensive negotiations in which the teacher unions would have several strategic advantages. The unions would represent an entrenched permanent constituency that knows what it doesn't want. In contrast, the supporters of choice are likely to be a highly diffuse group without any strong incentives to achieve their objectives. These parents who feel strongly about choice are more likely to enroll their children in private schools than to invest their time and energies in what is likely to be an unsuccessful effort to achieve it in public schools. Also, many parents probably will be concerned about retaliation if they publicly oppose teachers on this issue. In my own experience, I have met many parents who were strongly opposed to teacher strikes or teacher positions in bargaining, but who refused to express themselves publicly because (rightly or wrongly) they feared teacher retaliation if they did so.

The weakness of choice within public schools is especially evident when problems of scale are considered. Currently, some of the largest school districts operate specialized high schools. For example, the New York City school system operates the Bronx High School of Science, the High School of Music and Art, and several other specialized academic and vocational high schools. It is practically impossible for the overwhelming majority of school districts to do so; although many of their students might wish to attend specialized schools, the number of such students in most districts is insufficient to establish them. On the other hand, a voucher system could overcome this problem because specialized private schools could enroll students from several districts. "Choice within public schools" really has no solution to this problem, even though school districts occasionally operate specialized schools that enroll students from other districts. The vast majority of such schools serve disabled students; the schools are not a response to parental choice but to school district efforts to avoid excessive costs for facilities serving a small number of students. In these situations, however, parents from the sending districts cannot withdraw their children or vote in a school board election in the receiving district.

Let me cite one additional reason why choice solely within public schools is not likely to be effective. The rationale for choice assumes that the service providers will have strong incentives to respond to parental wishes. For the reasons just outlined, these incentives become highly attenuated—if they do not disappear altogether—when choice is limited to public schools. Public schools that can keep their market share regardless of parent preferences are not likely to change very much.

These drawbacks to choice within public schools are not merely speculation. The Office of Economic Opportunity tried to conduct an experiment with educational vouchers in the early 1970s. The experiment, conducted in the Alum Rock, California, school district, provided choice only in public schools and then only insofar as school facilities would permit. In addition, teachers were protected against any loss of employment or compensation as a result of parental choices. Even under these and other crippling limitations, the results were not clearly negative as far as vouchers were concerned. On the other hand, they were not dramatically favorable either, so they did not lead to increased support for vouchers.[4] Ironically, public school leaders currently urging support for choice solely within public schools conveniently overlook this experiment, which supposedly demonstrated that such choice would not lead to educational improvement.

Paradoxically, the prospects for choice within the public schools may depend partly on private school reactions to the idea. For the most part, state organizations of teachers, school administrators, and school board members oppose choice legislation, even when choice is restricted to public schools. These organizations do not necessarily fight such legislation to the bitter end, but they are not enthusiastic supporters of it.

At the same time, such legislation presents a dilemma for private school leaders. Their rhetoric supports choice, but choice only within public schools is disadvantageous to private schools. Such choice provides parents with options that cannot help and may even be disadvantageous to private schools. In the absence of the legislation, parents seeking certain courses or programs might find them available only in private schools. By making it possible for students to enroll in such courses in other public school districts, the legislation weakens private school attractiveness. Indeed, some of the leading proponents of choice within public schools have explicitly cited this as a reason for their position.[5]

Generally speaking, the private schools have some influence in the state legislatures. Consequently, choice legislation limited to public schools presents a dilemma for at least some proponents and opponents of choice. The private school proponents may be faced with a plan that strengthens choice, but in part to their disadvantage. At the same time, the public school opponents of choice legislation must now decide whether to join the private school opposition to it or support the legislation as a way of avoiding policies that would facilitate choice of private schools.

Choice Within Public Schools: Tactic or Policy?

Measures to provide choice within public schools receive widespread publicity and may be widely enacted. The ostensible purpose of these measures is to foster greater flexibility and responsiveness to consumer preferences. Other things being equal, however, this objective would be far better served by resort to the private sector; the record of private sector superiority on this criterion is persuasive, to say the least. At bottom, choice within public schools is an effort to incorporate the features of a market system in government provision of service. Unfortunately, such efforts usually fail, no matter what service or country is involved.

The naivete of these efforts should also give us pause; for example, a recent study supportive of choice within public schools asserts that it is "based largely on a free market concept" and "stems from the free market ideology of Adam Smith developed over 200 years ago."[6] I suspect that Adam Smith would be startled to read that choices offered by a public sector monopoly illustrate his "free market ideology."

As we have seen, voucher critics contend that vouchers providing schools of choice would lead to ethnic, religious, economic, and social class isolation and stratification. Wouldn't choice within public schools have the same effects? It would unless choices are different, which is clearly the case. This undermines the idea that choice in public schools can replace choice of public or private school. Regardless, educational literature is replete with references to the public school problems of tracking, that is, to problems resulting from students choosing or being assigned to different educational or career objectives. Tracking is not due solely to student choice, but the expansion of choice within public schools unquestionably will lead to more of it. On the other hand, the way to reduce tracking is to reduce the choices that lead to it.

The tracking problem reveals a fundamental dilemma of choice within public schools. Essentially, it fosters the same outcomes of self-selection which are deemed reprehensible if they result from choice of a private school. To make matters worse, by catering to a wide range of choice, public schools end up trying to be all things to all parents. Inevitably, they cannot provide choices as attractive as those available in schools which focus on particular choices. Anyone who doubts this should consider what choices of automobile would be available if limited to those made by a single monopolistic automobile manufacturer.

Some supporters of family choice view choice within public schools as progress toward voucher plans that would provide choice of school.[7] A little reflection suggests something is remiss here. The public school establishment is adamantly opposed to private school participation in voucher plans. If choice within public schools were a step in that direction, would the AFT and NEA support it? Are these organizations unwittingly moving us closer to private school participation in voucher plans? Any such conclusion underestimates the political sophistication of the teacher unions. Their support for choice within public schools should be viewed as a blocking maneuver, not as an incremental step toward family choice plans. For better or for worse, however, legislative action in the next few years is likely to focus on choice within public schools.

The Political Paradox of Vouchers

An ironic aspect of the voucher controversy is the fact that it would be most feasible to introduce vouchers in those states in which there is the least political support for them. This is due to the fact that since some students are already enrolled in private schools, the states would have to pay out substantial amounts before transferees from public schools would result in savings in total state expenditures for public education. If the voucher amount is low, it will be less of a drain on public expenditures, but fewer parents will use it; the fewer who use it, the less likely it is that transferring students will compensate for the voucher expenditures to students already enrolled in private schools. On the other hand, the higher the voucher, the more students will transfer, but the amount that must be recouped by transfers from public to private schools is also much larger.

A hypothetical example will illustrate the difficulties. Let us assume that states A and B, each enrolling 1 million students, desire to enact a voucher plan. State A has 30 percent of its total enrollment in private schools; state B has only 5 percent in private schools. The amount of the voucher is $2,400, or half the cost of educating a student in the public schools. We assume further that per-pupil costs in public schools average $4,800, and that 10 percent of the students would transfer from public to private schools.

On these assumptions, we could expect the following results:

STATE A		STATE B
1,000,000	total number of pupils	1,000,000
700,000	pupils in public schools	950,000
300,000	pupils in private schools	50,000
$4,800	average per-pupil cost, public school	$4,800
$3,360,000,000	total cost of public education	$4,560,000,000
$2,400	amount of voucher, one-half per pupil cost in public schools	$2,400
$720,000,000	voucher costs for pupils already in private schools	$120,000,000
70,000	number of pupils who transfer from public schools (10% of public school enrollment)	95,000
$552,000,000	state gain or loss is 10% transfer out of public schools (costs for pupils already in private schools plus net savings from transferees)	$108,000,000

In other words, state A would be spending an additional $552 million in order to allow one public school student out of ten to exercise choice of school. In contrast, state B would show a net gain of $108 million if 10 percent of its public school students transferred to private schools. In state A, all taxpayers would have their taxes raised so that 70,000 pupils could go to private school; even if we subtract the 300,000 families with children in private schools, tax losers outnumber winners by a substantial margin. In state *B,* however, all the families would be tax winners, regardless of whether their children are in public or private schools. State *B's* total expenditures for education would be reduced from $4.560 to $4.452 billion. All taxpayers would enjoy a slight tax reduction; in addition, the 145,000 families sending their children to private school would be the beneficiaries of a $2,400 voucher.

The Vermont Experience: Reality Confounds Rhetoric

By and large, the debate over vouchers has ignored the existence of a voucher-type system in Vermont since 1869. The Vermont system shows that the reality of a voucher system may be quite different from the plans or rhetoric of both supporters and opponents.[8]

Technically, Vermont has a tuition, not a voucher, system. School districts are allowed to pay tuition for their students in schools in or out of the state. Parental choice is thus subject to school board approval; however, even school districts that include high schools are allowed to pay tuition for schooling outside the district, which often happens.

Initially, the Vermont system resulted from the existence of several school districts without high schools. Beginning in 1869, these districts were allowed to pay public or private schools, in or out of the state, an amount based on the per-pupil costs in neighboring districts. Over the years the legislation was amended and clarified so that in 1984–85, Vermont paid almost $8.6 million to send 2,857 secondary school pupils to private schools. Parents absorb the additional costs, which in some cases are considerable.

Vermont does not allow local districts to pay for tuition elsewhere at the elementary level. Legislation to authorize the practice failed to be enacted in 1985 after the State Board of Education, State Commissioner of Education, and Vermont Education Association opposed it in the Vermont House of Representatives. Even school districts without elementary schools are not allowed to pay the tuition for their elementary pupils in private nondenominational schools. As a result, in some cases parents pay the full cost of tuition in a private school below the seventh grade, but their school district pays for it in the same school from the seventh grade up.

The status of tuition payments to denominational schools in Vermont is especially interesting. In a 1961 case, the Vermont Supreme Court held that tuition payments to a parochial school violated the First Amendment. Nevertheless, several religiously oriented private schools have continued to receive tuition payments. For instance, three prestigious Episcopal schools, with Episcopal clergy on their boards and which hold chapel once or twice a week, have continuously received tuition payments; thus the extent of religious sponsorship, control, or orientation that is permissible remains unclear. This issue will be important if voucher plans are enacted. Some denominational schools are legally controlled by lay boards, not religious organizations or religious leaders. The issue is whether such schools are treated legally in the same way as schools formally under religious control.

The amount of the tuition payment to private secondary schools is based on the actual cost, up to a ceiling amount. The latter is the average tuition cost in Vermont's union high schools for the year of attendance; any amount over this must be paid by the parents, as well as the costs of transportation or other expenses resulting from a decision to enroll in a private school.

Another interesting feature of the Vermont system is the flexibility provided local districts. The latter can decline to pay for tuition elsewhere if they so choose. They can designate the school or schools eligible for payment (from a state-approved list). Or, as often happens, a district may allow parents to choose any school, in or out of the state, from the state-approved list. Thus Londonderry, a community with a population of 1,510 in 1984–85, paid for tuition for eighty-eight students in that school year. Of these, forty-six were enrolled in public high schools, at a cost of

$3,288 per pupil. Another forty-two were enrolled in forty-two private schools in Vermont, Connecticut, New York, Massachusetts, and New Hampshire, with the district paying $2,862 per pupil.

As noted, vouchers are not used in Vermont; eligible schools in or out of the state simply bill the sending district for the state-approved amount for students choosing their school. This arrangement has functioned efficiently, avoiding the problems that would arise by using vouchers with an identical face value. In the latter case, reimbursements would be necessary if tuition in some schools were less than the voucher amount.

The flexibility of the plan is especially interesting. Most voucher discussions assume that the state will pay for the voucher. The Vermont plan renders payment a local option, a feature that has received relatively little attention from voucher analysts. The Vermont experience also suggests that providing educational choice need not create difficult administrative problems. Paradoxically, parents in districts without high schools may have virtually unlimited choice, while parents in districts with several public and private schools may have none. Although local option inevitably results in such anomalies, there is much to be said for it, especially from a political standpoint. By leaving the issue in the hands of local school boards, legislators may find it possible to avoid voting on a statewide voucher or choice plan that would be costly politically, no matter what the vote. To be sure, public school organizations, especially NEA and AFT, would oppose this type of plan, but legislators could argue that they were voting for local autonomy, not for vouchers per se.

Overall, the Vermont experience is generally favorable to voucher plans. It shows that they need not involve closer regulation. Indeed, since the plan extends to out-of-state schools, close regulation of participating schools is not possible. Even the initial standards for eligibility are relatively innocuous. The plan has no effects on integration, especially when the students served are from school districts without a high school of their own. Parents do add funds to the voucher, strengthening the conclusion that vouchers would lead to greater total spending for education. Whether the benefits go to the affluent is not an issue; the students eligible for vouchers are defined in such a way that any result on this issue would be fortuitous. If local school boards should have the option of "making" or "buying" education, the Vermont system provides a unique combination of contracting out with parental choice.

THE POLITICS OF VOUCHERS

Writing more than ten years after Milton Friedman's first voucher proposals, Stanford professor Henry J. Levin concluded that they would have "deleterious consequences." He then inquired into how the market approach might be adapted to the needs of ghetto children, and answered his own inquiry by recommending that:

. . . the state provide tuition payments—and thus schooling alternatives—only for children of the poor. These family allowances ". . . would allow that one section of our population that suffers most seriously from segregated schooling—the poor—to move, at their own initiative, and if they want to, into schools of their choice outside their neighborhoods." This specific application of the Friedman proposal appears to be politically feasible and it is likely to spawn both the private and social benefits that we discussed above.[9]

Almost twenty years later the Reagan administration twice attempted to provide poor children, and only poor children, a voucher. On both occasions the effort was decisively defeated in Congress.[10] Whatever their educational merits, the proposals were clearly not "feasible politically." On the contrary, the entire public education establishment condemned them in the harshest terms, and they did not come close to enactment on either occasion. Significantly, although the Reagan administration supported the proposals as a way to help economically disadvantaged students and parents, organizations representing these beneficiaries were not actively supportive.

There is a wide gap between support for vouchers in public opinion polls and such support in legislative arenas.[11] Private school leaders are deeply divided over the issue; many fear increased government regulation, which they regard as inevitable under a voucher plan.[12] Although most private schools are denominational, none of the largest Protestant organizations officially supports government aid to religious schools. Except for some small Orthodox groups, Jewish organizations are opposed to it, and Catholic ones are ambivalent or divided. Inasmuch as the non-denominational private schools serve a relatively small group of students, drawn disproportionately from affluent parents, government aid to such schools is not a popular political position at this time. The upshot for many private school leaders is a tacit acceptance of the status quo: minimal public financial support but also minimal state regulation of private schools.

Despite the unfavorable history of voucher initiatives, Americans for Educational Choice, a national coalition seeking to enact voucher plans, was established in the fall of 1988.[13] Although composed predominantly of denominational schools and politically conservative organizations, the coalition hopes to launch a major effort to develop a broader base of political support for vouchers. In my opinion, however, its most difficult task is not changing the views of voucher opponents; it is achieving legislative and political unity among voucher supporters. Let me elaborate on this critical point.

In controversies over vouchers, there is a tendency to view the arguments as additive or cumulative. This is understandable but erroneous. Those who support vouchers on religious grounds might do so even if vouchers resulted in higher taxes or a less efficient educational system. These negative consequences might be seen as the price that has to be paid to protect religious rights.

As previously noted, voucher proposals may differ on a

host of issues: who is eligible, the amount of the voucher, the kinds of expenses covered, the standards to be met by schools that redeem the vouchers, and state regulation of voucher schools, to cite just a few of the issues.

Needless to say, changes in voucher plans that would overcome one objection are likely to create new ones. If a voucher is too small to provide genuine choice, increasing it solves the problem, but only by intensifying its fiscal problems. If a proposal is deemed too expensive for taxpayers to accept, reducing the tax burdens also reduces effective choice, especially among low-income parents. If a voucher is tied to increased regulation of private schools, some voucher proponents will oppose it; if there is little or no regulation, the proposal will be criticized for giving away public funds without adequate safeguards. And so on.

These considerations explain why public opinion polls exaggerate the level of support for family choice. Family choice, like any other policy, cannot be implemented as an abstraction. On the contrary, it must be implemented by legislation that deals with specifics which may weaken its support.

In my opinion, the extent of dissatisfaction with public education will be a key to whether voucher plans will be enacted widely. Inasmuch as I regard the educational reform movement as hopelessly futilitarian, I expect voucher support to increase among the public at large. As we have seen, the "partisan poor" (which includes a substantial proportion of black voters) support vouchers more heavily than any other major constituency in either the Democratic or Republican parties.[14] Such support raises an interesting political question. Black voters are predominantly Democratic. So are the teacher unions that are overwhelmingly opposed to vouchers. As I shall explain in chapter 11, the political influence of teacher unions is likely to decline; conceivably, voucher issues could play a role in this development. By emphasizing vouchers, conservative candidates could presumably appeal to black voters. Indeed, it is not at all clear why they have failed to do so; perhaps the perception of vouchers as a Catholic issue has been a factor.

Concern over alienating teachers who might otherwise support conservative candidates may also be a consideration. Nevertheless, if a significant proportion of black voters support voucher efforts, voucher prospects will be greatly enhanced.

In certain contexts, our political system responds more generously to failure than to success. For this reason, attitudes toward vouchers may be dominated by perceptions about their beneficiaries. If their beneficiaries are perceived to be low-achieving or low-income students and their parents, their prospects will be enhanced. If the beneficiaries are perceived to be private schools, the dominant reaction may be not to appropriate funds to schools that are functioning effectively. Political strategy and tactics may play a more important role than substance in shaping these perceptions.[15]

U.S. Supreme Court decisions will play a critical, perhaps even decisive role in the future of voucher plans. Currently, voucher plans are blocked by Supreme Court decisions prohibiting assistance to denominational schools except under narrowly defined circumstances. These decisions are based on the First Amendment clause prohibiting the establishment of religion. Faced with an appropriate case, the Supreme Court would probably uphold voucher plans as government aid to *parents* on a nondiscriminatory basis. The constitutional precedent for such a decision is *Mueller* v. *Allen,* which upheld tax deductions for educational expenses for all parents, even though the overwhelming majority taking the deductions were parents of students in denominational schools.[16]

Another possibility is that the Supreme Court will hold that compulsory education, in conjunction with parental inability to pay for private education, violates the free exercise of religion clause in the First Amendment. Constitutionally, government must show "a compelling state interest" to justify interference with religious freedom. Understandably, voucher opponents have no difficulty identifying such interests, but the legal argument for their existence is clearly vulnerable.

The constitutional issues related to denominational schools may be clarified in the near future. As this is written, day care legislation is the subject of intensive controversy in the U.S. Congress. The controversy involves several constitutional issues raised by education vouchers. This is evident from the debate over the Act for Better Child Care Services of 1988, widely known as the ABC Bill or the Dodd-Kildee Bill.[17] As initially drafted, the ABC Bill included stringent restrictions on participation by religious organizations and a strong emphasis on day care in public schools. Inasmuch as the NEA, AFT, and AFSCME hope to organize day care employees in public schools, these unions were among the 90 organizations that supported the bill by November, 1987. Although some religious organizations supported it, most were strongly opposed, as were several other organizations for a variety of reasons.

Subsequently, Representative Dale Kildee of Michigan introduced a substitute bill which included the following provisions relating to participation by religious organizations:

Sec. 19. LIMITATIONS ON USE OF FINANCIAL ASSISTANCE FOR CERTAIN PURPOSES.

(a) Sectarian Purposes and Activities.—No financial assistance provided under this Act shall be expended for any sectarian purpose or activity, including sectarian worship and instruction.

(b) Facilities.—

(1) New Facilities.—No financial assistance provided under this Act shall be expended for the construction of a new facility.

(2) Existing Facilities.—No financial assistance provided under this Act shall be expended to renovate or repair any facility unless— . . .

(B) if such provider is a sectarian agency or organization, the renovation or repair is necessary to bring such facility into compliance with health and safety requirements imposed by this Act. . . .

(b) Religious Discrimination.—A child care provider may not discriminate against any child on the basis of religion in providing child care services in return for a fee paid, or certificate redeemed, in whole or in part with financial assistance provided under this Act.[18]

Although some critics of the original bill characterized these changes as cosmetic, various public school organizations withdrew their support for it. Inasmuch as President Bush is expected to veto legislation that excludes religious providers, such legislation is not likely to be enacted. If it is, the constitutional issues would not be precisely the same as those arising under compulsory education statutes; still, if day care legislation is enacted, the Supreme Court will probably have to decide the constitutionality of non-preferential government assistance to religious organizations to fulfill secular purposes. Perhaps as education voucher opponents fear, a Supreme Court decision upholding such assistance could lead to widespread state voucher legislation. One way or another, however, developments in day care are likely to play a major role in the future of voucher plans.

Minivouchers

In the immediate future, perhaps the most effective way to advance the voucher concept is to deemphasize the idea that vouchers should pay for enrollment in a school. Instead, serious consideration should be given to "minivouchers," or, vouchers that could be used for subjects or activities that do not require a change of school. For instance, minivouchers might be available for Russian or sculpture or other courses not available in the school of enrollment. Such vouchers would have several advantages over vouchers that can be used only in connection with a choice of school.

1. Minivouchers would be less threatening to the public school establishment. Also, if teachers were allowed

to be service providers in their off-duty hours (as is the case in Japan), a significant number might support minivouchers. This would weaken union opposition to vouchers. In any event, teacher jobs would not be threatened by minivouchers as they would be if vouchers could be used for students to transfer from public to private schools.

2. Minivouchers would not justify any additional regulation of private schools. The latter would not benefit directly from minivouchers, but they could hardly be opposed to choice proposals that did not involve greater regulation of private schools. Even if there were some regulation of the vendors providing services under minivouchers, it would be difficult to use such regulation as a backdoor way of opposing minivouchers.

3. Minivouchers can more easily avoid the separation of church and state issues that thwart conventional voucher proposals.

4. Some services purchased by minivouchers could be made available in schools outside the regular school day. This could have several desirable side effects— for example, it would reduce the building capacity needed during the regular school day.

5. It would be more difficult politically to oppose minivouchers than choice-of-school vouchers. First, minivouchers would avoid the major objections to conventional vouchers, such as the criticism that they would turn the public schools into a dumping ground. Second, political leaders might view minivouchers as a way of meeting the demands for choice without disrupting public education. Parents who cannot or do not interact effectively with the public schools might welcome opportunities to become involved in specific educational matters affecting their children; at least, parents would have no reason to oppose minivouchers.

6. Minivouchers offer opportunities to frame choice issues in ways more favorable to promoting choice.

Currently, "choice" is viewed as choice of school. In the real world, however, choice of program, course, activity, or teacher may be more important. To put it another way, choice of school may be irrelevant to the specific choices that parents seek; neither the public nor the private schools may offer the course or activity parents would like to choose. The more we can separate choices and offer them independently of each other, the less reason parents will have to be dissatisfied with the system.

Whether vouchers providing a choice of school will fulfill the expectations of their supporters is an open question. It seems to me, however, that incremental strategy is essential to achieve such vouchers. Voucher proponents often accept this point, but they tend to think of it solely in financial terms. Their strategy has been to enact a voucher plan that treats choice of school as the critical decision parents must make. In order to enact the legislation, the financial benefits are deliberately held to a minimum; the thought is that in future years, it will be easier to increase the amount of the voucher. Essentially, the strategy is to enact acceptance of the voucher principle and to rely on an incremental approach to increase the voucher amount.

In my view, this strategy is flawed for two reasons. First, voucher opponents are acutely sensitive to it. For this reason, they are determined to defeat voucher proposals no matter how small the initial amount of the voucher. Strategically, they are right to do so, so we can expect their continued opposition to choice-of-school vouchers.

The second flaw in current incremental strategy is its self-defeating nature. If the dollar amount of the voucher is low, the vouchers will benefit only the parents who already are sending their children to private schools in the absence of vouchers. I am not contending that such help is undeserved but am simply calling attention to its political consequences. If assistance to parents who already send their children to private schools is tne main outcome of the initial voucher plans, other states are less likely to adopt such plans. As previously noted, OEO "experiments" in educational performance contracting and educational vouchers were so flawed that they could not provide an adequate test of either idea. By proceeding with these flawed "experiments," however, the OEO unwisely and unfairly discredited the very ideas giving rise to them.

Conventional voucher proposals are especially vulnerable in this regard. As in Alum Rock, efforts will be made to modify voucher proposals so that their failure is assured. Minimizing the dollar amount of the voucher is one way to achieve this objective.

Minivouchers have a much better chance to avoid this outcome. A voucher amount that is too small to affect the choice of school may nevertheless be large enough to affect a choice of course or activity outside the regular school day. Concretely, a voucher worth $250 may affect only a minuscule number of school choices, but it could affect a much larger number of choices relating to specific courses or activities.

As a matter of fact, in 1985 Minnesota enacted a Postsecondary Enrollment Options Act (PSEO).[19] Under PSEO, public school students in grades eleven and twelve can enroll in nonsectarian courses offered by public or private postsecondary institutions of higher education on a course by course basis. State aid on a pro rata basis goes to the institutions offering the courses. Public school organizations did not oppose this form of choice as strongly as they did voucher plans funding full enrollment in private secondary schools. As previously noted, the Reagan administration proposed minivouchers for remedial services, and Congress crushed such proposals. We should be careful, however, not to draw the wrong lesson from this experience. When vouchers were perceived as a Catholic issue, they were losers politically. When they were oriented solely to the disadvantaged, they were also losers. These failures are instructive. To be enacted, voucher plans must appeal to several constituencies. These constituencies have not as yet reached consensus on a voucher plan that is both politically viable and acceptable. To do so, they will have to agree on the specifics so that the voucher coalition does not break up when a concrete proposal is introduced. Agreement on pie-in-the-sky specifics is easy to achieve but politically futile. The crucial issue is what compromises voucher constituencies are willing to make to achieve a voucher plan that can be enacted.

9

Education for Profit:
Big Business or
Cottage Industry?

The scale of education for profit is important from several standpoints. Large companies support research and development in ways that small ones cannot. More efficient facilities and equipment may require large-scale use to be profitable, so small companies may not be able to take advantage of such opportunities. National or regional companies may adopt policies or practices that would not be appropriate if only a local market is considered. I do not mean that privatization in education must develop *in toto* as either a cottage industry or as large-scale enterprise. Some dimensions might follow one pattern while others followed a different pattern.

My objective in this chapter is to explore various patterns of development in education for profit. In doing so I do not assume that "big" is necessarily "better." Nor do I question the fact that large-scale enterprise has unique disadvantages or advantages. My objective here is simply to identify and analyze some of the factors that will affect the scale of education for profit.

257

Initially, it may seem that instruction will be a small-scale enterprise. Education is a service; unlike products, which can be shipped around the world, services must ordinarily be delivered to customers. Barbers in New York can't cut your hair if you are in California. Doctors can't operate on patients not at hand. Granted, some kinds of teaching, especially at higher grade levels, can be carried on through television and radio, but the interaction and feedback required for effective teaching usually requires a closer relationship between teacher and students.

Yet although most educational services require such proximity, we must avoid confusing the size of the delivery unit with the size of the firm. McDonald's is a multibillion-dollar company, even though none of its service outlets remotely approaches this dollar volume. Financial service conglomerates provide an extremely broad range of financial services across state and national borders. In fact, although the costs of health care have already reached over 11 percent of gross national product, some analysts have speculated that by the end of the century most health care will be controlled by twenty to thirty corporations. In short, the fact that education is a service does not necessarily mean that education for profit will be a small-scale industry.

Although I have already discussed developments in health care, a few additional comments on that subject may be helpful. The five largest companies dominate the hospital chains: Hospital Corporation of American (HCA), Humana, American Medical International (AMI), National Medical Enterprises (NME), and Lifemark. These five chains owned about half the hospital beds owned by all for-profit hospitals in 1981.[1] (These proportions have changed considerably since then as a result of mergers and acquisitions in the hospital industry.)

Several differences between the leading hospital chains might be applicable to education. Unlike Humana, HCA does not limit itself to operating only its own hospitals; HCA also manages a large number of hospitals under contract. AMI and NME stress diversification. NME owns nursing homes and provides construction, purchasing, and other services for other hospitals. AMI sells a variety of special services to other hospitals: laboratory, dietary, and pharmaceutical services; respiratory therapy; mobile CAT scanners; and alcohol recovery centers. There is no obvious reason why similar developments cannot or should not emerge in education. For that matter, the leading companies providing food, maintenance, and other noninstructional services typically provide management services, not the entire complement of employees required to provide the service. This fact raises an interesting and perhaps highly important issue. Why do school districts buy management services for noninstructional but not for instructional services? For that matter, why isn't school district management ever contracted out? After all, governments often contract out hospital management, not merely this or that aspect of it.

The possibilities of contracting out a particular service is rarely raised in education. One recent development, however, suggests that it may become an urgent practical issue in the near future. A number of states, most notably New Jersey, have enacted legislation authorizing state takeover and operation of local school districts for various reasons. If and when such takeovers occur, it will become imperative to find management capable of managing the school districts. Educational management companies could conceivably meet this need, just as hospital management companies do in the field of health care. Whether or not takeover legislation triggers such a development, the possibilities of contracting out school management or the management of instructional services should be explored thoroughly.

Educational Testing and Market Size

Private companies provide a wide variety of testing services. Although most of these companies are for profit, the largest is Educational Testing Service (ETS), a nonprofit company based in Princeton, New Jersey. Established in 1947 as a nonprofit corporation, in 1986 ETS revenues were almost $200 million.

Like most other national companies that are active in education markets, ETS provides services to a wide variety of noneducational clients as well. For example, its Center for Occupational and Professional Assessment (COPA) provides job-related tests for more than fifty occupations. Clients include government licensing agencies, trade associations, employers, and institutions of higher education. The services offered can include job analysis; test development, administration, and scoring; and score reporting. Similarly, ETS also tests proficiency in English for government agencies, business firms, and educational institutions.

In education, ETS is best known for the development and administration of the Scholastic Aptitude Test (SAT), a test taken by about 1.5 million high school juniors and seniors every year. The SAT is a prime example of economies of scale; although SAT development cost several million dollars, students paid only $11.75 each in 1988 to take the test and have the scores sent to three institutions of higher education. The large number of students who pay for the test every year funds a level of technical support that no single institution could finance solely from its own funds.

In one respect, however, the growth of ETS seems to contradict my argument that nonprofit schools would not expand rapidly under an educational voucher plan. The rapid growth of ETS is not to be ignored but hardly demonstrates that nonprofit status is irrelevant to expansion. Many of the services ETS provides are in noncompetitive markets. Its tests are used primarily to guide educational transitions—high school to college or college to graduate or professional schools. Other test companies sell mainly achievement and various sorts of noncompeting programs. Interestingly enough, although ETS officials have not tried to change its nonprofit status, they do not express any strong opposition to such a change.[2]

FOR-PROFIT LEARNING
CENTERS

Learning centers operated for profit raise several significant issues related to educational reform. These centers provide supplementary educational services for students in public and private schools. In 1988 the three leading companies in this field were Sylvan Learning Corporation (based in Montgomery, Alabama), Huntington Learning Centers (based in Oradell, New Jersey), and American Learning Corporation (based in Chicago, Illinois).[3] The latter operates centers under the name The Reading Game in the West and under the name Britannica Learning Centers elsewhere.

The following discussion will focus largely on Sylvan Learning Corporation, which is a Delaware corporation in the business of diagnosing learning needs and offering individualized instructional services to meet those needs. Essentially, the company provides supplementary educational services for children in school. Reading, mathematics, and writing were the initial supplementary services, but others, such as study skills, have been added.

Sylvan's growth has been impressive, to say the least. The company was established in 1979 under the name Achievement Centers Inc. The founder was a high school teacher who still serves as chairman of the company's board of directors. Starting with one center in Portland, Oregon, the company began to franchise centers in September 1980. The company was reorganized as Sylvan Learning Centers in 1981 and was purchased by Kinder-Care, the nation's largest provider of day care services, in 1984. Subsequently corporate headquarters moved to Montgomery, Alabama, where Sylvan shares a new office building with Kinder-Care. By 1987 the parent corporation had over four hundred centers under license or direct operation. Despite increasing competition, Sylvan expects to increase both the number of centers and the services offered for many years to come.

Sylvan sells three types of franchises; the differences are

mainly in the number of school-age children and the demographics of the franchise territory. The most common is an "A" type franchise, which normally includes 20,000 to 25,000 school-age children. Total start-up costs are estimated to be from $97,000 to $110,000, including a franchise fee of $35,000. Franchisees are required to be open for business within 120 days from the date they have paid for the franchise, and they must maintain a minimum level of operation to avoid revocation of their franchise rights. In addition, franchisees must pay a 1½ percent national advertising fee and 8 percent of gross revenues to the franchisor.

A learning center staff normally consists of a director (owner/franchisee), an education director, a receptionist, and teachers. Most teachers are certified, although not necessarily by the state of current residence. Many are retired or individuals seeking only part-time employment. Others are deemed qualified despite the absence of certification. Each teacher teaches a maximum of three pupils at a time; the floor plans are designed to enable four teachers to work with three students each at any given time. Depending on the area, the subject involved, and other factors, the teachers are paid $6 to $10 an hour; the centers charge $20 to $30 an hour, with the difference going for salaries and benefits for full-time staff, rent, utilities, advertising, and other expenses.

Parents usually pay $800 to $1,000 for a program of thirty-six instructional hours provided over three to five months. The franchisees are not allowed to add programs or services or sell products not approved by Sylvan. Instruction is limited to three students per teacher; typically a student receives instruction for an hour a day, two days a week, after regular school. Parents transport the children to and from the centers, which are usually open about five hours a day during school days. Some centers are open on Saturdays; all operate during the summer.

The franchise agreements require franchisees to comply with company standards applicable to staffing, curriculum, accounting, and management methods. Some items, such as classroom furniture, may be purchased from the franchisor; franchisees can also purchase other items on the open market if they wish to do so. Franchise sites and floor plans must also be approved by Sylvan, but the criteria for approval are made available prior to purchase of a franchise. Sylvan also reserves the right to cancel the franchise arrangement for specified reasons, including conduct that would harm the company's reputation. Sylvan continually develops and field-tests new products and services that would be new profit centers. In addition, franchise consultants (often former franchise owners) are available for assistance at any time, especially in the early stages of franchise development. For example, the franchise consultant works with the franchisee on site selection, advertising, school relations, and other business and educational problems. In addition, franchisees are required to participate in training programs, both in the preoperational stage and afterward as new services are introduced. Sylvan also provides several manuals on franchise operations to assist franchise owners with anticipated problems.

Although some of the requirements franchisees must meet may seem restrictive, three considerations suggest they are not unduly so. First, Sylvan has a significant stake in the financial success of its franchises. If franchises are not successful, Sylvan receives less revenue from them. Furthermore, Sylan's income from franchise fees would be less if franchisee income is not so attractive to prospective franchisees. Long-range growth both in franchise fees and royalties requires successful franchises.

Second, the franchisees have their own organization that represents their interests to the franchisor. This, of course, is not unusual in franchise operations; for example, automobile dealers have organizations to deal with automobile manufacturers. Third, the fact that an increasing number of franchises are purchased by existing franchisees suggests the restrictions are not unreasonably onerous.

Virtually every aspect of these operations provides significant economies of scale compared to freestanding local companies:

1. New programs and services can be developed and field-tested before being introduced on a large scale. A local operator considering the introduction of a new service would find it too expensive to develop and field test, hence the program is less likely to be educationally or financially effective.

2. Sylvan has developed newspaper and radio advertisements that are made available to franchisees. Because the same advertising copy is used in hundreds of centers, the cost per center of effective advertising based on extensive market research is relatively low. A free-standing local company cannot afford the expertise of national advertising agencies.

3. Just as leading fast food and automobile service stations develop expertise on site selection, so do educational franchisers. They are more knowledgeable about the factors associated with site selection than any solo operator could hope to be.

4. Sylvan has developed loan plans for both parents and franchisees. These loan plans are made available through Educational Finance Plans, Inc. (EFP), a wholly owned subsidiary of Sylvan. The plans enable parents who cannot pay the full tuition in a lump sum to stagger the payments. For example, if parents are willing to buy a $1,000 program subject to financing, EFP offers several financing options. Whichever is adopted, the franchisee gets $900 immediately and the franchiser and its bank absorb the risks of default for $100 and the interest on the loan. Most local operators could not develop and market such a plan; the costs would be prohibitive.

The foregoing economies of scale are illustrative, not exhaustive. Most are also evident in the operations of Huntington Learning Centers. The latter was founded in 1977 by Ray and Eileen Huntington, a couple seeking primarily to establish their own business. At the time, Ray Huntington was an analyst for American Telephone and Telegraph and Eileen Huntington was a high school teacher. Although the first center was successful, expansion in the next seven years was rather slow and limited to the Middle Atlantic states. In 1985, however, the company was reorganized to expand nationally, and it grew rapidly thereafter; in June 1987 it had exceeded fifty franchise agreements covering 111 territories in twenty-one states. By May 1989 it had approximately 100 centers, including sixteen that were company owned and operated. As was the case at Sylvan Learning Corporation, several franchisees had purchased exclusive rights to establish two or more centers in areas where none was operative.

In general, Huntington and Sylvan operate in similar ways. In both, franchise operations are affected by such factors as size and population density of the franchise, its geographic desirability, demographic characteristics of the population, residential and commercial characteristics of the franchised territory, and competitive factors. Both companies sponsor weekly meetings with potential franchisees and conduct intensive training programs for franchisees. Franchisees in both companies rely on both advertising and informal networks (guidance counselors, doctors, parents, etc.) for referrals. Both companies emphasize the importance of responding to telephone inquiries effectively and of converting such inquiries into parental visits to the center. Both require and charge fees for tests prior to recommending a plan of instruction. Finally, both companies use company-owned centers to field-test new services and plan to introduce additional services in the future. For the most part, the differences between the companies are significant primarily to potential franchisees or to parents. Some of these differences are as follows:

1. The Sylvan franchises are somewhat more expensive but also include more on-site consultation.

2. Sylvan franchisees are required to budget and sponsor a "grand opening"; Huntington franchisees are not required to do this.

3. Sylvan provides regional consultants; Huntington does

not, preferring to emphasize immediate telephone assistance.

4. Huntington uses the number of school-age children to set franchise fees; although the number of such children is obviously important, Sylvan relies upon multiple criteria in setting franchise fees.

5. Sylvan employs a national advisory board, whereas Huntington employs educational consultants as needed.

6. Sylvan uses plastic tokens to reward pupils for achievement; the tokens are redeemable in the "Sylvan Store." Huntington eschews this approach, relying instead on other ways of motivating pupils.

7. Sylvan only requires parents to purchase month-to-month blocks of hours of instructional time; Huntington offers a discount for large blocks of time paid in advance, but parents are allowed to withdraw their children at any time with a refund for the time not utilized.

8. Sylvan's advertising emphasizes a "guarantee" that students will improve to a certain extent. If they do not, the center provides additional instruction. Huntington advertising does not include such "guarantees"; company officials regard them as inappropriate.

In pointing out these differences, my intention is not to favor one company over the other, or to endorse any educational service provided by either company. Nor is it intended to be a criticism of the large number of independent educational service companies. My comments are meant only to illustrate how educational franchising works and the economies of scale that are available to large scale educational providers. How effectively companies take advantage of these economies of scale is a separate question.

I have tried to show that for-profit enterprise could play a more important role in instruction, whether by contracting out or through vouchers. These two modes differ in several important ways; for example, a voucher plan would involve parents in a very different way than contracting out instruction. In principle, there should be no objection to using for-profit enterprise in either mode of privatization; on the contrary, utilization of for-profit enterprise is essential to either mode if it is to bring about educational improvement.

I have further contended that contracting out instruction has several strategic advantages, at least in the short run. Unlike vouchers, it does not require new and highly controversial legislation. Also, contracting out does not require drastic changes in the governance structure, and there is ample precedent for it both in and out of the field of education. I do not contend that contracting out is a substitute for vouchers or that it would serve all of the same purposes. Instead, my contention is that for-profit enterprise should play an important role in either mode or both.

Finally, I have suggested that economies of scale apply to instruction as much as they do to support services and that because of this fact, greater reliance on for-profit enterprise is likely to result in the emergence of large companies that develop, sell, and/or manage educational services. None of these propositions commands widespread popular or professional support at this time. For this reason, let me comment briefly on a common reaction. Essentially, it is that the analysis fails to give sufficient weight to the actual school situation. More specifically, if there is no difference in principle between contracting out instruction and transporation, or food service, or whatever, why isn't instruction contracted out more often? The implication is that because instruction is rarely contracted out, it must be for a good reason.

With this criticism in mind, let us compare efforts to contract out language instruction with efforts to contract out custodial services. Efforts to implement these two decisions would differ in the following ways:

1. The legal obstacles to contracting out language instruction would be much greater. For instance, state law might require that language instruction be pro-

vided only by certified teachers; it is less likely to require that custodial services be provided only by licensed custodians or by school district employees.

2. If the affected employees object, the teacher union will be a more formidable opponent at the bargaining table. It is more likely to provide a full-time negotiator and more backup in terms of data and public relations.

3. If the decision to contract out would result in loss of jobs, the tenure protections for teachers would be more difficult to overcome than those for custodians.

4. There is less interaction between the custodians and students than between teachers and students. For this reason, parents are less likely to be concerned about contracting out custodial services.

5. Contracting out instruction may require or be facilitated by continuity in the teacher-student relationship. It is more likely that providers of custodial services can be changed with little or no harm to the service.

I am not suggesting that these differences are exhaustive or that they always apply or are always important. State laws and local collective bargaining agreements vary widely, as do the circumstances giving rise to the desirability or viability of contracting out. In general, however, the obstacles to contracting out instruction are primarily legal and political, not economic or educational. There is no public policy reason why school districts that can contract with ServiceMaster for custodial and maintenance services, or ARA for food services, or Burns International for security services, or ETS for testing services, or for dozens of other noninstructional services should not have the same right to contract for instructional services. Whether a district wants to exercise that right, or when, how, and why, are separate issues.

The obstacles just mentioned do not explain why instructional services are rarely contracted out. Managerial incentives, or the lack thereof, are probably the most important reason why for-profit companies are used more frequently to provide noninstructional than instructional services.

To see why, consider the situation in hundreds of school districts in which for-profit learning centers have been established. The public school buildings close in the afternoon, let us say at 3:30 P.M. Down the street, the learning center, which charges $25 an hour for instruction, opens its doors at the same time. The public schools could hire the same teachers; because the facilities are already in place and there is no need to earn a profit, the public schools could provide the same service for $10 instead of $25 an hour. My assumption is that if a teacher is willing to teach for a private corporation for $8 an hour, he or she would be willing to teach in the public schools under the same conditions for the same hourly rate. Actually, it appears that the public schools could pay higher wages to the supplementary teachers, include an override to pay for any increased costs to the school system, and still offer the service for less than half of what private companies are charging.

Note that if teacher union opposition is a problem, the public schools need not employ the after-school teachers. Instead, they could disseminate to parents lists of teachers, rates, and qualifications; parents could pay the teachers directly for supplementary services, with the teachers paying the school district to cover its costs.

Ostensibly, the learning centers for profit reflect a failure to utilize public facilities efficiently, a failure that appears to be very costly to parents. Note also that if the cost of supplementary services were drastically reduced, the services would be available to a much larger number of students. Why then do school districts accept a situation that forces parents to pay $25 an hour for instructional services that the districts could make available for $10?

School administrators answer this question in a variety of ways. In general, however, the answers do not point to anything that would deter a district determined to provide such a program. Partly for this reason, I believe the most adequate explanation is one that is never given: There are no personal incentives for school administrators to initiate such a program. On the contrary, most have disincentives to do so, especially insofar as the programs are devoted to remedial instruction. First of all, administrators would be initiating programs that imply public school failure. Obviously, no such implication results from contracting out noninstructional services. Also, if public schools make remedial programs available, parents will feel that the school districts should pay for them. Such demands could create financial or equity or union problems that school management would just as soon avoid.

The bottom line is that school officials have no financial or political incentives that outweigh the disincentives for initiating the change. Of course, if officials objected on educational grounds to supplementing services for profit, such objections could justify their inaction, but this is seldom the case. The learning companies obviously want school cooperation (and referrals), but they appear to be prepared to function without it if necessary. One indication of this is their employment of leading educators as advisers; former Secretary of Education Terrel H. Bell is chairman of Sylvan Learning Corporation's advisory board.

In practice, the learning companies assert that they are only doing what school districts would like to do but cannot—provide instruction on a one-to-one or tutorial basis. Most school districts also express this view. Still, their rhetorical acceptance of it does not really explain their inactivity on the issue.

The Future of Learning Centers

Franchised learning centers may develop in several ways; it is still too early to predict their long-range development, educationally or financially. It appears, however, that in the next five to ten years, they will emphasize enrichment instead of remediation. As large as is the market for remedial services, it is much more limited than the market for helping average or superior students in a wide variety of subjects. Conceivably, centers devoted to performing arts, foreign language, mathematics and science, or sports might have widespread appeal to parents seeking ways to improve their children's education.

As we have seen, a number of social and demographic trends are resulting in diminished opportunities for desirable child-adult interactions—that is, to a decline in social capital. Viewed in this context, the learning centers may play a role that is much broader than remediation. Indeed, the basic idea underlying such centers may eventually be applied to large numbers of students during the regular school day. On the one hand, millions of students lack any means of interacting with adults outside the context of discipline or remediation. On the other hand, there exists an enormous pool of potential part-time instructors: retired persons, college students, and persons seeking or willing to accept only part-time employment. The physical facilities for bringing these two groups together are largely in place. Large numbers of students could be taught for at least a few hours a day with three or four to one student/teacher ratios. Such arrangements might have beneficial effects that go far beyond remediation in school subjects. Granted, the approach would not be applicable everywhere, but it may be in a large number of districts.

The development of franchised learning centers suggests that "cottage industry" and "large-scale industry" are not necessarily mutually exclusive, even with respect to the same service. Franchised learning centers are small businesses, requiring an investment of about $100,000 overall. The franchisors are much larger corporations that can provide funds for research and development and aggressive growth policies. In a franchise agreement, small-scale and large-scale business are highly interdependent; the profitability of each type is directly dependent on profitability in the other. This pattern will not be predominant in every type of education for profit, but it is very likely to be in many fields. From a broader perspective, this should not be surprising. Franchising is a major source of economic growth in our economy; the reasons are just as applicable to education as to other franchised services.

10

Thinking
the Unthinkable:
Load Shedding

Thus far, privatization has been discussed in terms of separating government support for education from government operation of schools. Some proponents of privatization do not regard such a change as desirable. They point out that private contractors can and do lobby for increased government appropriations to pay for their services. They also emphasize that private monopolies can be as harmful as government-operated monopolies. Thus a change from public to private operation does not necessarily result in the beneficial consequences associated with privatization.

To some, therefore, "privatization" consists of load shedding—government shedding of support as well as operation of public services. At first glance, the idea of withdrawing government support from education may seem to be hopeless, even quixotic, regardless of any abstract merits it might have. My position, however, is that any such dismissal of load shedding is unrealistic, especially if taxes for education were reduced proportionally. Many adults without children, a rapidly growing segment of the population, would be receptive to it. So would many parents who send their children to private schools. Another group likely to support load shedding consists of parents who educate their children at home. Thus there are important interest groups that are, or have reason to be, sympathetic to some degree of load shedding.

The Emergence of Education at Public Expense

To understand the possibilities for load shedding in education, it will be helpful to review briefly the emergence of education at public expense. This is related to but not the same as compulsory education. Strictly speaking, compulsory education does not necessarily require education at public expense; governments often require that certain things (such as waste removal) be done while costs must be borne privately. As a practical matter, however, compulsory education has been closely tied to public support for it.[1]

Although taken for granted now, compulsory education was not widespread in the United States prior to the Civil War; in 1852 Massachusetts was the first state to enact a general compulsory education statute. By 1900, thirty states and the District of Columbia had done so, but the statutes often mandated only part-time attendance while providing very little enforcement machinery. Illiteracy rates revealed by our nation's entrance into World War I led to greater emphasis upon compulsory education.

In practice, compulsory education was tied very closely to child labor; in fact, the two types of legislation were frequently interdependent. Prohibitions of child labor were widely enacted after the Civil War. Nevertheless, by contemporary standards, these prohibitions were very limited. Most applied primarily to manufacturing; agricultural and domestic work was exempted. To be eligible for work in manufacturing industries, children had to be at least twelve years old and could not be required to work more than ten hours a day. Parental statements concerning age were accepted perfunctorily and rigorous enforcement was exceptional.

To avoid economic competition on the issue between states, efforts to limit child labor emerged in Congress. Eventually these efforts succeeded by restricting the sale of goods made with child labor. In any event, compulsory education was more the result than the cause of child labor prohibitions. The interrelationships between these policies is evident from the fact that the maximum school age and minimum work age were often the same. School officials were usually delegated responsibility for enforcing child labor laws, and work requirements often included minimum education requirements, such as completion of the sixth grade.

Perhaps the most important implication of this brief summary is that repeal or substantial easing of compulsory education laws per se might not result in any major changes in school attendance. For this to happen, it may be essential to repeal or amend the legislation that prohibits or restricts youth employment. As will be discussed shortly, pressures to do that can be expected to intensify in the near future.

HOME SCHOOLING

Some parents have done more than urge government withdrawal from funding and delivery of educational services. These parents have taken it upon themselves to educate their children at home. These parents, and the situation regarding home schooling, provide an interesting point of departure for our analysis of load shedding.

"Home schooling" is not easily defined, legally or practically. In the following analysis, the phrase refers to any effort to meet compulsory education statutes by instruction in a family residence. In other words, "home schooling" refers to both a process and a site. The nature of the process is subject to debate and litigation, but it presumably differs from the informal instruction that takes place in any home with children.

The 1925 Supreme Court decision in *Pierce* v. *Society of Sisters* held that a state cannot require children to attend public school.[2] States can require children to attend school but, subject to reasonable regulation, parents have the right to enroll their children in private schools. A major point of constitutional uncertainty is the determination of reasonableness in state regulation; at some point, regulation could be so onerous that it would negate the rights of private schools or parents wishing to enroll their children in such schools.

Within this constitutional context, all states have compulsory school attendance or education laws. The distinction is significant. If a state requires compulsory school attendance, home schooling may be justified on the basis that the home qualifies as a school. As of 1983, thirty-eight states had enacted compulsory school attendance laws.[3] The absence of a statutory definition or statutory criteria for defining a school may render some of these laws vulnerable to legal challenge; in five states—Wisconsin (1983), Georgia (1984), Iowa (1985), Minnesota (1985), and Missouri (1985)—compulsory school attendance laws were held to be unconstitutionally vague for this reason. In all of these states except Iowa, the aftermath of the court decision was legislation that was rather favorable to home schooling.[4]

Compulsory *education* legislation avoids the need to define "school," but it faces a different problem: What activities constitute "education" in a compulsory education law? Needless to say, the legal definitions of "education" vary about as much as the legal definitions of "school." In addition, courts are not always consistent in applying the same definition to a given factual situation. Parenthetically, we might note that the legal definitions have implications besides those directly related to education. For example, schools may be tax exempt or be allowed to operate in residential areas despite local opposition. Of course, the way "school" is defined reflects legislative or judicial policy toward home schooling; an expansive definition reflects more support for home schooling than a restrictive one. In recent years the courts that have been willing to construe the term judicially have been more favorable to home schools.

In one way or another, by 1987 every state permitted some type of home instruction.[5] A summary of the legal status of home schooling in 1986 revealed the following:

1. Twenty-three states had enacted some type of home schooling legislation in the years indicated: West Virginia, Vermont, and Minnesota (1987); Missouri (1986); Arkansas, Florida, Oregon, New Mexico, Wyoming, Washington, Tennessee (1985); Georgia, Virginia, Louisiana*, Rhode Island* (1984); Wisconsin and Montana (1983); Arizona and Mississippi (1982); Ohio* (1976); Colorado* (1963); Utah* (1957); Nevada* (1956).

2. Only Iowa, Michigan, and North Dakota required that a certified teacher provide the instruction in all home schools.

3. Twenty-four states and the District of Columbia required home schools to be approved by the local school district or school board.

4. Seven states (Connecticut, Indiana, Kansas, Maine, New Jersey, Nevada, and South Carolina) required the instruction in home schools to be "equivalent" to public school instruction. The "equivalent" requirement has been successfully challenged on grounds of vagueness in Iowa, Minnesota, and Missouri.

5. Three states (Maryland, Delaware, and Rhode Island) required home school instruction to be "regular and thorough."

6. Idaho and Michigan required home school instruction to be "comparable" to public school instruction.

7. Seven states (California, Hawaii, Kansas, New York, Ohio, Pennsylvania, and South Dakota) required

---

*These six states still give local superintendents or school boards the authority to "approve" home schools.

home school teachers to be "competent," "qualified," or "capable of teaching."

8. Home schools could operate as private or religious schools in Alabama, California, Illinois, Indiana, Kansas, Kentucky, Michigan, North Carolina, Nevada, North Dakota, Oklahoma, and Texas.

9. Home schools may possibly be allowed to operate as private or religious schools in Arkansas, Colorado, Delaware, Maine, New York, Ohio, and Pennsylvania.[6]

Although changes in the legal status of home schooling will undoubtedly occur, there is little likelihood of state uniformity on the subject; if anything, state legislation may vary even more in the future than it does now.

The Number of "Home Schoolers"

How many children of school age are educated at home? The estimates vary widely. Raymond S. Moore, a leading advocate of home schooling, has made what appear to be the highest estimates.[7] His estimates, however, include a substantial number of migrant and disabled children who do not attend formal school. Including these children, Moore estimates that the total of home schoolers is well over 1 million and may run much higher. Although his estimates may be accurate for the most part, his figures really refer to the estimated number of school-age children who are not in school; they are not an estimate of the number of children being educated at home pursuant to a compulsory education statute. Most children of migrant workers who are not in school are not receiving an education at home; they are not receiving an education from any source. Although the education of such children is an important problem, they are not "home schoolers," or students undergoing a planned program of instruction at home pursuant to a parental decision that such instruction is preferable to education in a public or private school.

Michael Farris, director of the Home School Legal Defense Association, has estimated that about 200,000 families and 500,000 pupils were involved in home schooling in 1987.[8] This estimate suggests that slightly more than 1 percent of the school-age population is being schooled at home. Because of the restrictions on home schooling, underreporting may have been widespread in the past, but the trend toward legalization and accommodation is probably resulting in more accurate data.

There is no doubt that the number of home schoolers increased in the 1980s. It is difficult to say where the increase might level off; some observers believe that home schooling will be a major trend in American education, reflecting the broader social trends of self-help as opposed to reliance on institutions to deliver services. Realistically, however, several factors are likely to curtail any major increase in home schooling. Much of its growth has resulted from devout Protestant parents unhappy with public schools. Many of these parents are likely to abandon home schooling as Protestant schools continue to expand.

While the legal climate for home schooling has improved in recent years, this could change as the number of children educated at home increases. The recent increases, small as they are in absolute terms, led the National Association of Elementary School Principals to adopt a resolution critical of home schooling. The resolution is quoted here in its entirety because it summarizes the objections to home schooling:

Compulsory School Attendance

NAESP believes that education is a cornerstone of American democracy and that, in order to guarantee an enlightened electorate capable of governing itself, the American people must ensure quality education for each citizen.

NAESP asserts that this is most effectively done through cohesive organization in formal settings in which resources can most beneficially be brought to bear and a compulsory attendance policy employed.

NAESP views with alarm the increasing number of

individuals and groups who are avoiding education in the traditional setting in favor of at-home schooling. Such schooling:

1. deprives the child of important social experiences,
2. isolates students from other social/racial/ethnic groups,
3. denies students the full range of curriculum experiences and materials,
4. may be provided by non-certified and unqualified persons,
5. creates an additional burden on administrators whose duties include the endorsement of compulsory school attendance laws,
6. may not permit effective assessment of academic standards of quality,
7. may violate health and safety standards, and
8. may not provide the accurate diagnosis of and planning for meeting the needs of children with special talents, learning difficulties, and other conditions requiring atypical educational programs.

Therefore, NAESP reaffirms the value of compulsory school attendance. The Association urges local and state associations to support legislation which enforces compulsory school attendance and prohibits at-home schooling as a substitute for compulsory school attendance.

NAESP further urges local and state associations to address these issues as important educational concerns.[9]

Other public school organizations may adopt a similar posture toward home schooling. We can expect these organizations to publicize home schooling deficiencies or instances of child abuse during home schooling. Supporters of home schooling may contend that the instances are isolated, or that children are abused whether or not they attend regular school. On the merits of accommodating home schooling, I side with the home schoolers, but the merits are not the point. It is simply that any increase in home schooling will inevitably evoke opposition and negative publicity, justified or not.[10]

In home schooling, the burden of educating children falls mainly upon their mothers. The fact is, however, that over half the mothers of young children work outside the home, a proportion that is likely to increase in the future. For a variety of reasons, more women are seeking economic security in careers outside the home than in homemaking. Also, many parents who educate their children at home do not continue past the first year. In short, despite some contradictory factors, the number of pupils educated at home is not likely to change drastically in the next five to ten years. Patricia Lines, an attorney who has made a careful study of home schooling issues, projects the continued growth of home schooling, but at a slower rate than in the early 1980s.[11]

Who Are the Home Schoolers?

The parents who educate their children at home are not a homogeneous group, either demographically or in the reasons why they prefer home schooling. On the contrary, virtually the only characteristic children educated at home and/or their families have in common is that the children are not enrolled in a regular school.

Let us first summarize the demographic data on home schoolers. Several efforts have been made to develop profiles of this population. Brian D. Ray, a home schooling activist who summarized these studies in 1986, found that despite considerable ethnic, religious, and socioeconomic diversity among home schoolers, the studies agreed, or at least did not contradict the conclusions that:

1. The female parent was mother/housewife/home-maker.
2. The male parent was a professional or skilled worker. . . .

5. Various religious backgrounds were represented, including some very untraditional ones; with 64% regularly attending religious services.

6. Parents were average socializers.

7. It was a family enterprise, usually operated by both parents. . . .

10. Informal, child-centered, and relatively flexible programs for learning were used.

11. The programs were effective and interesting to children (as perceived by parents). . . .

13. The school formally convened for 3–4 hours per day.

14. Children studied on their own an average of 2.7 hours per day.

15. The home school was approved by local authorities.

16. Most often instructional materials prepared by the parents were used. . . .

18. The curriculum covered a wide range of conventional course offerings (with math, reading, and science as the three most often stressed).

19. The home school was operated for more than two years.

20. Families decided to home school for various reasons, which follow in order of their importance: (a) concern for moral health of children, (b) concern over character development of their children, (c) . . . excess rivalry and ridicule in conventional schools . . . (d) overall poor quality education in public schools, and (e) desire to enjoy children at home in early years of their lives.[12]

Although Ray's summary did not include all the demographic profiles of home schoolers, it is consistent with those not included. For example, Earl W. Gladin's doctoral dissertation involved a study of home schoolers based on a 6 percent random sample of 6,850 families in eleven states, using the Bob Jones University Press home school mailing list. The questionnaire included thirty-seven questions and was returned by 253 of the 416 recipients. The major conclusions were as follows:

1. The father's occupation was primarily professional or self-employed; over 50 percent of the fathers were ministers (14.0); in construction (11.2); in management (10.7); salesman (7.8); or in computers (7.8).
2. Both parents had graduated from high school; a surprising 45.4 percent had at least four years of college. Again, these percentages refer to the educational level of both parents.
3. The mean annual income was $30,972.
4. Over half (51.3 percent) of the families lived in the suburbs and an additional 12.0 percent lived in urban areas.
5. Over 72 percent of the respondents characterized themselves as evangelical or fundamentalist in religious orientation; the average home school family attended religious services two or three times a week.
6. According to their questionnaire responses, home school families tended to watch television only 1.7 hours a day, compared to the national average of 3.7 hours a day. The responses also indicated that oral reading and library visits by home schoolers greatly exceeded national averages.[13]

In terms of why they support home schooling, home schoolers appear to fall into two major categories. One views home schooling as predominantly a religious or philosophical issue; researcher Jane Ann Van Galen has characterized the parents in this group as the "ideologues." The second major category consists of parents who believe home schooling is superior from an educational point of view; in Van Galen's study, such parents were categorized as the "pedagogues."[14]

Although useful as an effort to describe a highly diverse group, the ideologue/pedagogue breakdown has at least two major limitations. First, most home schoolers cite more than one reason for their preference; many cite both ideological and pedagogical reasons. Second, the variations within the major categories are sometimes more significant than the differences between them.

Understandably, the studies of home schoolers agree that the latter are highly supportive of their children's education. Although the number of home schoolers may not be very large anywhere, it would be a mistake to view their absence from the public schools primarily in quantitative terms. Home schoolers include a disproportionate number of the kind of parents who are normally expected to provide leadership in improving education. For whatever reason, they have used the exit instead of the voice option with respect to public schools. In conjunction with the much larger number of parents who enroll their children in private schools, they reflect an erosion of the leadership needed to improve public education.

The Rationale(s) for Home Schooling

In some cases home schooling is justified by the unique circumstances or characteristics of individual children. For instance, the parents may believe their child is too bright to profit from conventional schooling. At the other extreme, a child may be so disabled that conventional instruction, even in special classes, may be futile or impractical. Children may be experiencing difficulty in adjusting to classmates or teachers. In other situations parents may feel a need to protect their children from harassment or ridicule because of appearance, disability, dress, or some other idiosyncratic factor.

Aside from such situations, let us consider the arguments for home schooling that are not so dependent on the special characteristics, actual or assumed, of pupils being educated at home. One way is to compare the arguments for home schooling with the arguments for vouchers.

The basic arguments for educational vouchers are that they would: (1) protect the religious freedom of parents and students; (2) result in taxpayer savings; (3) minimize social conflict; (4) be a civil rights protection; and (5) result in improving educational services.

Clearly, the first four arguments are also applicable to home schooling. Its proponents also contend that it results in better education, albeit their reasons are different from those adduced to support vouchers, and they assert other educational arguments which do not apply to vouchers.

As was the case with vouchers, the foregoing arguments for home schooling are often viewed as cumulative although they may be inconsistent with each other. For the most part, however, anyone who found one or more of these reasons persuasive in the voucher context would be likely to find them persuasive in the home schooling context as well. In some situations these arguments are more persuasive regarding home schooling; for example, the taxpayer savings resulting from home schooling are likely to be larger than the savings from enrollments in private schools, with or without vouchers. Since parents who have religious objections to regular schools may not have access to an appropriate school, home schooling constitutes the only feasible way to accommodate some religious objections to public school. Home schooling would also accommodate parents who reject formal schooling, public or private.

I do not mean to suggest that the rationale(s) for vouchers are equally applicable to home schooling, or that acceptance of an argument for vouchers necessarily implies its acceptance for home schooling. One can plausibly believe that the problems of regulating private schools are so different from those of regulating home schools that policies appropriate in one area are not in the other. Nor do I intend to denigrate the importance of those arguments for home schooling that are not considered here. Again, my focus is on educational improvement. For this reason, the following discussion focuses on the educational improvement issues raised by home schooling. I shall consider whether or under what conditions, if any, home schooling would help to bring out better education—"better" from a secular, not a denominational standpoint.

It should be noted that the educational rationale for home schooling is based on dissatisfaction with private as well as public schools. In fact, a number of studies suggest that proportionally more home schoolers have been withdrawn from private than from public schools.[15]

Educational arguments for home schooling include the following:[16]

1. The family is (or should be, or both) the most important educative influence on children. Compulsory school attendance undermines this influence.

2. Children educated at school tend to succumb to peer pressures early on, because teachers cannot interact effectively and frequently with each child individually in a conventional classroom. The result is that children's character is formed by pressures from peers who necessarily lack (for reasons of immaturity) the values and attitudes essential for constructive personality development. For example, youthful peers are more likely than parents to sacrifice long-range objectives for short-range gratification. In contrast, when children are educated at home, they interact with and are guided by adults much more often than occurs in the school situation.

3. Proponents of home schooling also emphasize the importance of family relationships in social and emotional development. It is asserted that compulsory school attendance results in maternal deprivation leading to negative emotional, social, physical, and cognitive effects on children.

4. Advocates of home schooling also assert that it fosters constructive social development. The contention is that a child who is educated at home will develop socially in a more positive way. Moore's argument is typical:

Parents and educators usually talk about sociability, but neglect to differentiate the kind of sociability they prefer. The child who feels needed, wanted, and depended upon at home, sharing responsibilities and chores, is much more likely to develop a sense of self-worth and a stable value system— which is the basic ingredient for a *positive* sociability. In contrast is the *negative* sociability that develops when a child surrenders to his peers.[17]

All of these reasons support, and are supported by, the social capital hypothesis discussed in chapter 7. Even if the reasons do not add up to a unified theory, there is considerable evidence to support them. To be sure, there is some contrary evidence. For instance, while proponents of home schooling cite evidence that children are required to attend school too soon, its critics cite evidence that allegedly supports lowering the age of compulsory school attendance, or at least providing for earlier schooling for parents who want it.

The stakes involved in these issues are very large indeed. For example, if the age at which children must begin school were raised one year, the supply of teachers would be greatly increased. It would be more difficult for teacher unions to increase teacher salaries; union income and influence would be diminished by the reduction in the demand for teachers. By the same token, lowering the age of compulsory school attendance would have the opposite effects.

Interests aside, the evidence on home schooling generally supports it for those who choose this option. In at least one respect, this is a surprising conclusion. Despite the relatively small number of home schoolers, they are an extremely diverse group. As we have seen, some are motivated by religious considerations, some are not. Even among the latter, a wide variety of secular considerations are involved. Some home school parents object to the competition they see fostered by regular school; others believe that schools do not adequately emphasize the free enterprise system. Some home school parents believe that schools are too distracting and too directive; others believe they can provide better guidance and direction at home. These and other differences in motivation and rationale are reflected in the diverse curricula and pedagogical procedures found in home schools. Some curricula emphasize acceptance of authority (mainly supernatural and parental), whereas others emphasize the importance of questioning all authority. Once you get beyond the idea that home schooling and heavy parental involvement is preferable to formal schooling, there is little if any unanimity among home school families. Thus from this standpoint, it seems surprising that children educated at home compare favorably to those educated in regular schools. The research is not systematic or comprehensive, but enough is available to place the clear burden of proof on the opponents of home schooling.[18]

From another standpoint, the evidence on home schooling is not surprising. Previously I referred to research on the "effects of education." The leading studies, such as those conducted by Coleman, point unambiguously to the family environment as the most important variable affecting educational achievement. Consequently, we might expect children educated at home to do well—not necessarily because they are educated at home but because their families are most supportive of educational achievement. For example, according to one study, 90 percent of the Connecticut children who begin a program of home instruction are already at or above their grade level.[19]

One might argue, therefore, that even though children educated at home achieve at a higher level than those educated in regular school, the home schoolers still do not make as much progress as they would in a public or private school. Theoretically, this is possible; politically, it would be difficult to restrict home schooling for this reason.

Actually, we can expect much better data on the effects of home schooling in the future. One reason is that fourteen states either require testing or allow local school districts to test as part of the procedures for approving home schooling. As Lines points out, cooperative relationships between public school officials and home schoolers could advance our understanding of the effects of one-to-one instruction; the effects of peer pressure; the value of teacher certification and more frequent contact with adults; and of other matters of interest.[20] Needless to say, the conclusions might embarrass both public and private school leaders.

The evidence on the social development of children educated at home is very limited; what there is, however, supports the conclusion that home schooling results in superior development. This is somewhat surprising, but there is a plausible basis for it, besides the obvious importance of substantial parental involvement. Home school families are not necessarily or predominantly hermits or isolated. They may participate in a wide range of community activities while educating their children at home. As a matter of fact, some home schoolers participate in school-based field trips or special activities.

Very few children are educated at home for their entire elementary and secondary careers. The research available does not provide an adequate basis for evaluating the effects of home schooling over various periods of time, such as one, three, five, or seven years. Evaluations of the effects of Catholic schools are mired in controversy over the duration of the effects; some researchers assert the Catholic school advantage disappears over the long term. Home schooling may present the opposite situation—no visible effects over the short term but clear-cut effects over a longer period of time. Unfortunately, research is inadequate to resolve these issues now.

It should be noted that the compulsory school attendance laws were enacted long before there was research on child development, maternal bonding, peer pressures, or any of the other issues now thought to be relevant to the age of compulsory attendance. It would be serendipitous indeed if the research supported the mandated age requirements; unfortunately, the compulsory education statutes have greatly strengthened the groups with a stake in their perpetuation. For example, kindergarten and first-grade teachers have a bigger stake in the perpetuation of early compulsory school attendance than others have in postponing it. As so often happens, the "evidence" on the issue has not played a major role in shaping the policies on it and may not do so in the future.

Some arguments for home schooling are arguments against public education per se. Others, however, are essentially arguments for raising the age of compulsory school attendance. For the most part, the home schooling movement owes its existence to the fact that the compulsory education statutes require school attendance at a highly debatable early age. The overwhelming majority of children educated at home attend school at one time or another, especially as they become older. Home schooling is primarily an elementary-level phenomena, as even its most articulate supporters concede. For this reason, the home schooling movement per se would be greatly diminished if the age of compulsory school attendance were raised; in that case, there would be no legal obligation on parents to operate a home school for children age six to eight, just as there is no such obligation now to educate children under the age of compulsory attendance. To be sure, some of the arguments for home schooling would still come into play, but the number of their supporters would be greatly diminished.

Although recent statutory trends have been more supportive of home schooling, wide variations exist and several issues are not resolved. The major regulatory issues involve fire, health, and safety; curriculum and instructional materials; teacher licensing; time devoted to instruction; testing and reporting student progress; and whether home schools need be licensed. Some of these issues have arisen because statutes that apply to private schools did not anticipate the existence of home schools. For instance, statutes requiring fire drills and firefighting equipment in private schools might be inappropriate if applied to a home school. With the growing acceptance of home schooling, its supporters are likley to intensify their efforts to have home schools treated differently from conventional schools.

THE FUTURE OF EDUCATIONAL LOAD SHEDDING

Perhaps the strongest argument for load shedding is one parents seldom make. If parents pay for the education of their children from their own income, they are much more likely to insist on performance from their children and from educational producers. In this respect, load shedding is a more desirable public policy than vouchers; with vouchers, the parents would presumably exercise choice, but it would be choice in using a credit provided by government for a specific purpose. Parents would not be forced to choose between more or better education and more or better food, shelter, medical care, transportation, and other goods and services. Load shedding would require such choices; undoubtedly parents and children would show a different attitude toward education if it were paid for from personal instead of government funds. The student who wastes time in school or cuts classes would be wasting family funds, not "the government's."

The evidence that higher levels of effort and achievement would result from education paid from personal instead of public funds is overwhelming, in and out of education. For example, the dropout rate is much lower in private institutions of higher education, where students have to bear a higher proportion of the costs, than it is in public institutions, where government subsidies greatly reduce the amounts paid by students. Where employees are required to absorb or share the costs of medical services, they are much more prudent in using them; it makes a difference whether the insurance company or the patient has to pay the hospital bills. If your car is damaged in an accident, the first question asked in estimating the repair bill is likely to be who will be paying it. Unfortunately, public education has severed the connection between the payor and the consumer, to the point where the latter lacks adequate incentives to monitor the services provided.

While parents do have incentives to evaluate educational services because their children are involved, these incentives are rather weak. Parental resources are not at stake, and the difficulty of taking remedial action gravely weakens the incentives for parental involvement. The underlying question is who should be the decision-making consumer of educational services: the family or an appropriate government agency? Inasmuch as education is both a collective and an individual benefit, the answer depends on which way of resolving the issue will maximize desirable outcomes. Approached in this way, the case for load shedding may be much stronger than its low level of political support would suggest.

One objection to home schooling may be the substantial transaction costs it would impose on parents. Most parents may not want to grapple with a myriad of decisions about the education of their children. Load shedding may be attractive to a small group of activists who know what they want educationally; to others it may mean being forced to make decisions they prefer to avoid. Whether or not this is the case, load shedding would require greater transaction costs than any other educational policy.

As previously noted we could maintain compulsory education while withdrawing government support for it. The financial impact of such a policy on parents is debatable. Compared to the amounts parents currently pay in school taxes, some would pay more, some less, and some would just about break even. The main reason some parents would pay more is that the costs of tax-supported schools are shared by people who are not parents of school-age children. On the other hand, parents would also avoid the costs of educating other children, and the costs of educating their own would be limited to their years in school. Interestingly enough, an analysis of this issue in Great Britain strongly suggested that even a working-class family with two children in school would not be demonstrably worse off by paying for education from personal funds if their taxes were reduced proportionately as the result of educational load shedding.[21] Although the study is outdated and was based on survey data from another country, it suggests that state-supported education is not as favorable economically to low-income groups as is commonly assumed. Public education is no exception to the proposition that the affluent are usually better able to reap economic advantages from our political system.

Indisputably, our tax supported schools have always been characterized by severe inequalities of educational opportunity. The rhetoric of equality of educational opportunity obscures the fact that tax support for education benefits the middle class and upper classes much more than the poor. Middle- and upper-class children tend to stay in school longer. Public funds support the education of large numbers of marginal middle-class students who would withdraw except for the government subsidy. Their culture calls for a high school diploma and a college education. As a result, they tend to extend their education regardless of their ability to profit from it; tax-supported education meets their needs very nicely. Financing the education of able students from lower economic strata is not difficult; the major problems arise because public funds are used to finance the education of hordes of students from all economic strata who should be working.

At the present time, the existence of inequality of educational opportunity is thought to be illustrated by the fact that a lower proportion of students from the lower economic levels stay in and graduate from high school and enter and graduate from college. Efforts to achieve equality focus on raising the proportion of low-income youth who continue and/or complete their education at various levels. Because of the political and media influence of the education lobbies, the possibility of achieving greater equality by decreasing the proportion of economically favored youth who stay in school is ignored; it will continue to be ignored as long as the value of secondary and higher education is shielded from scrutiny and publicity.

The concerns frequently expressed over the number of high school and college dropouts reflect the economic interests of the education lobby far more than any genuine concern for the disadvantaged. High school diplomas and college degrees are symbols of time serving, not of significant educational achievement. In many cases, staying in school retards rather than fosters the skills, attitudes, and habits required for civic, social, and economic competence. The fact that the education lobby opposes objective standards for awarding diplomas or degrees illustrates that it is more concerned about enrolling students than educating them.

In effect, public policy on education operates on the principle that "more is better." The upshot is a vicious circle characterized by the most benign rhetoric. To raise the proportion of the economically disadvantaged who stay in school, larger tax subsidies are provided. The subsidies do not and cannot eliminate the alleged inequities that led to their enactment; instead, they increase the actual transfers of funds to middle- and upper-class families. Meanwhile, given the fact that states rely heavily on regressive taxes to finance education, the burden of support falls more heavily on those least able to bear it.

The way higher education is financed illustrates how the rhetoric of equal opportunity is used to rationalize public subsidies that go largely to the nonpoor. On the one hand, higher education is advocated as an "investment" in future earnings. On the other hand, institutions of higher education vigorously promote increased government absorption of the costs of such education, especially of student loans.

Clearly, something is amiss here. If the "investment" in higher education is worth it to the students, they should be able to pay back the loans. If there is a repayment problem, perhaps the reason is that the investment was not a good one. At the secondary level, however, taxpayers make the poor investment. As a result, there is less concern at the family level about its costs and benefits. Meanwhile teachers and professors benefit, even if the students do not.

The importance of investment in education is often justified by relying upon the distinction between public and private goods. Education supposedly contributes to both. If investment in it is based solely upon the private benefits, underinvestment in education will result. To be candid, however, this argument is not consistent with the rhetoric directed at students. They are urged to stay in school for their welfare, not society's. To put it mildly, candor on this issue is not widespread.

In brief, we have strong reason to be skeptical of equity reasons as an objection to load shedding. We can always provide for those unable to pay for education. Education lobbies are opposed to the use of a means test, allegedly because they seek to avoid stigmatizing the poor. This argument might have made sense fifty years ago, but its relevance in the age of food stamps is questionable. Arguably at least, the avoidance of means tests in education protects affluent taxpayers more than the sensitivities of poor families.[22]

Home Schooling Implications for Load Shedding

Home schooling is an anomaly. It does not reflect a government decision to withdraw support for or provision of education. Instead, it reflects a consumer decision that the service is not wanted or needed. Whereas vouchers maintain the principle of government support, home schooling does not—at least, home schoolers have not sought state aid. In some respects they appear to have at least as strong a case for it as conventional private schools. If a home school qualifies as a school, the case for state aid to home schools would be even stronger. Such aid might also be justified as an element of a family rather than an educational policy. Of course, if home schooling is subsidized, it would no longer be load shedding.

The most significant point about home schooling is its message that load shedding in education need not be total. As an all-or-nothing policy, load shedding is not of any practical importance, at least for a long time to come. Nevertheless, as we saw with voucher proposals, the basic idea can be implemented incrementally, and the possibilities for doing so add significantly to the practical value of the idea. The history of public education in the United States underscores this point.

Public education as it exists today was not created de novo by a single legislative enactment. The idea of government-supported education was not widespread, even as an idea, when our nation was founded.[23] On the contrary, education was regarded as a family and church responsibility. The moral dimensions focused on religious themes, not civic virtues. Contemporary writers who quote a founding father as supporting public education overlook the fact that such a view was a distinct minority, both conceptually and in practice. Legislatures first enacted compulsory primary education; subsequently compulsory education was extended to higher and higher grade levels. Today public support for higher education is more common and more substantial than support for secondary or even elementary education was earlier in our history.

We should also note that public schools frequently add (but seldom drop) various educational programs. None of our early high schools offered consumer education or sex education. Over the years high schools have added a wide variety of programs and courses; computer education and AIDS education are two recent examples. Home schooling raises the question of whether the incremental expansion of government support for education can be transformed into incremental contraction of it. Many home schoolers believe that children should not be required to attend conventional school until age eight to ten, instead of five or six as is the case now. In effect, this is an argument that government should shed financial support for educating children below the age of eight.

Let us pursue this line of thought briefly. We have seen that fourteen states require or allow testing as part of the procedures for resolving requests to educate at home. For the sake of discussion, suppose that the tests show that conventional schooling for children age five to seven has no lasting effects for normal children whose parents are willing to educate them at home. Then withdrawal (or at least diminution) of government support for primary education would be a feasible political objective. Conceivably, government might provide financial incentives to encourage home schooling while continuing to support primary schools for parents who do not exercise the home schooling option. It is not difficult to think of several other possibilities. Higher education is too large a target to be attacked *in toto,* but some elements of it offer good prospects for incremental load shedding. It is ridiculous for government to be subsidizing the costs of training physicians who will earn several million dollars over their professional careers. Whether government guarantees fewer student loans, requires higher interest rates and more stringent payback provisions, and/or imposes stiffer penalties for fraud, it should shed or reduce its financial support for these future millionaires.

In brief, incremental load shedding in education can be implemented by program as well as by grade level. Driver education is a perennial candidate for load shedding, and many others could be cited. All over the United States students are required to take "physical education" courses. These courses consist largely of normal physical exercise or athletic activity similar to that which students undertake on their own after school. In many cases students in physical education courses are simultaneously active members of school athletic teams and simply use the courses for team practice. In this connection, note that the for-profit sector has played a much more significant role than schools in promoting exercise and fitness. The explosion in health and fitness services and equipment has occurred independently of school programs in physical and health education.

In short, if load shedding is viewed as an incremental process, not as a revolutionary educational and political change, its usefulness and political prospects would be greatly enhanced. No matter how strong the case for load shedding, it will never happen as long as its supporters overlook the need for an incremental approach. Because the all-or-nothing approach forces the public to shed activities which it is not prepared to give up, it forgoes opportunities to shed the clearly indefensible. Citizens who would be receptive to raising the age of compulsory school attendance, or requiring future millionaires to pay the cost of their medical education, nevertheless balk at total load shedding of public support for education. I am not arguing here that total load shedding of education is desirable. Whether it is or not, it can only be achieved by shedding public support for education on an incremental basis. Obviously, any such strategy should focus on the grades, subjects, and programs most vulnerable to public scrutiny.

Finally, the all-or-nothing approach unites the public

education lobby in opposition whereas it might be deeply divided by an incremental approach. In our analysis of contracting out, we noted the crucial importance of achieving the support or neutralizing the opposition of public employees and their unions. Load shedding obviously presents the same problem, and the same flexibility is required to deal with it. Suppose, for example, that secondary teachers were offered a 20 percent wage increase, contingent upon the elimination of the first grade or shedding physical education with adequate benefits for incumbent PE teachers. Such approaches might have some prospects for success. Incremental load shedding can be implemented flexibly as circumstances require; the all-or-nothing approach cannot.

Efforts to end government support for specific educational activities can be justified without reference to load shedding. If a case can be made for withdrawing government support, there is no need to relate it to broader objectives, if any. This ambiguity is one of the strengths of an incremental approach to load shedding. It focuses attention on specifics that are favorable to it. In contrast, efforts to shed public education per se inevitably focus on ideology, a battleground in which load shedding is at a severe disadvantage. Most citizens simply are not prepared for any such drastic change, and advocacy of it is likely to be counterproductive for a long time to come. Nevertheless, incremental load shedding in education could become a significant development within the next few decades.

In considering the future of load shedding, we need to consider the milieu in which the issues will emerge. It is especially essential to avoid the assumption that the relevant conditions will be the same in the future as they are now. The reactions to the spread of AIDS illustrates this point. Compared to only a few years ago, we now have a different situation concerning sexual ethics, medical examinations, advertising, and sex education, to cite just a few areas of rapid change. Policies, such as those on condom advertising, have been suddenly raised and resolved in ways that would have been out of the question only a short time ago.

Changing attitudes toward marriage illustrate how attitudes toward public education may also change in the near future. Support for public education declines among senior citizens. Yet changing attitudes toward marriage are leading to declining support among young adults as well. The average age of persons first married in 1983 reached 26.8 for men and 24.5 for women, reflecting a long-term trend toward postponing marriage. About one in every eight Americans remains unmarried for life. In recent years the divorce rate has exceeded the marriage rate; marriage is clearly declining as a lifetime commitment.

The consequences of the decline of marriage are highly adverse to public education in several ways. Adults who are not married or who marry later tend to have fewer children. Partly for this reason, the political objectives of unmarried or childless adults differ markedly from those of married adults with children. The latter seek low taxes, affordable homes, and good schools. The unmarried, or the adults who marry frequently, tend not to be so interested in home building or schools. Furthermore, single-parent and nonfamily households require heavier expenditures for nonschool social services, such as police protection and health care. In short, the decline in marriage results in fewer children, less parental interest in public education, weakened political support for good schools, and more spending for nonschool public services.[24]

Load Shedding and Equality Issues

Chapter 6 noted that rising standards of living generate support for consumer choices. In the educational context, such support encourages load shedding, at least to some degree. This is evident from the patterns of choice when public and private sectors provide the same or similar services.

Both the public and private sectors provide food, housing, and medical services. In these cases, and many others that can be cited, the private sector provides a much greater variety of choices. To put it bluntly, the superiority of the private sector in this regard is indisputable. It is unrealistic to ignore this fact, or the sectoral factors which underlie it.

Essentially, rising economic levels generate a dilemma for public education. Its supporters emphasize the danger that public schools will serve only the poor if educational services are provided by market processes. Even if the factual premise is valid, the objection is not clearly persuasive. With food and shelter and medical care, government provides services primarily for those who cannot afford to purchase them. Dumping ground rhetoric notwithstanding, why not follow a similar policy in education? Equalization requires funding, and we cannot fund complete equality for all services. We cannot fund it even for one service, unless we are prepared to limit private expenditures for it. Outside of education, however, the issue is not perceived or treated as one of equality. Instead, it is what level of service should be made available to those who cannot purchase it in the market. In setting this level, educators give education a high priority. In fact, they give it a higher priority than the disadvantaged themselves often deem appropriate. The latter often prefer a higher level of protection from crime or a higher level of shelter over a higher level of educational funding. It is not at all clear, at least to me, why such preferences are irrational or shortsighted.

The suggestion that avoidance of market processes is a cause of our educational difficulties is obviously anathema to public school educators; any such suggestion appears to threaten their economic security. Among academics, especially in the educational reform industry, the suggestion is just as odious, since it challenges the value and intellectual level of much of their work over many years. Difficult as it may be, a significant shift to privatization, if otherwise desirable, must avoid being held hostage to these obstacles.

The Graying of the Population

Our population is becoming older. From year to year the increases are incremental; yet over a few decades the increases constitute changes of enormous magnitude. In 1900, 4.1 percent of the population was sixty-five or over; by 1980 this group was 11.3 percent of the total population, and it is projected to reach 13.1 percent by the year 2000. By 2010 one of every seven Americans will be sixty-five or over; the number of persons eighty-five and over may double to 6.8 million, a remarkable 2.4 percent of the total population.[25]

These changes are likely to affect education in several important ways. The needs and interests of senior citizens differ from those of children and/or younger parents. Thus as the elderly become a larger interest group, they generate heavy pressures on public budgets for services. It has been estimated that from 1960 to 1979, the average government expenditure (local, state, and federal combined) for each person over sixty-five was about triple the expenditure for each child. Because the expenditures for the elderly started at a higher absolute level, maintaining the three-to-one ratio meant that expenditures per elderly person increased more in absolute terms than expenditures per child. Since 1979, moreover, the disparity has increased substantially. Major federal programs for children, such as federal aid to education and Aid to Families with Dependent Children (AFDC), have been reduced whereas those for the elderly are still growing. In 1987 the federal government spent at least ten times as much per senior citizen as it did per school-age child; the 1987 rush in Congress to provide assistance for catastrophic medical situations suggests that the disparity is not likely to be reduced in the near future.[26] Likewise, congressional and presidential reluctance to cap Social Security entitlements in order to reduce the budget deficit (even though most of the elderly are not poor) reinforces this conclusion.

The enormous changes in the age composition of the population do not fully convey the declining political future of public education. Public opinion polls show that the elderly are more likely to vote but are not as supportive of education as younger citizens. A 1983 Gallup poll asked whether respondents would support higher taxes for schools if asked to do so by their local school board. Among those under fifty, the answers were evenly divided; among those over fifty, the responses were 62 to 28 percent opposed.[27]

A 1988 referendum in Arizona dramatically illustrates the declining support for public education among senior citizens. Prior to the referendum, Arizona retirement communities that were not part of any school district did not pay taxes for school district operations. As a result of the referendum, retirement communities are required to pay them. Several communities are taking legal and political action to avoid or reduce the school taxes they will otherwise have to pay.

Significantly, some retirement communities opposed to paying school taxes are quite large. For example, two such communities in Sun City do not accept residents under fifty or children under eighteen, yet have over 60,000 residents. Only a handful of children under eighteen, deemed hardship exceptions, are permitted to live in those communities. Obviously, the situation also illustrates the points made in chapter 7 about age segregation in American society.[28]

By and large, the elderly include lower proportions of disadvantaged minorities than the population as a whole. On the other hand, the black and Hispanic proportions of the school-age population is increasing dramatically. Thus in addition to the conflicts resulting from age related needs and interests, the elderly will include a much lower proportion of citizens with family ties to school-age children. This is likely to exacerbate the problems of financing public education. Challenges to public spending for education will become politically advantageous at a much lower expenditure level. The ideology of public education will come under increasing scrutiny. Its claims to foster basic skills, good citizenship, racial and social integration—all such claims will encounter a more skeptical if not a more hostile audience.

The graying of the population is especially likely to affect labor markets and the Social Security system in ways that will be conducive to shortening the period of compulsory tax-supported education. First, employers are experiencing greater difficulty in recruiting employees for entry-level jobs. Historically, young people have been the major source for such employees, but the supply of teenagers relative to the demand is decreasing substantially. Despite greater utilization of senior citizens and immigrants as sources of unskilled labor, our nation is being forced to reconsider its basic policies concerning youth employment. It may well be concluded that a great deal of the protective legislation concerning youth employment actually works against their short- and long-range interests as well as against the interests of the larger society.

Another consideration is less immediate but potentially significant in the long run. Our Social Security system is essentially based on intergenerational stability. Recipients are not paid from their prior contributions but from the contributions of current and future employees. Consequently, as the proportion of recipients increases vis-à-vis the proportion of contributors, the aggregate amount of claims will exceed the aggregate amount of contributions; any excess of contributions over payments from past years will not maintain the system's stability.

Undoubtedly, several policy changes will be required to maintain the solvency of the Social Security system. One such policy change will almost inevitably be lowering the age restrictions on gainful employment. Having large numbers of young people contribute to Social Security for three or four years more than they do now will be an important step. Of course, it will be argued that earlier participation in the labor force is a poor long-range investment for young people and for society. With some young people the issue can be easily resolved one way or the other. For large numbers, however, the value of maintaining their formal education at present levels is far from clear. In view of the pressures to increase the work span, we can anticipate heavy pressures to reduce the extent of compulsory education. In other words, just as compulsory education resulted partly from the prohibition of child labor, it may decline under pressure to increase youth participation in the labor force. While educational organizations, especially teacher unions, will adamantly oppose earlier entry into the labor force, the demographic pressures to increase years of work are likely to be decisive.[29]

Changing Attitudes Toward Children

Children are more and more being viewed as the outcome of deliberate "consumer" decisions whose economic costs should be borne by those who make the decisions. In my opinion, we are at the beginning, not the peak, of this change. Nevertheless, I believe the change is an irreversible one that is certain to weaken support for public education.

First of all, the feminist emphasis on a woman's unqualified right to abort reinforces a "consumerist" attitude toward children. Education is the major public expenditure for children. If the decision to have children is a personal and individual one, it is more difficult to contend that government is obligated to absorb the costs of raising children. Why should everyone else pay if the decision is a personal one? As we have seen, the 1987–88 estimated per-pupil cost in public schools was about $4,800. On this basis, the average public cost of educating a child through high school will exceed $100,000 in a few years. If the decision to trigger those costs is a personal one, it will occur to many that perhaps the costs should be also. Sooner or later, one suspects that the feminist orientation of teacher unions, with their emphasis on choice in matters related to pregnancy, will be seen as inconsistent with their anti-choice approach to education.

Here again we must consider the politics as well as the substantive dimensions of the issue. When bearing children and raising a family were the normal career patterns of women, including the more affluent and better educated ones, the political decision to support public education was easy to make. Intentions notwithstanding, the feminist movement weakens the consensus underlying public education. For one thing, it weakens the economic incentives for marriage as a career. As divorce has become easier to implement and more common, more and more women seek economic security in careers instead of families. Inasmuch as children may be an obstacle to careers outside the family, it is not surprising that birth rates have declined precipitously; in 1984 the fertility rate among women twenty to twenty-four years of age declined to an all-time low, despite a sizable increase in the percentage of babies born out of wedlock among all age groups.[30] A critical factor has been the decline in fertility among women oriented to careers outside of homemaking. The thrust of the feminist movement has gone far beyond the elimination of discrimination against women; while downgrading the economic benefits of marriage, it has increased the economic opportunities for women outside the home. Indeed, to the extent that we move to greater economic equality between men and women, we will experience increased declines in fertility rates, at least among women who make a conscious choice between homemaking and other careers. More and more women who formerly would have been active in the PTA are pursuing careers that exclude such activity.

At or near the other end of the economic order, the birth rates among teenage mothers have increased or remained relatively stable. Just as our policies have weakened the economic incentives for marriage and for raising children among the affluent, they have strengthened the incentives to bear children among poor teenage females; the United States now has by far the highest teenage birth rate of any western industrialized nation. These higher rates are not primarily a racial phenomena; while the birth rate for white teenagers in the United States is not as high as for blacks, it is still higher than for any other industrialized nation.[31] In 1985 about 8.8 million single mothers were legally entitled to child support. Only about half were receiving the amounts awarded. About a quarter were receiving less and a quarter were receiving none. In 1987 four million children needed to establish paternity to receive child support but only 260,000 paternities were established nationwide. About one in eight children are conceived by parents who are not living together; in these cases, the fathers seldom provide support of any kind.[32]

Thus as contraception and abortion make it easy to avoid child bearing, decisions to have children at all economic levels are increasingly made independently of paternal obligation or responsibility. I see no reason to assume that fathers who pay no child support will pay for their children's education. Federal legislation enacted in September 1988 is intended to require them to do so, but the effectiveness of the legislation has yet to be demonstrated. The probability is that the long-term decline in paternal support will not be made up, or made up fully, by government or by legal actions against absentee fathers; instead, there will be a decline in the standard of living of single parents (mostly females) and their children. This decline, or the threat of it, will exert negative pressure on birth rates, especially among more affluent and better educated women. In short, the demographics indicate an erosion of support for public education among the groups that formerly provided much of its political support and leadership.

To repeat, making these observations does not imply approval of them. Indeed, I regard them as cause for deep concern. Nonetheless, the underlying realities have a momentum of their own that cannot be ignored. Public education emerged from a confluence of several factors: small, homogeneous communities, widespread acceptance of traditional family styles and structures, relatively little pressure on early labor force participation, and high expectations about the effects of education. These factors may have changed or may change too much to enable public education as we know it to survive.

The Decline in Teacher Unions

As we have seen, the National Education Association and the American Federation of Teachers constitute the major political obstacle to privatization in any form. AFSCME must also be viewed as an obstacle, even though its efforts may focus on support services. In general, we can expect these unions to actively oppose privatization of either instructional or noninstructional services.

The political importance of this opposition will vary widely from state to state and district to district. In some northern states, especially in large urban districts, their opposition will prevail, at least during the early 1990s. Yet elsewhere their opposition will be negligible, mainly in some southern and western states. Probably in most states their opposition will be significant but not necessarily decisive. In the long run, however, these unions are likely to be less influential than they were in the 1980s. In fact, such a decline is already under way. Although its end point is unpredictable, it is virtually certain to bottom out at a much lower level of union influence in political matters. A complete analysis of the reasons unions are losing influence would take us too far afield, but a brief discussion may suffice to show why we can anticipate this outcome.

First of all, the union movement per se is experiencing a substantial decline. Union membership has declined from an all-time high of 36 percent of the labor force in 1945 to 18 percent in 1986. Only 12 percent of college graduates employed full time on a year-around basis belong to a union. The AFL-CIO itself has sponsored several studies of the causes and possible remedies for its declining membership and influence. Although some changes in union programs and policies may help to stabilize union membership, the basic reasons for the decline do not seem amenable to union control. For example, the tremendous increase in part-time employment and employment at home renders union organization much more difficult. Competition from foreign companies means that unions have much less latitude to negotiate restrictive work rules. As their ability to negotiate such rules declines, so does an important reason for their appeal to employees.

Some but not all of the reasons for union decline in the private sector apply to teacher unions. One is that teachers are becoming more dissatisfied with their unions. A study by C. Emily Feistritzer, director of the National Center for Education Statistics, showed that although 75 percent of teachers with twenty-five to twenty-nine years of experience are NEA members, only 55 percent of those hired in the last five years are members. Thirty-eight percent of teachers with less than five years of experience were not members of either NEA or AFT, whereas only 14 percent of teachers with twenty-four to twenty-nine years of experience were not union members. In the poll one-third of the teachers were dissatisfied with their national union, 27 percent with their state union, and 21 percent with their local union.[33]

Although some factors underlying union decline in the private sector do not apply to teacher unions, one potentially critical factor raises the possibility that teacher unions will decline faster than private sector ones. In the private sector, there is usually no organizational alternative to unions. The decline in unionization results from demographic or economic factors, not from competition with nonunion organizations. In education, however, teacher unions may be seriously weakened by the growth of nonunion teacher organizations. The potential for such growth and its implications for privatization and choice issues require some elaboration.

In 1988 there were about twenty state nonunion organizations of teachers. Although most enrolled less than one thousand teachers, several enjoyed a much higher membership. The independent Missouri State Teachers Association enrolled more members than the state affiliate of either NEA or AFT; in Texas, Georgia, Louisiana, and South Carolina the nonunion organizations enrolled a substantial number of teachers, despite the fact that many teachers in these states do not join any teacher organization.[34]

A critical issue is whether nonunion teacher associations can increase their membership substantially in states with teacher bargaining laws. I believe this is possible, but the outcome depends on several factors that are unpredictable at this time. In membership, resources, and political support, the nonunion associations are in a much stronger position than was the AFT at the advent of teacher bargaining. Although they are not likely to support privatization, their positions on it are likely to depend primarily on whether proposals along these lines actually threaten teachers in service. As we have seen, this will depend largely on the specifics of the proposals and the way they are introduced. Expansion of nonunion associations would facilitate efforts to involve the private sector in more effective ways. Minimally, the nonunion associations are not likely to act as if the skies are falling every time vouchers are mentioned.

As the proportion of parents with school-age children declines, so will the proportion of teachers in the labor force and the political influence of teacher unions. The latter are trying to maintain their numbers and influence by organizing day care centers, but it is doubtful whether their efforts along this line will be successful. To solve their own problems of declining enrollments, institutions of higher education will encourage earlier entry into higher education, thus weakening the ability of teacher unions to maintain the market for teachers below the college level. Everything considered, teacher unions will be hard pressed to maintain their share of a shrinking market for classroom teachers.

Load Shedding and the Day Care Movement

On its face, the day care movement seems to contradict my analysis of load shedding. Clearly, day care supporters in both major parties are seeking to expand government functions. As we have seen, the major obstacle to federal support for day care is whether parents or public agencies should control how the funds would be spent. Over the past fifty years, government has been replacing the family as the major source of support for the aged, the ill, the disabled, the unemployed, and other special populations. In this sense, the day care movement reflects a longtime trend toward government displacement of families as a source of financial support. I do not believe, however, that the day care movement invalidates my previous analysis. Education is an enormous institution which is constantly characterized by some countercyclical trends.

Government financial support for day care is contrary to load shedding but might nevertheless encourage privatization. If federal support for day care is made available through vouchers or tax credits, its overall effect would be to strengthen these policies for school-age children. Such an outcome would reconcile the apparent willingness of the American people to increase spending for social services with their distrust of government as the service provider.

Finally, the possibility remains that private delivery of educational services funded by government may be far less effective than is anticipated. In brief, the major criticisms of both public education and voucher systems may have merit. What then? By a process of elimination, we may be forced to reconsider whether education should be treated differently from food, clothing, shelter, and other necessities which parents buy for their children. Eventually, we may conclude that parent purchase of educational services from parent funds is preferable to either the existing system or the alternatives currently receiving the most attention.

11

Ethical and Policy Issues
in Education
for Profit

Teaching is widely regarded or referred to as a "profession." Ideally, professionals act in the best interests of their clients. In business, however, the welfare of the customer is secondary. A doctor who recommends surgery because he would profit thereby would be considered unethical, regardless of the effect of such surgery on his practice. In contrast, an automobile salesman who persuaded customers to purchase expensive but unnecessary optional equipment is ordinarily considered a successful salesman, not an unethical one. The business firm may guide customers away from unwise purchases, but it does so to retain the customers or avoid damage to its reputation. For this reason the operative principle in business is the welfare of the seller, not the customer.

The extent, if any, to which professional ethics differ in practice from business ethics is a matter of dispute.[1] Clearly, however, public opinion assumes that professions adhere or should adhere to a higher standard of conduct than business firms. Education is one of the professions that is expected to adhere to such higher standards, imprecisely defined as they may be. Consequently, we need to consider the ethical or professional implications of any trend toward education for profit.

Most ethical problems in the professions involve conflicts of interest, situations in which action on behalf of one party is actually or potentially contrary to the interests of another party. Financial gain or loss is not always an issue. Teachers who devote classroom time to one student may be acting contrary to the interests of others with greater need for individual attention.

For our purposes, the most important conflicts of interest are those involving teacher or owner interests on the one hand and student/parent interests on the other. Such conflicts already exist under public operation of schools. Student welfare may call for individual attention after school; teacher welfare calls for teachers to be released from service immediately after the last regular class.

In the commercial world, the existence of conflicts of interest is taken for granted, as is the presumption that each party will, or has the right to, maximize its own interests. Even in the commercial world, however, in some situations conflicts of interest are not tolerated or must be resolved in certain ways. The rules prohibiting "insider trading" illustrate this point; corporate officials are prohibited from purchasing or selling stock in their corporation on the basis of information not available to shareholders generally.

All of the established professions have adopted rules or codes of ethics that are intended to avoid or mitigate conflicts of interest. Attorneys are not normally allowed to represent both parties in legal transactions; to do so would raise the possibility that one party or the other would not receive the full benefits of representation. Currently, the NEA code of professional ethics and the codes of several of its state affiliates state that "Educators . . . shall not use professional relationships with students for private advantage." Such rules are enforced, however, by school management, if they are enforced at all.

Public opinion often treats the differences between professional and business ethics as a matter of individual character. That is, the differences in conduct are ascribed to differences in the kind of individuals who enter various occupations. In this view, professional workers are more idealistic or more dedicated to service than their business counterparts; the latter are supposedly driven by greed or profits. This attitude is common among teachers, who often assert that they prefer helping children grow over earning a higher income.

Such rhetoric notwithstanding, there is little justification for the idea that "professionals" are a different breed. As far as teachers are concerned, it is very doubtful whether their conduct is any less self-serving than the conduct of businesspeople; as pointed out in chapter 6, teachers have frequently exploited their students not only in strike situations but in other contexts as well. More important, and aside from the fact that business ethics sometimes provide better consumer protection than professional ethics, any differences in conduct between the professions and business are due to occupational structure and culture, not personality factors. This point does not contradict my previous comment that sectoral status is not a reliable guide to individual conduct.

If adherence to professional standards was mainly due to personality factors, the change from a professional to a business context would not matter very much. Presumably, the individual who places client welfare above personal gain would continue to do so regardless of context. If, however, context is the controlling factor, changes in it can be expected to have significant implications for relationships with service recipients, whether they are labeled "customers" or "clients."

On several occasions I have cited developments from health care that appear to shed some light on educational issues. Perhaps no aspect of medical practice is more useful in this regard than the effects of a business orientation on medical ethics and practice. Medical ethics are widely regarded as a model of professional conduct. At the same time, for-profit enterprise has become the dominant mode in many aspects of health care. For these reasons, and with the usual caveats about analogies, it will be helpful to review the changes in medical ethics for their educational implications.

Let me first illustrate the kinds of problems that would raise concerns about greater reliance on for-profit organizations. A brief historical note may provide a helpful point of departure.[2] The first teachers in western culture (the Sophists) were fee takers; Protagoras, the most renowned among them, waived his fees for students who swore that his instruction had not been helpful. Needless to say, few if any contemporary teachers would accept such a standard. In any case, this bit of history suggests that education for profit has some roots in the educational practice and traditions of western civilizations. Second, it also suggests that for-profit enterprise is not necessarily characterized by standards of conduct that are morally inferior to "professional" standards.

Neither business nor professional ethics condones outright falsehoods. There appear, however, to be significant differences in the duty of disclosure. Businesspeople are not ethically obligated to disclose the negative features of their product or service. In contrast, physicians are expected to inform patients about the disadvantages of a treatment that might lead a patient to reject it. What policy would govern teachers in schools for profit?

A physician who sees another physician using a wrong procedure is obligated to alert the erring practitioner. Similarly, teachers also would do so in the normal course of events. Suppose, however, several for-profit educational companies are competing for students. Company *A* realizes that its competitors are relying on outdated information or teaching methods. If the welfare of students is paramount, company *A* should inform its competitors. From a business standpoint, however, the company would say nothing; it would be to its advantage to have its competition rely on outdated information or ineffective procedures. To cite another likely scenario, a profit-making school would enroll students in a certain program even though a competitor has a better one, thus working contrary to the students' best interests.

Historically, medical practice has not always been clearly distinguished from commercial practice. Anglo-American medical ethics has always held that physicians should act in best interests of patients; this principle can be traced all the way back to the Hippocratic tradition. At the same time, nothing in our medical traditions requires physicians to provide their services on a philanthropic basis. While physicians could ethically decline to provide service, once they elect to provide it, the patient's welfare was to be the guiding criterion. Interestingly enough, physicians in ancient Greece avoided hopeless cases that would damage their reputations and jeopardize the market for their services.

In American medical history, the potential conflicts between the service and commercial dimensions of medical practice were largely ignored until the twentieth century. When such attention emerged, it prohibited or warned against treating medical practice as a business. In fact, even the appearance of commercialization was condemned. Thus the AMA's first code of ethics, adopted in 1847, prohibited advertising, the holding of patents, and the dispensing of "secret nostrums." At the same time, however, the purpose of the code was not to control physician behavior. Instead it was to distinguish physicians from quacks and charlatans who engaged in the practices proscribed by the AMA.

Whatever its origins, hostility to business practices is no longer evident in the AMA code of professional ethics. In many cases the code now accommodates business practices that were previously prohibited. Some examples follow.

Advertising The prohibition against advertising has been changed to a provision that physicians "should not solicit patients." This change occurred in part as a reaction to a lawsuit against the AMA by the Federal Trade Commission, alleging that its prohibition of advertising was a restraint on competition. Regardless of any legal issues, a shift to for-profit companies in education might change the content of advertising but not its utilization. Public and nonprofit schools and organizations already advertise extensively; in fact, the longest running advertisement in the field of education is probably a weekly column in the Sunday *New York Times* sponsored by the American Federation of Teachers.

Patents The AMA's initial position, adopted in 1847, asserted that "It is derogatory to professional character . . . for a physician to hold a patent for any surgical instrument or medicine." In 1981 the AMA adopted a completely opposite provision: "It is not unethical for a physician to patent a surgical or diagnostic instrument."[3] Analogously, such a provision would allow educators to patent teaching devices, diagnostic instruments, or any other otherwise patentable product used in schools. Inasmuch as no restriction now exists, no change in practice would be involved.

Dispensing Pharmaceuticals Obviously, if physicians are allowed to sell the drugs they prescribe, they might prescribe and sell drugs on the basis of their own profit, not patient welfare. Since 1957, however, the prevailing principle has been: "Drugs, remedies or appliances may be dispensed or supplied by the physician provided it is in the best interest of the patient."[4] Needless to say, this is not much of a restriction as long as the dispensing physician is the one who decides what is "the best interest of the patient." In education, this posture would allow teachers or education companies to sell various products to students; for example, music teachers could sell instruments. Where restrictions on such sales currently exist in education, they are due to school board policies, not to the policies or standards of teacher organizations.

Fee Splitting Fee splitting is a pervasive issue in medical practice because general practitioners often guide patients to specialists. Is it ethical for a specialist to compensate a general practitioner from fees paid the specialist? Despite some earlier emphasis on the evils of secrecy rather than fee splitting per se, the practice itself is still deemed unacceptable in the AMA code. In this respect, the prohibition against fee splitting, which seems to be weakening, is an exception to the tendency to ease the restrictions on business practices.

A prohibition against fee splitting would prohibit teachers from receiving compensation for referring students to educational specialists. This would be a significant limitation.

Ownership of Health Facilities Physician ownership of hospitals has always been accepted. In recent years physician ownership of pharmacies, hospitals, nursing homes, and laboratories has increased considerably.[5] At the same time the AMA deems it unethical for physicians to allow their practice to be influenced by such ownership. The outcome has been rather ambiguous. Currently physicians can share in the profits of facilities they own (in whole or in part), but their compensation as physicians ethically cannot be geared directly to their referrals as physicians. Many observers view this as a distinction without a difference, or much difference.

For several years the AMA emphasized the importance of professional control over hospitals; its Judicial Council held at one time that "A physician should not dispose of his professional attainments or services to any hospital, corporation, or lay body by whatever name called or however organized under terms or conditions which permit the sale of the service of that physician by such an agency for a fee." This language was deleted from the AMA code of ethics in 1981; no reason was offered for the omission. Obviously, any restrictions on teacher-owned schools, camps, learning centers, testing preparation facilities, and other profit-making centers could be a major limitation on education for profit. Experience in health care, however, suggests that such limitations are not likely to survive a large shift to privatization.

As Georgetown University ethicist Robert M. Veatch points out, the ethical obligations of physicians increasingly are being defined in terms of patient rights instead of patient welfare or interests. There is a heavy emphasis on physician control of medical decisions, including fees, but business involvement is acceptable if physicians maintain such control. In Veatch's words, "Nowhere in all of the professional literature of Anglo-American medical ethics is there any condemnation of the profit motive in the practice of medicine. In fact . . . the AMA has viewed the question of whether an institution is making a profit on the physician's services as irrelevant to whether the arrangement is ethical."[6]

The changes in medical ethics just discussed raise a question that soon may become important in education: Did the changes in medical ethics precede and pave the way for changes in practice, or did the changes merely ratify irreversible changes that had already occurred? Undoubtedly both patterns have been operative, but it appears that the ratification pattern was predominant. For example, as the result of changes in medical technology and the sources of medical revenues (especially the tremendous growth of payments by government and insurance companies), more doctors enjoy more opportunities than ever before to earn substantial income from practices previously prohibited or discouraged. It has become increasingly difficult for the AMA to maintain ethical standards that conflict with the interests of a larger and larger proportion of its members. In effect, the standards could not survive the opportunities of doctor-owned profit centers, such as laboratories, testing centers, and nursing homes. Granted, some of the changes in medical ethics are not desirable from a client point of view. Again, however, it must be emphasized that we are dealing with system issues. If education for profit plays a larger role in the future, competition and disclosure may protect students and parents just as adequately, if not more so, than reliance on professional ethics. Let us see why this may be the case.

Competition Versus Regulation as a Student Safeguard

Within the public school establishment, regulation by state and local authorities is viewed as the primary means of safeguarding student interests. Whatever goes or might go awry is supposed to be brought to the attention of state and local public officials. These officials will then remedy the problem by administrative or regulatory measures, including legislation if need be. Regulation is also viewed as the means of safeguarding the interests of children in private schools. The nonprofit, especially denominational, status of private schools is also deemed to protect students.

At the same time, competition as a means of protection is virtually ignored, especially when denominational considerations are paramount. As previously noted, consumer ability to compare price and quality is an essential element of competition. We have also seen that it is more difficult to compare the quality of human services than of products, such as television sets or vacuum cleaners. On the other hand, whether choice in education is feasible depends on its own circumstances, not the fact that services are more difficult to compare than products (if indeed they are). Most people believe they can recognize the difference between good and poor teachers. Granted, this is not equivalent to recognizing the difference between good and poor schools, but it is surely an important component of such recognition.

In any event, our difficulties in comparing schools may be partly due to the lack of incentives to make such comparisons. The vast majority of parents have no practical incentive to compare schools. If you cannot afford either a Mercedes or a Rolls-Royce, you are less likely to have any interest in, and therefore any capability of, comparing and choosing between them. If your comparison was intended to lead to a purchase, you would undoubtedly become better informed about the options. By the same token, the ability of parents to compare and choose among schools might be greatly enhanced if the choice was intended to lead to action.

The analogy may not be persuasive. Persons who can purchase $35,000 automobiles are usually quite able to look after their interests in such matters. What about individuals who have to buy an inexpensive subcompact or a used car? There appears to be heavy competition for such purchases, yet some states have recently enacted "lemon laws" to protect car buyers from unscrupulous car salesmen. Indeed, it might be argued that fierce competition has made it so difficult to earn a profit that salesmen have had to adopt unethical tactics.

Although the preceding point has merit, it does not necessarily mean that competition among schools would lead to undesirable outcomes. Some car salesmen can survive by squeezing every penny from one-shot deals in which the customer is virtually defrauded. It would be much more difficult for a school to survive this way. Even if they did not withdraw their children immediately, most parents would not reenroll their children in a school that exploited to the hilt every short-term possibility for maximizing profits. Furthermore, it would be very difficult for such a school to attract a new complement of students every year at every grade level.

For that matter, we can question the assumption that competition must be at the school level. Theoretically at least, we could leave the structure of public education largely intact while fostering competition among teachers. To see how, suppose that instead of employing teachers, school boards rented space in school buildings to them. Suppose also that teachers were free to set their own fees; teachers who were in great demand could charge more than teachers who were not. Such a system might be tied to a plan for divisible vouchers, so that part of the voucher credit could be used to pay mathematics teachers, part to pay science teachers, and so on.

Such a system could stimulate competition among

teachers—most of whom would be adamantly opposed to it for that reason. Needless to say, teacher unions would be also. Nonetheless, such a system might be more efficient and more desirable than competition at the school level. Among its potential advantages are the following:

1. It would attract more resources into education under conditions conducive to their more efficient use. Parents who may be willing to pay more for particular teachers may be unable to do so if their choice is limited to schools.
2. Class size and room size could be coordinated more efficiently.
3. Parents would probably devote more effort to deciding what they want from education and how much they are willing to pay for what they want.
4. Teacher accessibility to and cooperation with parents would be greatly enhanced. Teachers would have no interest in collective bargaining contracts that limit their accessibility to parents to a few evening and/or afternoon meetings a year.
5. Teachers would have greater control over their work and work schedules.
6. Insofar as the market would be an accurate guide, better teachers would be paid more; others would be paid correspondingly less.

A major objection to such a system would be that enrollments might reflect the entrepreneurial instead of the educational abilities of teachers. I regard this as more of a short- than a long-range problem, but the danger exists. Probably the other major objection would be that such a system would lead to greater social class segregation than exists. Although such an outcome is possible, it is by no means certain. More important, the increased efficiency and productivity of the system as a whole might justify any negative change along this line.[7]

From a public policy perspective, we can say that both competition and regulation have a role to play in consumer protection. I do not mean to imply that the affluent rely on competition and the less affluent on regulation, although consumer protection in some situations follows this pattern. In education, however, we rely almost exclusively on regulation to protect students and taxpayers. The possibility that competition might be a more effective way to provide such protection is virtually ignored. Even discussions of vouchers and tuition tax credits do not address seriously the role of competition. Because most family choice proponents are from the nonprofit sector and envisage assistance to private schools, not competition among them, they have also failed to present the case for competition in a serious way. On both sides, "competition" is a slogan, not an idea worthy of serious analysis.

This is unfortunate, especially because most citizens do not realize how ineffectual educational regulation has turned out to be. If more courses in science and mathematics are required for a high school diploma, school districts relabel courses so the latter can be counted to meet the requirement. If a certain grade-point average is required for athletic eligibility, grading standards are lowered to avoid the requirement. If schools must be open a certain number of days, "days" are interpreted very liberally. If a district can employ noncertified teachers only in an "emergency," "emergency" is interpreted very loosely. If textbooks are required to be up to date, publishers make cosmetic changes and change the copyright date.

In short, the regulatory approach is frequently characterized by loopholes and inadequate enforcement—and it is doubtful whether rigorous enforcement without any loopholes would improve matters. I am not asserting the desirability of completely avoiding regulation. Instead, my point is that the effectiveness of regulation is widely exaggerated, and that competition in some situations may be a more effective way to achieve the objectives of educational regulation.[8]

A critical point, often overlooked, is that the absence of regulation does not affect denominational and independent schools in the same way. Denominational schools are accountable to their parent denominations. Independent private schools, however, enjoy freedom from both state and denominational regulation. The upshot is that such schools operate under minimal safeguards of any kind.

In many quarters, independent private schools are regarded as "elite" institutions of elementary and secondary education. No doubt some of these schools are outstanding, but reason and personal experience suggest that our worst schools, public or private, are private independent schools.[9] The deficiencies in these schools tend to escape public scrutiny; they would be less likely to do so if voucher plans were enacted. On the contrary, we could expect some exposés followed by demands for increased regulation of private schools.

Nevertheless, I do not accept as foreordained the idea that vouchers would automatically lead to greater state regulation of private schools. There was no significant increase in regulation of grocery stores or medical practice as a result of food stamps or Medicare. Many public institutions of higher education are not closely regulated; even private ones receiving substantial support from government are not subject to close state or federal regulation. Significantly, there is the least regulation of private schools in some states which provide the most government assistance for them. Increased regulation under a voucher system may not result from demands for greater accountability. Such demands will be made and they will be a factor. The main problem, however, would be the political objections to funding both public and private schools while closely regulating only the former. In other words, the inconsistency in regulation might have to be resolved by increased regulation of private schools, regardless of any need for it.

Another possibility is to tie the degree of regulation to the level of government support. As noted in chapter 2, the President's Commission on Privatization recently recommended this approach and some nations have adopted it. Apart from the specifics, it is not feasible to assess such policies, but they may receive more attention than in the past. In any event, the nonprofit status of private schools may lead to increased regulation of them, independently of government financial support for them. Because of its growth, the nonprofit sector is coming under greater scrutiny and regulation. As a result, public policy may evolve in the direction of a comprehensive rather than an industry-by-industry approach to nonprofit organizations. Any such trend would probably affect nonprofit schools adversely. When regulation is industry by industry, the regulated industries are better able to control, or strongly influence, the regulatory agency. For example, if occupational licensing is regulated by separate agencies, the occupations regulated have more influence over the agencies that concern them than if a single state agency regulated all licensing. The 1987 scandals concerning certain television ministries may well result in greater scrutiny and skepticism concerning nonprofit organizations generally. Historically, once public attention begins to focus on a neglected area, the fallout is much broader than the initial focus of attention.

Although the possibility is seldom discussed, family choice plans might lead to less regulation of public schools. The reason is that the absence of regulation may be an important factor underlying any private school educational superiority.[10] The policy implication is to reduce the regulation of public schools, whether or not family choice plans are enacted. Of course, no matter how desirable in theory, deregulation would be difficult to achieve. It would be necessary to identify those aspects of regulation which impair public school effectiveness. At that point, influential interest groups with a stake in the status quo would oppose deregulation. That is probably the main reason why it receives so little attention from legislators. The latter are searching for what may not exist, a way of improving education that does not arouse influential interest group opposition.

The Outlook for Regulation by "the Profession"

Some observers believe that the deficiencies of government regulation point to the need for a different kind of regulation—*self-regulation* by teachers as a profession. This point of view is expressed in a variety of ways, such as the need to "empower teachers" or "to replace bureaucratic control by professional control," or by some other phraseology that suggests teachers should control education.[11]

Although arguments for teacher control usually strike a responsive chord among teachers, careful analysis suggests several major objections to any such development. In the first place, delegating responsibility for policy and administrative decisions to teachers as a group creates an insoluble dilemma. All individuals in the group cannot be held accountable for group action since some individuals may have opposed it. For accountability to be meaningful, individuals must be responsible for their own actions, not for the actions of others. Thus to avoid being unfair to individuals in the group, collective responsibility often deteriorates into collective irresponsibility.

Second, arguments for "empowering teachers" or self-regulation by teachers rely on the fee-taking professions as models. Such reliance ignores the fact that the need for a viability of self-regulation in fee-taking professions differs significantly from its need and viability for salaried professionals subject to single employer supervision. A fee taker may have dozens, even hundreds of clients (employers); it is simply impractical for any one employer to supervise professional workers. This is not the case when one employer (the school district) employs a large number of professional employees (teachers). The notion that supervision of teachers is unwarranted because professionals should not be supervised merely avoids teacher accountability under the rhetoric of professionalism.

An impressive body of evidence indicates that self-regulation by the professions has been used as much or more to advance the professionals' welfare as to advance the public interest.[12] Whatever one's assessment of this evidence, self-regulation is likely to be even less effective in education. In the first place, teachers do not have an affective code of ethics or a tradition of observing one. Generally speaking, it is school management's responsibility to ensure that teachers do not engage in conduct prejudicial to student interests. For example, school boards and school administrators, not teacher unions, are responsible for ensuring that teachers avoid commercial relationships with their students. Turning over this responsibility to teachers (in effect, to teacher unions) would leave the public without any feasible way of preventing or remedying abuses.

Despite contentions that teachers are stifled by state legislation, most such legislation affecting teachers promotes their welfare. Legislation on teacher tenure, retirement, leaves, and collective bargaining illustrate this point. State legislation restricting teaching methods or materials is virtually nonexistent. The limitations on teachers that do exist are usually the result of limitations on school officials. For example, if a state requires that textbooks be selected from a state-approved list, teachers will necessarily be limited in their choice of textbooks. Realistically, however, very little state legislation infringes on the freedom of teachers in the classroom.

The alleged desirability of developing an autonomous, self-regulated teaching profession fails to take account of the implications of teacher unionization. Teachers are heavily unionized, perhaps more so than any other major occupational group in our nation. Legally and practically, teacher unions exist to represent teachers on wages and terms and conditions of employment. The union role is very similar to the role attorneys play in our legal system. Attorneys represent clients and client interests, not the public interest; likewise, unions represent employees and employee interests. This does not mean that unions always act in the short-range interests of the employees they represent, any more than lawyers always act to maximize the short-range interests of their clients. Regardless, we should not allow special interest groups or organizations to exercise legal authority over policies affecting the public interest.

Here again, a bit of history is instructive. Prior to the advent of collective bargaining in the early 1960s, the NEA and many of its affiliated state associations had adopted codes of professional ethics.[13] Although code enforcement was minimal at best, there was at least a symbolic recognition that "professionals" were supposed to adhere to a higher standard of conduct than ordinary employees.

Collective bargaining put an end to this line of thought. Legally and practically, teacher unions are the defender and promoter of teacher interests. As such, they should not also be accorded the legal authority to represent the public interest. Although the rhetoric of teacher unions portrays them as protector of the public interest, adherence to the rhetoric would lead to intractable problems. Teachers do not pay hundreds of dollars annually in union dues so that unions can discipline or dismiss unethical or incompetent teachers. When an accused person employs an attorney, the latter is not expected to help public authorities send the person to jail.

By the same token, teachers pay the union to protect their interests; protection of the public interest is management's job. The principles involved are not affected by the fact that teacher unions sometimes support policies which are in the public interest. Attorneys sometimes assert correctly that their clients are "not guilty," but occasional congruence between client interest and public interest does not justify giving defense attorneys the authority to decide cases involving their clients.

In practice, teachers support student interests when it is in the teachers' interests to do so, but not otherwise. Thus teachers support smaller class size ostensibly as a student benefit; at the same time, they oppose any weakening of tenure protections, no matter how indefensible they may be. The problem is not merely that the union role of defender of teacher interests fundamentally conflicts with the role of the public interest. It is that as matters stand, teachers, acting through their unions, have far too much power to veto or eviscerate changes to which they are opposed. The reasons for this conclusion have been spelled out in considerable detail elsewhere, and I shall not repeat them here.[14] It should be noted, however, that the advocates of "teacher empowerment" or "self-regulation by the profession" rarely specify what actions teachers cannot take that justify self-regulation. Insistence on straightforward answers to this question would go a long way toward resolving controversies over it.

Finally, and most important, teacher self-regulation violates the concept of democratic representative government. Whether we are referring to the state or local level, educational policy is public policy. Public policy should be made by duly elected representatives of the public, not by representatives of an interest group with the most to gain from its control of public policy. Although this objection to teacher self-regulation is implicit in some of the preceding comments, it needs to be stated explicitly. Even if teachers were not unionized, self-regulation by teachers, whether of personnel matters or educational policies, is inconsistent with the underlying principles of representative government.[15]

Information Issues in Education for Profit

As this is written, the U.S. Department of Transportation has required airlines to publicize the percentage of flights from specified airports that arrive and depart on time. Airline companies with a favorable ranking in these data are already doing so in their advertisements. This example shows that government can play an important role in fostering effective competition. In education, this role calls for three basic policies. First, government has to create a market for competing educational suppliers. Second, it must provide for sectoral neutrality; specifically, it must avoid placing conditions or restrictions on education for profit that create competitive advantages for nonprofit schools. Finally, government policy should require, or at least encourage, disclosure of relevant data from all schools, public and private.

In dealing with these issues, we must recognize that the parents' information needs differ to some extent from those of educational policymakers. The latter may want to know how much public revenue is lost because of tax exemptions for nonprofit schools; parents choosing a school are not likely to be interested in this issue. Parents may be interested in whether a school requires tuition to be paid in advance in full or if it can be paid in monthly installments; policymakers are not likely to get involved in such issues.

In medicine, prior disclosure of the risks associated with a course of treatment is extremely important. The doctor who does not inform patients of the risks of treatment may be inviting a malpractice suit. Life-threatening or crippling situations are relatively infrequent in education; even incompetent teachers do not kill or irrevocably cripple students for life.

Parent information needs would fall into three major categories. First, information is needed to help parents decide which school offers the best value for the money. Second, parents need information to identify and protect their interests in conflict-of-interest situations. Finally, parents need information that will help them evaluate school performance as it affects their children.

In both business and the professions, mandatory disclosure of conflicts of interest is often used to protect consumers and clients. Although not a comprehensive solution, mandatory disclosure would certainly be an important safeguard in some situations. For example, whenever a school or teacher recommends an outside product or service vendor and also receives a commission or rebate from those vendors, prior disclosure of this fact should be required.

Mandatory disclosure would have two desirable outcomes. First, it would help parents decide for themselves whether seeking a better deal elsewhere would be worth the effort. For example, if a school recommends a transportation service, parents would be more likely to investigate alternatives if they knew that the school received commissions from the service. Second, parents would be in a better position to negotiate improvements in service or costs if they were aware of any kickback arrangement. Mandatory disclosure of such arrangements need not necessarily replace other measures to protect parents, but it could be a major step in this direction.

Disclosure and School Performance

To some extent, parents and policymakers do have the same or similar information needs. Just as car buyers and government agencies have an interest in automobile mileage ratings, parents and government agencies (local, state, and/or federal) have an interest in the performance of schools.

Unfortunately, it is extremely difficult to judge school performance. What data about schools would serve the same purpose as the mileage data about new cars required by the EPA? The EPA data is not all car buyers consider, and its importance varies from one buyer to another. Still, the data provide a relatively clear-cut and important standard available to anyone interested in buying a new car.

Student achievement would not be a very useful indicator of school performance for several reasons. First, it is affected more by nonschool factors than by school ones. Second, the technical problems in distinguishing school from nonschool effects are extremely difficult, especially in the short run or on a school-by-school basis. Furthermore, even if these problems are resolved satisfactorily, the answers may not be helpful as a guide to parental choice. For example, it may be that school X has performed very well in recent years. Suppose, however, that several teachers who taught at school X have recently retired or accepted employment elsewhere. In that case, even accurate judgments about school performance in the past might not be reliable guides to future performance.

The technical issues in comparing school performance are formidable enough, but the political ones may be even more troublesome. To see why, consider the political differences between EPA and school officials as they relate to performance indicators. The EPA does not manufacture automobiles. Its performance as a public agency is based on the accuracy of its ratings, not whether cars are gas guzzlers or are highly fuel efficient. In contrast, the school authorities who control the data collection process have a very large stake in the test scores they report. In effect, they are being asked to provide data that can be used to challenge their own performance. As a matter of fact, when the National Assessment of Educational Progress was established in 1980, state superintendents of education successfully insisted that test data not be used to compare educational achievement on a state by state basis. This opposition to disaggregating national data on a state basis persisted until 1985, when the Council of Chief State School Officers (CCSSO) voted to support such comparisons.[16]

Even the state comparisons are likely to be suspect if they reveal average test scores for school districts or individual schools. Certain categories of students who are likely to receive low scores—for example, non-English speaking children—may have been excluded from the test sample. When this happens, it may be impossible to know whether an increase in average test scores is due to better teaching or to the greater selectivity of the test sample. The importance of this point is underscored by the fact that approximately one-half to two-thirds of the decline in test scores on the Scholastic Aptitude Test from 1964 to 1975 was due to the fact that a larger number of low-ability students took the tests after 1964.[17] Taking this into account, a former U.S. Commissioner of Education has even argued that the overall decline in SAT scores conceals educational *improvement* rather than reveals educational deterioration, as contended by virtually all of the reform reports.[18]

What information should schools be required to disclose? Despite the possibility, even the likelihood, of some abuse, I believe data on student achievement should be disclosed. In addition, I would require aggregate data on, among other things, student grades, the number and duration of suspensions and expulsions, the number of years teachers have taught at the school, the number of days teachers and students have been absent, employment and college admission data, and class size. I cite these merely as suggestions, in the expectation that experience will lead to improvements in the data used to evaluate schools. Of course, the information should be available on a school-wide, not an individual basis.

While disclosure issues are important, it is not feasible to analyze them here in detail. Before leaving this topic, however, let me suggest some basic considerations that should guide our policies toward the subject. First, it should be recognized that public school organizations have themselves created some of the problems that arise out of disclosure. In the face of overwhelming evidence to the contrary, the educational community has repeatedly claimed that what schools do is the major factor affecting educational achievement. Yet according to the evidence, nonschool factors, especially family and home conditions, play a much more important role than school factors in educational achievement.[19] When school data reflects low achievement, teachers and school officials fear that they will be held accountable for results they cannot control. This would not be a problem, or so much of one, if public school rhetoric had been more realistic in the past. In seeking public funds, the educational community asserts that good schools will produce literate graduates, skilled workers, and well-informed citizens. When the evidence is clear that substantial numbers of students cannot read after twelve years of schooling, lack skills and habits essential for employment or higher education, and are unprepared to participate in civic affairs, the educational community naturally wants to blame nonschool factors. If educators had been realistic about their limitations in the first place, they would have much less to fear from disclosure of negative information about school achievement. The educational community believes schools are being treated as scapegoats because they cannot overcome the harmful educational effects of adverse social conditions. In fact, the educators' tendency to exaggerate the influence of schooling, especially in their quest for larger appropriations, is a major cause of unrealistic public expectations about schooling.

Concern over disclosure often fails to distinguish between long-term and short-term effects. If disclosure reveals low achievement that is not due to poor schooling, subsequent events will bear this out. In the not so long run, effective schools will be recognized as such, regardless of the student body they enroll. Some disclosure opponents fear that teachers in ghetto schools will be criticized because their students do not achieve as well as those in affluent suburban schools. Of course, it might be unfair to draw any conclusions about teacher competence and dedication from such comparisons. The problem is, however, that we cannot find out whether one ghetto school is better than another, or whether one suburban school is more effective than its counterparts, without looking at comparative data. Even in the absence of competition for students, disclosure requirements might make a major contribution to education. They could do so not by showing which schools were better or worse, but by fostering a realistic attitude toward the relative importance of school and nonschool factors in educational achievement.

In considering disclosure issues, it should be noted that "disclosure" per se is not tantamount to consumer awareness. Advertising may be essential for the latter regardless of disclosure requirements. On this issue, developments in health care may be predictive of things to come in education. When hospitals first began to advertise, they emphasized "We care" advertisements intended to create a favorable image in the community. This appears to be changing. Now hospital advertising is rapidly becoming similar to advertising for commercial services generally; the emphasis is on why you receive better service at a lower cost in the advertising hospital instead of a competing one.[20]

Cross-subsidization Issues

As we have seen, proposals to privatize education are often criticized on egalitarian grounds. The criticisms allege that privatization will exacerbate problems of equality of educational opportunity. Essentially, the criticism is that leaving the quantity or quality of education to market forces means that the affluent will get a better education than the poor. This would be contrary to equality of educational opportunity. A related argument is that since race correlates highly with economic status, reliance on market forces will intensify racial segregation in education.

As I have previously discussed these criticisms, I shall discuss only one additional issue here—"cross-subsidization," or the practice of using the excess revenues from the more lucrative services or clients to subsidize services or clients that do not pay their way. I use the phrase "excess revenues" instead of "profits" because nonprofit as well as for-profit organizations engage in cross-subsidization. For example, either type of hospital may use the excess revenues from insured patients to pay for services to the indigent. Or either may use excess revenues from one service to subsidize another that is not profitable. Actually, cross-subsidization is an issue at the individual as well as the organizational level in health care. Doctors as well as hospitals are commonly supposed to provide some service to patients unable to pay for it. It is widely thought that many physicians charge high fees to cover the costs of their time with indigent patients.

Inasmuch as education is publicly supported, public school teachers need not be concerned personally about charging some students more to finance the education of those who cannot afford to pay. Nor do private school teachers face the issue as individuals. Decisions to admit students to private schools are made at the school, not the individual teacher, level. For this reason, cross-subsidization will be considered here only at the school level. It should be noted, however, that fee-taking professionals do not seem to provide an impressive amount of service for those unable to pay.

With respect to cross-subsidization, there is at least one basic difference between education and other services. Outside of education, the indigent do not receive the service in the absence of cross-subsidization. When a doctor or a hospital provides service to a patient who cannot pay for it, the assumption is that the patient would otherwise not receive the service at all. Obviously, this is not the case in education. If a private school does not admit a student, the latter still has the option of attending public school.

Nevertheless, private schools are confronted by cross-subsidization issues. First, it is often contended that for educational reasons, private schools should enroll some less affluent students. The rationale is that students should not be segregated in their schools by race or socioeconomic status. In order to enroll a diversified student body, private schools should cover the costs of students who cannot pay by whatever means are available.

Cross-subsidization has also been advocated as a way to achieve increased financial support for Catholic schools. Thus in a recent address then Secretary of Education William J. Bennett urged Catholic schools to enroll a significant number of the most difficult to educate students, even if such students could not pay for private schooling. Bennett urged that this be done to demonstrate the effectiveness of Catholic schools and to strengthen their case for increased government financial aid. Strictly speaking, therefore, he was recommending cross-subsidization as a temporary strategic policy, not as a permanent policy to be adopted on its merits.[21]

Another argument for cross-subsidization in private schools is based on their impact on public schools. If private schools do not enroll any poor students, a disproportionate number will be in public schools. Inasmuch as such students do not perform as well educationally as middle- and upper-class students, public schools will be stigmatized as schools for less able pupils; consequently, the public schools will lose students from the middle class and eventually political and financial support as well. To avoid these consequences, whether or not family choice measures are adopted, private schools are urged to enroll "their share" of students from poor families.

Because the underlying issues are much the same, it will be helpful to comment briefly on the cross-subsidization issue in health care. Several efforts have been made to compare government, nonprofit, and for-profit hospitals on the extent to which they provide care for the indigent. Although the data and procedures used in these comparisons are far from ideal, perhaps two important conclusions can be drawn from the studies. One is that in both nonprofit and for-profit hospitals, uncompensated care amounted to less than 5 percent of total charges in 1982 and 1983 (the two years for which recent data was available). Most of the studies report little or no difference between for-profit and nonprofit hospitals in this regard. On the other hand, public hospitals show a higher proportion of uncompensated health care than either nonprofit or for-profit hospitals.

Perhaps this is as it should be. Cross-subsidization is clearly an inefficient and inequitable way of distributing or sharing the burden of providing medical services for those unable to pay. The doctors and hospitals near depressed areas would inevitably have to assume a heavier burden than their counterparts in difficult-to-reach affluent areas. Even if it is assumed that doctors and/or hospitals have collective responsibilities in the matter, there is no commonly accepted way to allocate the burdens. The ability of hospitals to absorb any costs of indigent care is affected by dozens of factors which vary over time and geographic areas. Hospitals that tried to provide as much indigent care as possible would have to charge higher fees to others; it is not at all clear why a limited group of patients should be the ones to subsidize the free care. Furthermore, acceptance of such a burden when other competing hospitals, profit or nonprofit, may not be doing so could jeopardize a hospital's competitive position and even ability to survive.

These objections are supported by our experience in providing other basic necessities to the poor. The grocery stores that redeem food stamps are not expected to absorb the costs of feeding the hungry. Landlords are not expected to provide housing for the poor at their own expense (except perhaps in New York City!). Similarly, there is no special obligation on the part of private hospitals to provide health care for the indigent. In all of these cases, the costs should be shared by everyone—paid for through taxes, not by a series of fortuitous payors who provide a convenient excuse for the majority to avoid paying their share of the costs.

The same considerations appear to be just as applicable to private schools. While they may absorb the costs of some students who cannot afford to pay, their refusal or inability to do so should not be regarded as objectionable. The major educational argument to the contrary would be this: Unlike food or medical care, education cannot be consumed by freestanding individuals. Good education requires diversity among students, so they can develop awareness and appreciation of diverse backgrounds.

One problem with this argument is that it implicitly condemns most public schools. True, public school systems enroll students of every race, religion, and socioeconomic level. Individual public schools, however, enroll students from a relatively narrow socioeconomic strata. Thus if the objection is valid, it applies to so many public schools that any effort to require it of only private schools seems egregiously unfair.

Another objection challenges the argument on its merits. Public school classrooms may already be characterized by too much diversity.[22] Diversity can reach a point where it becomes impossible to provide quality service to most students within the classroom. The students can be so diverse in aptitude, achievement, incentives, family background, and other characteristics that whatever a teacher does to accommodate some will be inappropriate or less than optimal for most of the others. As a practical matter, whether there is too much or too little "diversity" in specific classrooms cannot be resolved by abstract appeals or rejections of it. If a class has fifteen nonreligious students, ten Protestants, and five Catholics, does it help to include a Jewish student? An atheist? A Confucian? Does the grade level and subject and educational level of the student matter? What if the addition of a student promotes diversity on some criteria but sameness on others—which is always the case?

In short, a policy that fosters diversity without regard to

its specific criteria is impossible to defend. So is a policy that fosters "diversity" on one criterion, such as economic status, without regard to grade level, subject, student ability or interests, or any other relevant factor.

"Increasing diversity" is often a euphemism for increasing the proportion of blacks and Hispanics. At the present time, certain kinds of private schools are trying to do this. Because the Catholic population is extremely diverse, Catholic schools as a whole are also, even though the diversity tends to characterize the system as a whole more than individual schools. With some other denominations (for example, Amish, Orthodox Jewish), the denominations are simply not ethnically heterogeneous, and there is no feasible way to maintain religious solidarity while introducing ethnic diversity.

The private independent schools present an interesting situation. They tend to be the most expensive schools and the most diversified on religious criteria. On the other hand, because of their high costs, they enroll proportionally fewer black and Hispanic students than the public schools. Although not interested in expansion, private independent schools are attempting to enroll larger numbers of black and Hispanic students. Their rationale is not especially clear; it probably includes a measure of noblesse oblige and some concern that the absence of such students leads to political vulnerability. Whatever the reason, however, their efforts are not necessarily cross-subsidization. The schools seek scholarship funds to finance the minority students. This means that the students are not funded from excess revenues but from donations that may or may not have been available for other purposes. If not, we do not have cross-subsidization; the school's financial situation would not be affected by who was enrolled in it.

Recent proposals in health care have some interesting implications for cross-subsidization in private schools. Some observers have proposed that hospitals be required to provide a certain amount of indigent care as a condition of tax exemption. The logic seems straightforward; if a tax exemption is granted because an organization will be performing services for those unable to pay, the organization should be required to demonstrate its performance of the services. Logical or not, the rationale seems less applicable to private schools. As we mentioned, while medical patients may have to go without service if it is not contributed, students are still entitled to attend public schools. Although private schools should not be allowed to discriminate on racial grounds, forcing them to enroll students to achieve diversity seems to be a highly questionable policy.

Cross-Subsidization in Education: A Caveat

Cross-subsidization can be implemented in several ways. As with other concepts I have discussed, there is the danger that criticism of one form of it may not apply to others. Still, cross-subsidization in education entails risks and costs which do not characterize the practice in most other fields.

First, requiring private schools to engage in cross-subsidization is likely to weaken their educational effectiveness. The reason is that student characteristics affect school effectiveness. A pupil surrounded by highly motivated, well-behaved, and talented students is likely to learn more than if enrolled with indifferent, disruptive, and less talented students. Public as well as private schools accept the underlying premise; for example, specialized public high schools, such as the Bronx High School of Science, do not accept students that weaken the school's reputation. In short, control over admissions is critical to school effectiveness and reputation, and hence to school prospects in the marketplace.[23]

In most fields, the cost of cross-subsidization can be estimated with reasonable accuracy. For example, a doctor would estimate the value of the time devoted to indigent patients. The services provided this way do not affect the quality of service to others, nor do they have a negative effect on the doctor's reputation; if anything, reputation would be enhanced.

In education, the costs and effects of cross-subsidization are more problematic. The characteristics of the students who are subsidized are more likely to affect school efficiency, reputation, and acceptability in the market. In this respect, the costs of cross-subsidization in education are more complex than the costs in other fields.

The students who are not wanted fall into two general categories. One category consists of students such as drug pushers, who adversely affect the education of others, regardless of school. The other category includes students who have no negative characteristics per se, but who would have negative effects on the educational objectives of particular schools. For example, a student who is not an Orthodox Jew would probably have negative effects on students in a school for Orthodox Jews. Even if cross-subsidization avoids the latter type of negative effects, it cannot avoid the former; no school can. As long as we have compulsory education, some students will adversely affect others, whether in a public or private school. Cross-subsidization cannot ameliorate this problem. If practiced only under threat of penalty or waiver of benefits, it is more likely to weaken private schools without any corresponding benefits to students in either public or private schools.

To avoid any misunderstanding, let me emphasize that I am not urging carte blanche for nonprofit schools. Public policy might justifiably require nonprofit schools to accept some of the burden of educating the disadvantaged or the disabled as a condition of tax exemption or some other privilege associated with the benefits of nonprofit status. This might be done in a variety of ways. My point is that these ways should not weaken the basic rationale for the nonprofit school. I would not require a school catering to the affluent to accept students from nonaffluent families; neither would I provide such schools with tax exemptions or any other benefits of nonprofit status. Most emphatically, I would not agree that saving the public treasury the cost of educating such students is an adequate quid pro quo for the nonprofit status of independent private schools.

A CONTRACTUAL APPROACH
TO EDUCATION

In conclusion, I would like to suggest that perhaps the strongest rationale for both vouchers and education for profit has not been articulated in the debate over educational reform. This rationale is based on the advantages of a contractual approach to education.[24] To illustrate its advantages, let us assume that everyone is agreed on the goals of education and on the curriculum designed to achieve it. In other words, we shall assume that there is no support for vouchers for religious or ideological reasons. Nevertheless, parents may still disagree on some important issues. To simplify the analysis, I shall confine their disagreement to a single issue: whether teachers should be paid for services or for results.

Some parents believe that tax dollars should be paid for services. In their view, it would be unfair and unrealistic to pay teachers on the basis of results. As long as teachers adhere to standards of reasonable care and competence, these parents are satisfied.

Other parents view the issue in a different light. As they see it, schools were established so that students would learn certain things. If the children don't learn, the teachers shouldn't be paid. These parents are willing to pay whatever it takes to achieve results, but they want to pay only for results, not services.

Other parents have still a third view. They believe that payment should be for services in some subjects but only for results in others. We could spell out several variations of these positions, but let us instead consider the issue from the standpoint of service providers.

First of all, payment for results, or according to results, is common in both the commercial world and among the professions. You can buy a television set with a warranty, but it costs more than if there were no warranty. When you rent a car, the rental agencies offer several insurance options covering things that might go wrong. You can rent a car (1) without additional insurance, (2) with insurance requiring the rental company to pay any amount over a specified deductible, or (3) with insurance that covers you against all claims. The costs of the insurance vary with the risks involved and the willingness of the parties to pay for various allocations of risk.

Arrangements for legal services also illustrate this flexibility. Ordinarily when you employ an attorney, you pay for legal services, not results. Nevertheless, payment to attorneys is sometimes explicitly based on results, not services rendered. Lawyers representing clients in personal injury cases may agree to accept a specific percentage of the award as their fee; if there is no award in their client's favor, there is no fee.

Note that contingent fee arrangements are extremely flexible. The client may pay the lawyers' direct expenses and the contingent payment may apply only to an award, if any. The contingent fees can vary, depending on the difficulty of preparing the case, the prospects for a large award, and so on. The fee arrangements can deal with the time required to resolve the case, including what happens if an award is appealed by either the plaintiff or the defendant. In contrast, medical and dental patients typically pay for services rendered, not results. The critical point, however, is not whether payment is typically for one or the other; it is that the parties can resolve the issue through contractual arrangements.

A contractual approach to education would, therefore, be consistent with practice in other professions as well as in the commercial world generally. In principle at least, such an approach would be feasible. This is not to say that payment according to results should or would replace payment for services rendered; "feasible" means that we could structure education so that the producers and consumers of educational services could decide for themselves what the basis of payment would be. Most payments to professional workers are for services, not results, and this practice would probably continue to be dominant in education. Unfortunately, we have no way to be certain of what would happen if other options existed.

Although the contractual rationale for vouchers is independent of the others previously discussed, it does not necessarily conflict with any of them. A contractual approach would tend to encourage parents to clarify what they expect from schooling, but the approach per se has no logically necessary relationship to any particular outcome. Similarly, a contractual approach has no inherent implications for taxpayer issues. Whether vouchers would result in taxpayer savings will depend on the factors previously discussed, such as the amounts of the voucher, eligibility for vouchers, the costs of public education, and the number of students who transfer to private schools. Whether parents contract for services or for results, or contract at all with their schools of choice, is not likely to affect taxpayer issues directly, one way or the other.

In one sense, a contractual approach can be viewed as a special case of the educational improvement rationale. Instead of competing on educational criteria, educational producers would compete on contractual criteria: Who offers the best contract? The competition would be similar to a situation in which two automobile dealers selling the same car compete on the basis of the warranties, not the automobile itself.

Conceptually, the contractual rationale can also be treated as a special case of the argument that vouchers are necessary to minimize social conflict over education. As previously pointed out, a major advantage of a contractual approach is that it would or could reduce conflict over educational issues. On the other hand, the conflicts that could be resolved in this way do not endanger social stability as much as the conflicts over religious issues in public education. That is, a contractual approach would tend to resolve conflicts that are important to individuals but do not involve powerful interest groups. This is why the argument for a contractual approach is not primarily its utility in reducing social conflict. Instead, the argument is that a contractual approach would create significant options that cannot emerge in the absence of a voucher system. Parents and citizens are not fighting over these options; they are not even aware of them in most cases. Nevertheless, if raised to the level of conscious choice, these options could set in motion a process that has genuine promise for improving education.

To see why, let us first consider the dynamics of this approach in a noneducation context. Let us assume that two automobile companies offer the same car for sale. One company charges less because it offers no warranty of any kind; the other company provides a warranty, so its price is higher. (Actually, one company could offer both options, which would eliminate any controversy over whether the cars were truly identical.)

At a given time, buying the car with the warranty might be the wise thing to do. Over time, however, the costs of making good on the warranty are identified and corrective measures are taken. If, for example, a certain part frequently becomes defective while under warranty, the manufacturer will devote resources to developing a more durable part or perhaps a way of avoiding any need for it. Thus the economics of the warranty stimulate improvements in the product; as the improvements are made, it becomes more practical to buy the cars without the warranty, or perhaps the cost of the warranty may be reduced. In any event, the contractual arrangements and the cost and quality of the product and the warranty interact.

Undoubtedly the same dynamics would emerge under a contractual approach to education. For the sake of discussion, let us assume that two schools offered the same program, quality of staff, and were otherwise indistinguishable on any educational criterion. Let us further assume that the only difference was that school A charged on the basis of services rendered, whereas school B charged more because it guaranteed the results; to make up for its losses when the results were inadequate, school B would have to charge more than school A.

Predictably, the students who did not achieve up to the level of the guarantee would be scrutinized carefully. These students, of course, would be analogous to the instances in which the automobile companies have to make good on their warranties. Several outcomes might be anticipated. Some students with certain characteristics might be identified as too high a risk for the money-back guarantee. As a result, school *B* might charge more for the guarantee or even refuse to offer it for such students. That school might also identify another group of students whose failure is remediable. By careful analysis of its losses due to warranty payments, school *B* may be able to reduce the cost of the warranty. This reduction in cost may enable school *B* to achieve a competitive advantage over school *A,* or over schools that charge more than *B* for the same educational guarantees.

Under a contractual approach, therefore, attention would necessarily focus on the educational needs and prospects of individual children. Market forces would distinguish high-risk from low-risk students. They would also encourage research into ways of reducing the incidence of high-risk students; schools would have financial incentives for their early identification and remediation.

Suppose, for example, that suburban parents wish to purchase a "money-back guarantee" of educational progress. Suppose also that an inner city mother of three children on welfare also seeks to purchase the same guarantee. A contractual approach would reveal the costs of equalizing the results. If no educational vendor was willing to offer such a guarantee at any price to the inner city parent, the implication would not be that the contractual approach was fostering racial discrimination or unequal opportunity. It would be that the demand for equal achievement was unreasonable. It would be comparable to a demand that a physician guarantee the results of a heart transplant for a ninety-year-old patient. Similarly, educators will accept the risks for some objectives with some types of students at some agreed-on price, whereas they will not be willing to do so in other situations. A contractual approach would enable a market system to sort out these situations; the equality issues could be resolved by public assumption of the costs where equalization of outcomes is feasible. What if certain parents determined to pay only for results could not find a school willing to educate on that basis? The outcome would be the same as when people can't find a lawyer to handle their lawsuits on a contingent fee basis; the parents would have to change their position on fees or go without educational services.

It should be emphasized that such a situation would be drastically different from school board efforts to pay teachers on the basis of results. There are enormous differences between payment to employees on the basis of employer-mandated standards and payment based on arrangements negotiated voluntarily by professionals and their clients. Payment based on results may or may not have a significant role to play in American education, but unsuccessful efforts to structure the practice on a school or class basis (such as those by the OEO discussed in chapter 4) have little or no relevance to its possibilities on a voluntary professional-client basis.

In some respects, private education already illustrates the advantages of a contractual approach to school-parent relations. In private schools, student discipline, suspension, and dismissal are matters of contract, not statutory regulation. Litigation over these issues is relatively infrequent, whereas it is pervasive in the public school environment. Of course, contract interpretation can lead to litigation; we cannot completely eliminate litigation and conflict by reliance upon a contractual instead of a statutory system of school-parent relations. Nevertheless, a contractual system is more likely to reduce conflict between schools and parents. Contracts can be revised and enforced more expeditiously than statutes as the need arises. Teachers and teacher unions would probably oppose a shift to a contractual system; ironically, they advocated teacher collective bargaining contracts precisely because the statutory protections for teachers were deemed inferior to contractual ones.

Education as Joint Production of Services

Whatever its potential, the option of contracting for services or results is only one illustration of the advantages of a contractual approach to education. To fully appreciate these advantages, it is essential to note some significant differences between products and services. Products can be accumulated and stored somewhere until they are sold or needed. Educational technology aside for the moment, services cannot be stored; they must be delivered to consumers.

Most products are made without reference to particular consumers. For example, on the whole, automobiles are manufactured without the intervention of specific consumers. Of course, manufacturers take into account consumer preferences, but they normally do so only on a large-scale basis. There is often interaction at the point of sale— the customer wants a blue automobile instead of a red one. At the assembly plant, however, the decision to assemble red or blue cars is made independent of individual consumer preferences.

In contrast, services are more often jointly produced. That is, the producer is more often required to adjust the service to individual consumers and to enlist their cooperation in its production. Physicians and patients have to adapt their schedules if the physician is to provide medical service. No such cooperation is needed to consummate the sale of most products.

Generally speaking, consumer/producer cooperation (that is, "complementarity") is more important in services than in products. This is not necessarily the case when the services are performed on products, such as television sets or watch repair. When, however, the services cannot be performed without the presence of consumers (including third-party service recipients), complementarity between producers and consumers becomes more important. In many situations, such as in education, consumers must play an active role if the service is to be fully effective. Furthermore, the consumer of services is not merely the recipient of directions from the producer; consumers often want to negotiate their own preferences into the service.

Of course, even in selling products, complementarity can be important, even essential. The effective use of computers or machinery may require user training programs. The important point here is the growing importance of complementarity in our economy and what it suggests for the delivery of educational services. To be sure, public school officials acknowledge its importance in principle. Much is made of the importance of school/parent cooperation and of parent involvement and support. Many educational organizations have sponsored publications intended to facilitate parental involvement, and no one denies its importance in principle.

Unfortunately, all such efforts are characterized by one major and perhaps fatal flaw. They urge complementarity, but for all practical purposes, it is on *their* terms, not the parents' or the result of negotiations between teachers and parents. To cite a common case, teacher collective bargaining contracts severely limit parent access to teachers. Most teachers are not normally available to meet with parents during evening hours, on weekends, or during the extended periods school is not in session. Often teachers are available only on a few specified days or afternoons after students are dismissed. Consequently, only those parents who can confer with teachers at the specified times have access to them. I am not contending that there should be no limits on teacher availability; I do contend, however, that such complementarity as exists in public education is almost entirely on producer instead of consumer terms. It would be astonishing indeed if a voucher system did not result in greater parent/teacher complementarity and therefore better education.

Whatever the advantages of a contractual approach to education, they cannot be achieved by governmental provision of it. In order for parents to contract, they must have the funds to pay for whatever it is they are contracting for. For this reason, large-scale contractual approaches will require a voucher system. In such a system, parents and schools could contract for services (or results) they mutually agreed on. There is no political interest in such an approach at the present time; political support for vouchers is based on religious or ideological, not contractual, considerations. The latter may come into play only if and when voucher systems are established on other grounds. Yet voucher legislation should be drafted carefully to maximize the potential benefits of a contractual approach to education.

Education for Profit: A Point of View

In concluding this analysis, let me suggest one final reason why education for profit may be our best hope for educational improvement. The reason receives no attention in educational reform literature or in the media, but it would be difficult to underestimate its importance.

Simply stated, the reason is this: The mass media (newspapers, television, and radio stations) do not understand and therefore cannot articulate the important developments and issues in education. This is a fatal weakness in the conventional approach to educational reform.

My assertion has two major components: the inability of media personnel to recognize important developments and issues and the importance of this inability, if it exists. Inasmuch as the latter component is less open to challenge, let me begin with it.

As emphasized throughout this analysis, educational reform requires sustained political leadership at all levels of government. Given the fact that educational reform is highly dependent on political processes, media dissemination of educational issues and developments is essential to reform. In many situations, such dissemination is critical, even decisive, as to whether any change takes place.

What, then, can be said about the educational sophistication of media personnel, whether they are education reporters or generalists who decide what education news is worth reporting? The vast majority know very little about such matters as how education is financed, who benefits from it and how, the relative weight to be given factors that affect student achievement, the way tenure and teacher bargaining laws work, the state aid formulas, union dynamics and the provisions of negotiated agreements, the evidence on compensatory and bilingual education, or any other issue raised by conventional reform proposals. Media attention to how much students or teachers or citizens generally know is commonplace; media attention to what its own personnel know about education is nil. (At least I have been unable to find any data or analysis on the issue, and I have no reason to expect more attention will be paid to it in the future.)

What is "education news"? Going on the basis of what is now filtered through the media, "education news" is who is appointed or who gets fired from a superintendency or university presidency, the community squabble over sex education or the dismissal of a veteran football coach, commencement speeches, honorary degrees awarded, teacher strikes, high school athletics, government and foundation grants made or received—in short, news is defined in terms of what reporters can handle intellectually. If Smith replaces Jones as superintendent, you don't have to know anything about education to write the article. If some parents want sex education and some do not, that is what is reported. No understanding or even familiarity with the effectiveness (or lack thereof) of sex education is required to communicate a community controversy over it. When an article seems to require some understanding of a complex substantive issue, the solution is as near as the telephone. Unfortunately, the "experts" at the other end of the line have their own biases and agendas as well as their own shortcomings.

Media incompetence explains why political and educational leaders can establish reputations as educational statesmen on the basis of trivial and transparent educational initiatives. It also explains why the educational reform movement was a basket case from the beginning. Because the media lack an independent capacity to evaluate educational issues, a significant proportion of what the American people read, hear, and see about education is taken directly from news releases. Inasmuch as news releases do not typically announce failures and deficiencies, the process tends to result in benign treatment of the political leaders, organizations, and public agencies with the most effective public relations staff. Meaningful reform has not emerged from this situation, and it will not in the future.

Theoretically, the mass media could employ persons knowledgeable about the underlying obstacles to educational improvement. I would not bet on it, but it is a possibility. Even if this problem were solved, however, the structure and modus operandi of the mass media pose insuperable obstacles to educational improvement. Indeed, a major advantage of a market system over a political one for delivering educational services is that the former would be more likely to avoid reliance on haphazard media and political treatment of education. To be sure, the change to a market system must itself be achieved by political action; that is, it must overcome the obstacles just mentioned. For precisely this reason, the change may not occur. Still, there is an enormous difference between changes that reduce dependency on the hopeless governance structure of education and changes that do not. Both kinds have to run the same obstacle course, but the former holds more hope for introducing a process of continual improvement.

Notes

CHAPTER 1

1. The leading example is National Commission on Excellence in Education, *A Nation at Risk: The Imperative for Educational Excellence* (Washington, D.C.: Government Printing Office, 1983).
2. See Myron Lieberman, *Beyond Public Education* (New York: Praeger, 1986).
3. Reason Foundation, *Privatization 1986, Annual Report on Privatization of Government Services* (Santa Monica, CA: Reason Foundation, 1986). List on p. 10 reprinted by permission of the publisher.
4. Ibid.
5. See Peter Young, "Privatization Around the Globe," NCPA Policy Report #120 (Dallas: National Center for Policy Analysis, January 1986); "Privatization Around the World," in Steve H. Hanke, ed., *Prospects for Privatization* (New York: Academy of Political Science, 1987), pp. 190–206; Reason Foundation, *Privatization 1986,* pp. 28–32; and Cento Veljanovski, *Selling the State* (London: Weidenfeld and Nicolson, 1987).
6. Widely known statements of the public choice position include Anthony Downs, *An Economic Theory of Democracy* (New York: Harper & Row, 1957); James Buchanan and Gordon Tullock, *The Calculus of Consent* (Ann Arbor, MI: University of Michigan Press, 1962); William A. Niskanen, Jr., *Bureaucracy and Representative Government* (Chicago: Aldine-Atherton, 1971). For a recent criticism of the public choice approach to political analysis, see Steven Kelman, "Public Choice and Public Spirit," *Public Interest* (Spring 1987): 86–94; and Lawrence Iannaccone, "From Equity to Excellence: Political Context and Dynamics," in William L. Boyd and Charles T. Kerchner, eds., *The Politics of Excellence and Choice in Education* (New York: Falmer Press, 1988), pp. 49–66.

7. For a good, brief analysis of the reasons why the reform movement has reinforced instead of altered the educational status quo, see David N. Plank, "Why School Reform Doesn't Change Schools: Political and Organizational Perspectives," in Boyd and Kerchner, eds., *The Politics of Excellence,* pp. 143–152; and Lieberman, *Beyond Public Education.*

8. Ted Kolderie, *Two Routes to the Improvement of Education: Part II* (Minneapolis, MN: Hubert H. Humphrey Institute of Public Affairs, University of Minnesota, 1984), p. 3. See Ted Kolderie, "The Puzzle of the Public Sector and the Strategy of Service Redesign," Background paper prepared for the conference entitled An Equitable and Competitive Public Sector, November 25–27, 1984, St. Paul, MN; and "Education That Works: The Right Rule for Business," *Harvard Business Review* (Sept.–Oct. 1987): 56–62.

9. Discussions of education in Japan may be found in Benjamin Duke, *The Japanese School* (New York: Praeger, 1986); "Japanese Education Today," Report from the U.S. Study of Education in Japan (Washington, D.C.: Government Printing Office, 1987); and Merry I. White, "Japanese Education: How Do They Do It?" *Public Interest* (Summer 1984): 87–101. For an analysis that challenges my point of view about the role of competition in Japanese education, see Eric Bredo, "Choice, Constraint and Community," in Boyd and Kerchner, eds., *The Politics of Excellence,* p. 77.

10. For an excellent discussion of the double standard problem in educational policy analysis, see Bredo, "Choice, Constraint, and Community," pp. 67–78.

CHAPTER 2

1. John D. Hanrahan, *Government by Contract* (New York: W. W. Norton, 1982).

2. Privatization Task Force of the President's Private Sector Survey on Cost Control in the Federal Government, *Report on Privatization* (Washington, D.C.: Government Printing Office, 1983).

3. The Foundation for the President's Private Sector Survey on Cost Control, Inc., has been established to promote implementation of the Grace Commission report. For criticism of the report and rejoinders, see Steven Kelman, "The Grace Commission: How Much Waste in Government?" *Public Interest* (Winter 1985): 65–82; J. Peter Grace, "The Grace Commission Controversy," *Public Interest* (Spring 1985): 111–121; and Steven Kelman, "A Reply," ibid., 122–133.

4. Section 2(a), S. 265, 100th Congress, 1st Session, introduced by Senator Gordon Humphrey.

5. President's Commission on Privatization, *Privatization: Toward More Effective Government, Report of the President's Commission on Pri-*

vatization (Washington, D.C.: Government Printing Office, 1988), p. 95.

6. See Philip E. Fixler, Jr., and Robert W. Poole, Jr., "Status of State and Local Privatization," in Steve H. Hanke, ed., *Prospects for Privatization* (New York: Academy of Political Science, 1987), pp. 164–178.

7. See John Tepper Marlin, *Contracting Municipal Services* (New York: Ronald Press, 1984), for an excellent summary of statutory issues affecting contracting out.

8. George Fleischli, "Subcontracting and the Duty to Bargain in the Public Sector," *Information Bulletin* (Public Employment Relations Board, Albany, NY) (May–June 1979).

9. Philip E. Fixler, Jr., ed., *Privatization 1986, Annual Report on Privatization of Government Services* (Santa Monica, CA: Reason Foundation, 1986), p. 5.

10. This position is argued most ably in Madsen Pirie, *Dismantling the State: The Theory and Practice of Privatization* (Dallas, TX: National Center for Policy Analysis, 1985), pp. 17–23.

11. A large body of literature emphasizes the differences in incentives between public and private operation. Much of it emphasizes the disincentives to be efficient under public sector operation. In addition to the representative publications on public choice cited in chapter 1, see John Tepper Marlin, *Contracting Municipal Services* (New York: Ronald Press, 1984), especially pp. 7–8; Henry A. Butt and D. Robert Palmer, *Value for Money in the Public Sector: The Decision Maker's Guide* (New York: Basil Blackwell, 1985), especially pp. 130–136; and Steve H. Hanke, "Privatization: Theory, Evidence, and Implementation," in C. Lowell Harriss, ed., *Control of Federal Spending* (New York: Academy of Political Science, 1985), pp. 101–113. A discussion of the issue in education may be found in John E. Chubb and Terry M. Moe, *Politics, Markets, and the Organization of Schools,* Governmental Studies Discussion Paper #1 (Washington, D.C.: Brookings Institution, June 1986).

12. In addition to the references cited on teacher pensions in note 10, chapter 3, see Robert M. Fogelson, *Pensions: The Hidden Costs of Public Safety* (New York: Columbia University Press, 1984).

13. David L. Birch, *Job Creation in America* (New York: Free Press, 1987), p. 1.

14. Sven Rydenfelt, "Power and Peasantry: A Report from the Soviet Union," *The Freeman* (April 1987): 157.

15. For an extended analysis with references to primary sources, see Myron Lieberman, *Beyond Public Education* (New York: Praeger, 1985), pp. 86–167. See also Edwin M. Bridges and Barry Groves, *Managing the Incompetent Teacher* (Eugene, OR: ERIC Clearinghouse on Educational Management, University of Oregon, 1984).

16. For example, the Municipal Development Corporation (MDC) has two subsidiaries. One, James J. Lowery and Company, has been de-

scribed as "the nation's largest independent consulting firm." It advises local, state, and federal agencies on infrastructure financing. The other subsidiary, Lowery Resources, "develops, acquires, and manages facilities for public use which have traditionally been owned and operated by government agencies." One 1986 MDC proposal was to build and operate a toll road between Dulles Airport and Leesburg, Virginia.

Parsons Muncipal Services (PMS) is a subsidiary of Parsons Corporation, one of the nation's largest construction companies. PMS is also oriented to the development and operation of municipal infrastructure facilities (transportation, parking, waste disposal, roads, water purification, convention centers, etc.). See Reason Foundation, *Privatization 1986*, pp. 17–18, and 1986 Annual Report, Municipal Development Corporation, 180 Maiden Lane, New York, NY 10038.

17. Lieberman, *Beyond Public Education*, pp. 108–126.
18. The strongest criticisms of privatization, especially contracting out, are by Paul Starr, Robert W. Bailey, and Walter F. Baber in Steve H. Hanke, ed., *Prospects for Privatization* (New York: Academy of Political Science, 1987), pp. 124–163. A revision of Starr's article was published as *The Limits of Privatization* (Washington, D.C.: Economic Policy Institute, n.d.). The American Federation of State, County, and Municipal Workers, AFL-CIO (AFSCME) has sponsored several publications critical of contracting out.
19. See Marc Bendick, Jr., "Privatization of Public Services; Recent Experiences," in Harvey Brooks, Lance Liebman, and Corinne S. Schelling, *Public-Private Partnership: New Opportunities for Meeting Social Needs* (Cambridge, MA: Ballinger, 1984); Steve H. Hanke, ed., *Prospects for Privatization;* Philip E. Fixler, Jr., Robert W. Poole, Jr., and Lynn Scarlett, eds., *Privatization 1987* (Santa Monica, CA: Reason Foundation, 1988); James T. Bennett and Manuel H. Johnson, *Better Government at Half the Price* (Ottawa, IL: Carolina House, 1981); Henry A. Butt and D. Robert Palmer, *Value for Money in the Public Sector: The Decision Maker's Guide* (New York: Basil Blackwell, 1985); and John Tepper Marlin, *Contracting Municipal Services* (New York: John Wiley, 1984). The preceding publications cite a large number of studies.
20. Los Angeles study, Ecodata, "Comparative Study of Municipal Service Delivery," Draft of final report submitted to U.S. Department of Housing and Urban Development, September 20, 1983.
21. Ruth Hoogland De Hoog, *Contracting Out for Human Services* (Albany: State University of New York Press, 1984).
22. Ronald Fisk, Herbert Kiesling, and Thomas Muller, *Private Provision of Public Services: An Overview* (Washington, D.C.: The Urban Institute, 1978).
23. Marc Bendick, Jr., "Privatizing the Delivery of Social Welfare Services: An Idea to be Taken Seriously," in Sheila B. Kamerman and Alfred J. Kahn, eds., *Privatization and the Welfare State* (Princeton, N.J.: Princeton University Press, forthcoming).

24. AFSCME-sponsored publications critical of contracting out include *Public Hospital Takeover: An Uneven Record* (Washington, D.C.: AFSCME, n.d.); *Passing the Bucks: The Contracting Out of Public Services* (Washington, D.C.: AFSCME, 1983); *Private Profit, Public Risk: The Contracting Out of Professional Services* (Washington, D.C.: AFSCME, n.d.); J. Michael Keating, Jr., *Seeking Profit in Punishment: The Private Management of Correctional Institutions* (Washington, D.C.: AFSCME, n.d.); *Does Crime Pay: An Examination of Prisons for Profit* (Washington, D.C.: AFSCME, 1985); and *When Public Services Go Private* (Washington, D.C.: AFSCME, 1987).

25. One problem in comparing public to private school salaries is that the comparisons typically do not take into account factors that impact the comparisons in major ways. The comparisons typically omit fringe benefits; such benefits usually would increase the differentials in favor of public sector compensation. On the other hand, the gap between public and private school compensation is partially due to the fact that public school teachers usually have more training and years of experience than private school teachers. Thus at any given time, public school teachers as a group would earn less if they were teaching in private schools—but more than the private school teachers are actually earning. Similarly, if private school teachers were employed by public schools, they would earn more than they do as private school teachers, but less than the average public school teacher earns. See J. Chambers, *Patterns of Compensation of Public and Private School Teachers* (Stanford, CA: Institute for Educational Finance and Governance, Stanford University, 1985).

26. Eli Ginsberg, *Services: The New Economy* (New York: Columbia University Press, 1955), pp. 8–9.

CHAPTER 3

1. West's Annotated California Code, Reorganized, Sections 41375, 41376.

2. Although there is no California statute or state Supreme Court decision, decisions upholding teacher rights to decline extracurricular assignments have been upheld by the Commission on Professional Competence. Such commissions are ad hoc bodies established to hear teacher appeals in discharge cases; the deciding vote on such commissions is usually cast by a hearing officer designated by the state. In addition, a decision by California's Public Employment Relations Board held that a teacher could not be disciplined for refusing to perform duties receiving extra pay. See PERB Decision 291, Modesto Teachers Association v. Modesto City School District (1983).

3. West's Annotated California Code, Reorganized, Section 45136.

4. West's Annotated California Code, Reorganized, Section 41372(c).

5. State of California, Senate Bill 813, Section 35432(b), approved by Governor George Deukmejian, July 28, 1983. The estimated rate of

suspensions is based on data provided by the Office of Administrative Hearings, State of California.

6. See Amendment to the Regulations of the Commissioner of Education, Pursuant to Sections 207, 3004, and 3006 of the Education Law of the State of New York, repealing Section 80.18 of the Regulations of the Commissioner of Education and adding a new Section 80.18, effective September 1, 1987, approved March 20, 1987.

7. The estimates were stated to me informally in April 1987 when I was serving as a consultant to the New York City Board of Education.

8. For an earlier survey of state mandated inefficiencies, see Myron Lieberman, *Identification and Evaluation of State Legal Constraints on Educational Productivity,* Final Report, Project 3-0231, National Institute of Education, U.S. Department of Health, Education, and Welfare, June 1, 1975.

9. See Myron Lieberman, *Beyond Public Education* (New York: Praeger, 1986), pp. 108–126.

10. All the data on teacher pensions are taken from Robert P. Inman, "Appraising the Funding Status of Teacher Pensions," *National Tax Journal* 39 (1986): 21–33; and Robert P. Inman and David J. Albright, "Central Policies for Local Debt: The Case of Teacher Pensions," manuscript.

11. *New York Times,* October 10, 1986, p. B3; and May 13, 1987, p. 1, B6.

12. Mario M. Cuomo, *The Diaries of Mario M. Cuomo* (New York: Random House, 1984), especially pp. 162–296. For a comprehensive analysis of the political influence of teacher unions generally, see Maurice R. Berube, *Teacher Politics* (Westport, CT: Greenwood Press, 1988).

13. Sections 20 and 49, Chapter 53, Laws of 1986, State of New York, and Section 175.35 of the Regulations of the Commissioner of Education, Pursuant to Sections 207, 1950 (15) and 3612 (27) of the Education Law Relating to Excellence in Teaching, State Education Department, State of New York, May 12, 1986. Although Mayor Koch of New York City initially said he would reject the state aid and reiterated that there were "far better uses for the money," the New York City Board of Education applied for and allocated the funds for across-the-board salary increases—something the union president had emphasized in the 1986 union election. *New York Times,* September 17, 1986, p. B1.

14. *Education Week,* October 14, 1987, p. 1; also June 3, 1987, p. 1.

15. See Inman, "Appraising the Funding Status of Teacher Pensions," and Inman and Albright, "Central Policies for Local Debt."

16. See John Tepper Marlin, *Contracting for Municipal Services* (New York: John Wiley, 1987), for a good analysis of monitoring costs.

17. Herbert J. Walberg, "Learning and Life-Course Accomplishments," in Carmi Schooler and K. Warner, eds., *Cognitive Functioning and Social Structure over the Life Span* (Norwood, NJ: Ablex, 1988), pp. 203–229, at p. 208.

18. Ibid., p. 205.
19. Ibid., pp. 204–205.
20. I am indebted to Ted Kolderie, Hubert Humphrey Institute of Public Affairs, University of Minnesota, for materials bearing on leasing by department stores.

CHAPTER 4

1. *Education Daily,* October 1, 1975, p. 5.
2. The following discussion of the OEO project is taken largely from Edward M. Gramlich and Patricia P. Koshel, *Educational Performance Contracting* (Washington, D.C.: Brookings Institution, 1975); James A. Mecklenburger, *Performance Contracting* (Worthington, OH: Charles A. Jones, 1972); and Donald Richard, "Performance Contracting for Equal Opportunity and School System Renewal," Master's thesis, Graduate School of Education, Harvard University (August 1971).
3. The evidence on this point is summarized in Nathan Glazer, "Education and Training Programs and Poverty," and comment by Christopher Jencks, in Sheldon H. Danziger and Daniel H. Weinberg, *Fighting Poverty* (Cambridge, MA: Harvard University Press, 1986). See also Michael Morris and John B. Williamson, *Poverty and Public Policy: An Analysis of Federal Intervention Efforts* (New York: Greenwood Press, 1986), pp. 156–157.
4. Battelle Columbus Laboratories, *Final Report on the Office of Economic Opportunity Experiment in Educational Performance Contracting* (Columbus, OH: Battelle Memorial Institute, 1972), p. 142.
5. Gramlich and Koshel, *Educational Performance Contracting,* p. 66. See Mecklenburger, *Performance Contracting,* p. 83, for a summary of the differences in the contractors' approaches.
6. Charles Blaschke, *Performance Contracting: Who Profits Most?* (Bloomington, IN: Phi Delta Kappa Educational Foundation, 1972), pp. 28, 44–46.
7. Gramlich and Koshel, *Educational Performance Contracting,* p. 46.
8. Myron Lieberman, "Employment Relations Under Performance Contracting," manuscript. At the time of the OEO project, I lived in the Bronx and had several opportunities to discuss union reactions to the project with United Federation of Teachers leaders. These reactions are discussed in the paper.
9. Gramlich and Koshel, *Educational Performance Contracting,* pp. 29–30; Mecklenburger, *Performance Contracting,* includes several references to union opposition to performance contracting, including instances that occurred before as well as during the OEO project.
10. Gramlich and Koshel, *Educational Performance Contracting,* p. 26. Mecklenburger, *Performance Contracting,* pp. 84–87, shows not only how the lack of time rendered the results useless but that the twenty OEO project directors expressed their concerns on the matter in Janu-

ary 1972. As Mecklenburger comments, "OEO had not done several managerial things one might reasonably expect in such an effort. The OEO itself was primarily responsible for unsatisfactory efforts at pretesting, training staff, organizing nationally, and avoiding conflicts of regulations" (p. 85).

11. General Accounting Office (GAO), *Evaluation of the Office of Economic Opportunity's Performance Contracting Experiment, Report to the Congress by the Comptroller General of the United States, B-130515* (Washington, D.C.: General Accounting Office, 1973).

12. U.S. Office of Economic Opportunity Office of Planning, Research and Evaluation, *A Demonstration of Incentives in Education* (Washington, D.C.: Government Printing Office, 1972).

13. GAO, *Evaluation;* Mecklenburger, *Performance Contracting,* p. 97, also points out the very limited nature of the OEO results.

14. Battelle Columbus Laboratories, *Final Report,* on p. 142. Emphasis added. Reprinted by permission of the publisher.

15. Examples are Berlitz (foreign languages); Institute for Reading and Development (remedial reading); Performance Learning Systems, Inc. (teacher training); and scores of schools for exceptional students.

16. See Madsen Pirie, *Dismantling the State: The Theory and Practice of Privatization* (Dallas, TX: National Center for Policy Analysis, 1985); John Goodman, ed., *Privatization* (Dallas, TX: National Center for Policy Analysis, 1985); Stuart M. Butler, *Privatizing Federal Spending: A Strategy to Eliminate the Deficit* (New York: Universe Books, 1985); and John Kay, Colin Myer, and David Thompson, *Privatisation and Regulation: The UK Experience* (Oxford: Clarendon Press, 1986).

17. The leading proponent of the view that the school board's role as producer of educational services conflicts with its role as a consumer of them is Ted Kolderie, Senior Fellow and Director, Public Services Redesign Project, Hubert H. Humphrey Institute of Public Affairs, University of Minnesota.

18. *American School Board Journal,* 169 (October 1982): 26.

19. The discussion of IFBs and RFPs relies mainly on John Tepper Marlin, *Contracting Municipal Services: A Guide for the Private Sector* (New York: Ronald Press, 1984), and H. A. Butt and R. D. Palmer, *Value for Money in the Public Sector: The Decision-Maker's Guide* (New York: Basil Blackwell, 1985).

20. Marlin, *Contracting Municipal Services.*

21. William Lowe Boyd, "Public Education's Last Hurrah?: Schizophrenia, Amnesia, and Ignorance in School Politics," *Educational Evaluation and Policy Analysis,* 9 (Summer 1987): 85–100; John E. Chubb, "Why the Current Wave of School Reform Will Fail," *The Public Interest,* 90 (Winter 1988): 28–49. Thomas B. Timar and David L. Kirp, "Educational Reform and Institutional Competence," *Harvard Educational Review,* 57 (August 1987):1–24.

CHAPTER 5

1. There is an enormous body of literature on both vouchers and tuition tax credits. Most of the major references include bibliographies and are cited in chapters 5 to 8. Some interesting data and perspectives from Britain may be found in five articles in *Economic Affairs*, 6 (April–May 1986); Arthur Seldon, *The Riddle of the Voucher* (London: Institute of Economic Affairs, 1986); Mark Blaug, "The 'Pros' and 'Cons' of Education Vouchers," *Economic Review* (May 1987): 17–21; and C. K. Rowley, "The Political Economy of British Education," *Scottish Journal of Political Economy* 16 (1969): 152–176. For an interesting analysis of the earliest voucher proposals in Great Britain as well as in the United States, see Charles S. Benson, "Economic Analysis of Institutional Alternatives for Providing Education (Public, Private Sector)" in Roe L. Johns, Irving J. Goffman, Kern Alexander, and Dewey H. Stollar, eds., *Economic Factors Affecting the Financing of Education* (Gainesville, FL: National Educational Finance Project, 1970), pp. 121–172.
2. For a good discussion of this point, see Thomas H. Jones, *Introduction to School Finance: Technique and Social Policy* (New York: Macmillan, 1985), pp. 245–273; and Blaug, "The 'Pros' and 'Cons' of Education Vouchers."
3. Milton Friedman, *Capitalism and Freedom* (Chicago: University of Chicago Press, 1962), pp. 85–107.
4. Milton Friedman and Rose Friedman, *Free to Choose* (New York: Harcourt Brace Jovanovich, Inc., 1980) (London, Martin Secker and Warburg, 1980.)
5. Ibid., p. 152. Excerpt from *Free to Choose*, copyright © 1980 by Milton Friedman and Rose D. Friedman, reprinted by permission of the publishers.
6. ". . . most of the members of the National Association of Independent Schools would rather broaden the access of new segments of the society to the schools working within present frameworks, rather than increasing the total number of students overall." Letter from John C. Esty, Jr., President National Association of Independent Schools, to Myron Lieberman, March 13, 1987.
7. *New York Times*, June 12, 1987, p. B12.
8. National Association of Independent Schools, NAIS Statistics, Spring 1986; NAIS Member School Operations, 1984–85; NAIS membership, 1985–86 (Boston: National Association of Independent Schools, 1986), p. 7.
9. *Education Week*, March 11, 1987, p. 6.
10. Hansmann views the tax exemption for nonprofits as a device that compensates for the fact that they cannot resort to equity financing. See Henry B. Hansmann, "The Rationale for Exempting Nonprofit Organizations form the Corporate Income Tax," *Yale Law Journal* 91 (1981): 54–100.

11. Peter Earl, *Lifestyle Economics: Consumer Behavior in a Turbulent World* (New York: St. Martin's Press, 1986).

12. See Marc Bendick, Jr., *Privatizing the Delivery of Social Welfare Services* (Washington, D.C.: The Urban Institute, May 1985).

13. This is not a matter of dispute although the causes and consequences may be. See James S. Coleman and Thomas Hoffer, *Public and Private High Schools* (New York: Basic Books, 1987), pp. 28–56.

14. "Voters Like Vouchers," advertisement by *Times Mirror* in *New York Times*, May 8, 1988, p. E29.

15. Burton A. Weisbrod, *The Nonprofit Economy* (Cambridge, MA: Harvard University Press, 1988), p. 45.

16. See Thomas B. Timar and David L. Kirp, "Educational Reform and Institutional Competence," *Harvard Educational Review*, 57 (August 1987): 308–330; Eric Bredo, "Choice, Constraint, and Community," in William L. Boyd and Charles T. Kerchner, eds., *The Politics of Excellence and Choice in Education* (Philadelphia, PA: Falmer Press, 1988), pp. 67–78.

17. *Peter W. v. San Francisco Unified School District*, 131 Cal. Rptr. 854 (1976).

18. Judith S. Kaufman, Roger A. Boothroyd, and David W. Chapman, "Proprietary College Counseling: Problem or Solution?" Paper available from Dr. David W. Chapman, 325 School of Education, State University of New York, Albany, NY 12222.

19. A good discussion of this point generally, as well as of several others discussed in this chapter, may be found in J. D. Forbes, *The Consumer Interest* (New York: Croom Helm, 1987).

20. For an excellent discussion of information issues, see Blaug, "The 'Pros' and 'Cons' of Vouchers."

21. See Charles L. Schultze, *The Public Use of Private Interest* (Washington, D.C.: Brookings Institution, 1976); and Charles Wolf, Jr., *Markets or Governments* (Santa Monica, CA: Rand Corporation, 1988).

22. Albert O. Hirschman, "Exit and Voice: An Expanding Sphere of Influence," in *Rival Views of Market Society and Other Recent Essays* (New York: Viking, 1987), pp. 77–78.

23. Albert O. Hirschman, *Exit, Voice, and Loyalty* (Cambridge, MA: Harvard University Press, 1970), p. 17.

24. "Article XVI, Complaint Procedure," *NJEA Sample Agreement* (Trenton, NJ: New Jersey Education Association, 1983), pp. 161–162. The same proposal has been included for several years in model contracts disseminated to NJEA local affiliates, including several in Hirschman's county of residence.

25. See David L. Kirp and Donald N. Jensen, eds., *School Days: Rule Days: The Legalization and Regulation of Education* (Philadelphia: Falmer Press, 1986).

CHAPTER 6

1. In 1988, 204 private schools were members of the National Association of Private Schools for Exceptional Children. These schools enrolled over 20,000 of the most difficult to educate students. In addition, the association reported over 600 additional private schools serving such students. Cooper found that the number of private schools serving disabled pupils increased from 8 in 1975–76 to over 2,600 in 1983–84, when they enrolled about 300,000 pupils. The inclusion of denominational schools serving such pupils probably accounts for Cooper's larger estimate. Bruce Cooper, *The Changing Universe of U.S. Private Schools,* Executive Summary (Stanford, CA: Institute for Research on Education Finance and Governance, October 1984), p. 15.

2. See Nathan Glazer, "The Future Under Tuition Tax Credits," and Richard J. Murnane, "The Uncertain Consequences of Tuition Tax Credits," in Thomas James and Henry M. Levin, eds., *Public Dollars for Private Schools* (Philadelphia: Temple University Press, 1983), pp. 87–100, 210–222.

3. Glazer, "The Future Under Tuition Tax Credits," pp. 87–100.

4. Daniel C. Levy, "Private Choice and Public Policy in Nonprofit Education," in Daniel C. Levy, ed., *Private Education: Studies in Choice and Public Policy* (New York: Oxford University Press, 1986), p. 3; Westat, Inc., *Private Schools and Private School Teachers: Final Report of the 1985–86 Private School Study* (Washington, D.C.: Center for Education Statistics, Office of Educational Research and Improvement, 1987), pp. 11–12. Unfortunately, the National Center for Education Statistics (NCES), which conducts periodic surveys of private schools, does not disaggregate data on private schools into for profit and not for profit. Similarly, most states do not categorize schools as "nonprofit" or "for profit," so it is often impossible to ascertain the breakdown within states. Even the National Independent Private School Association (NIPSA), the national organization of proprietary schools, has been unable to develop reliable data on the issue. The Bureau of the Census also collects data on private school enrollments, but its data is probably not as accurate as NCES data. Regardless, the differences would not affect any conclusion or policy recommendation in this book.

5. Henry B. Hansmann, "The Role of Nonprofit Enterprise," *Yate Law Journal,* 89 (5) (April 1980): 835–836. For criticisms of Hansmann's analysis, see Ira Mark Ellman, "Another Theory of Nonprofit Organizations," *Michigan Law Review* 80 (April 1982): 999–1050.

6. The following data are taken from Burton A. Weisbrod, *The Nonprofit Economy* (Cambridge, MA: Harvard University Press, 1988). Weisbrod cites the primary sources.

7. Michael B. Katz, *The Irony of Early School Reform: Educational In-*

novation in Mid-Nineteenth Century Massachusetts (Boston: Beacon Press, 1968).

8. This discussion essentially follows Burton A. Weisbrod, ed., *The Voluntary Nonprofit Sector* (Lexington, MA: Lexington Books, 1977), especially the chapter by Marc Bendick, Jr., "Education as a Three Sector Industry," pp. 101–142.

9. Donald A. Erickson, "Disturbing Evidence about the 'One Best System,'" in Robert B. Everhart, ed., *The Public School Monopoly* (San Francisco, CA: Pacific Institute for Public Policy Research, 1981), pp. 393–422.

10. See Burton A. Weisbrod, *The Nonprofit Economy*, pp. 33–41.

11. California Education Code, Paragraph 45372 (C).

12. The data on hospital chains in this analysis are taken from Richard B. Siegrist, Jr., "Wall Street and the For-Profit Hospital Management Companies," in Bradford H. Gray, ed., *The New Health Care for Profit* (Washington, D.C.: National Academy Press, 1983), pp. 35–50.

13. Bradford H. Gray, Introduction, in Bradford H. Gray, ed., *For-Profit Enterprise in Health Care* (Washington, D.C.: National Academy Press, 1986), p. xviii.

14. Myron Lieberman, *Beyond Public Education* (New York: Praeger, 1986), p. 225.

15. The following discussion is adapted from Bendick, Jr., "Education as a Three Sector Industry."

16. Stephen M. Shortell, "Physician Involvement in Hospital Decision Making," in Bradford H. Gray, *The New Health Care for Profit*, pp. 91–92.

17. Robert Charles Clark, "Does the Nonprofit Form Fit the Hospital Industry?" in *Harvard Law Review*, 93 (May 1980): 1418. See also *New York Times*, July 15, 1987, p. A 1.

18. Clark, "Does the Nonprofit Form Fit the Hospital Industry," 1416–1489. See also Henry Hansmann, *The Evolution of the Law of Nonprofit Organizations.* Paper presented at Independent Sector Spring Research Forum, New York City, March 19–20, 1987; Roger D. Blair and James M. Fesmire, "Antitrust Treatment of Nonprofit and For-Profit Hospital Mergers," in Richard M. Scheffler and Lewis F. Rossiter, eds., *Advances in Health Economics and Health Services Research. A Research Annual* (Greenwich, CT: JAI Press, 1987), pp. 91–106. For a contrary view, see Gray, ed., *For Profit Enterprise in Health Care*, pp. 186–187.

19. *CAPE Outlook*, No. 130 (May 1987): 3–4.

20. As will be discussed in chapter 11, the President's Commission on Privatization recommended that state regulation vary with the extent of state aid.

21. Mark A. Kutner, Joel D. Sherman, and Mary F. Williams, "Federal Policies for Private Schools," in Daniel C. Levy, ed., *Private Education: Studies in Choice and Public Policy* (New York: Oxford University Press, 1986), pp. 57–81.

22. Richard J. Murnane, "Comparisons of Private and Public Schools: The Critical Role of Regulations," in Daniel C. Levy, ed., *Private Education: Studies in Choice and Public Policy* (New York: Oxford University Press, 1986), pp. 138–152.

23. *Marjorie Webster Junior College, Inc.* v. *Middle States Association of Colleges and Secondary Schools*, No. 23, 351, USCA (DC Cir.), June 30, 1970, 302F. Supp. 459. 432F. 2d 650. Cert. den., 91 S.Ct. (1970).

24. Brief for Appellant Middle States Association in the United States Court of Appeals for the District of Columbia Circuit, in Marjorie Webster Junior College, Inc., Plaintiff, vs. Middle States Association of Colleges and Secondary Schools, Inc., Defendant, the Complaint, Briefs, and Decisions (New York: Middle States Association, June 1971), pp. 34, 43–44.

25. Mancur Olson, Jr., *The Rise and Decline of Nations* (New Haven, CT: Yale University Press 1982).

26. *Education Week,* February 25, 1987 pp. 1, 14–25.

27. For a good discussion of this point, as well as the problems facing organizations when they go into competitive enterprise, see Edward Skloot, "Enterprise and Commerce in Nonprofit Organizations," in Walter W. Powell, ed., *The Nonprofit Sector: A Research Handbook* (New Haven, CT: Yale University Press, 1987), pp. 380–393.

CHAPTER 7

1. See Gerard V. Bradley, *Church-State Relations in America* (Westport, CT: Greenwood Press, 1987); Rodney K. Smith, *Public Prayer and the Constitution* (Wilmington, DE: Scholarly Resources, 1987); Lloyd P. Jorgenson, *The State and the Non-Public School* (Columbia, MO: University of Missouri Press, 1987); and Raoul Berger, *Government By Judiciary* (Cambridge, MA: Harvard University Press, 1977).

2. Lloyd P. Jorgenson, "The Birth of a Tradition," *Phi Delta Kappan* (June 1963): 407–414.

3. D. E. Boles, *The Bible, Religion, and the Public Schools* (New York: Collier Books, 1963), p. 53; J. K. Flanders, *Legislative Control of the Elementary School Curriculum* (New York: Teachers College Press, 1925), pp. 158–159. David Tyack, "Toward a Social History of Law and Public Education," in David L. Kirp and Donald N. Jensen, eds., *School Days, Rule Days; The Legalization and Regulation of Education* (Philadelphia: Falmer Press, 1986), p. 212; Jorgenson, *The State and the Non-Public School.*

4. Otto T. Hamilton, *The Courts and the Curriculum* (New York: Teachers College Press, 1927), p. 113.

5. School District of Abington Township vs. Schempp, 374 U.S. 203 (1963).

6. In one highly publicized Nebraska case, a fundamentalist minister re-

fused even to provide the state with the names of pupils attending the school sponsored by the denomination and asserted that education officials had no right to inspect the school, which was "God's property." State ex rel. Douglas vs. Faith Baptist Church, Nebraska, 301 N.W. 2d 571 (1981). For a good analysis of the case as well as the conflicts arising out of efforts to regulate Christian day schools, see James C. Carper and Neal Devins, "Rendering Unto Caesar: State Regulation of Christian Day Schools," manuscript available from the Department of Curriculum and Instruction, P.O. Box 5365, Mississippi State University, Mississippi State, MS 39762.

7. Cantwell v. Connecticut, 301 U.S. 296 (1940).
8. Mueller v. Allen, 463 U.S. 388 (1983).
9. Lemon v. Kurtzman, 403 U.S. 602 (1971).
10. Torcaso v. Watkins 376 U.S. 488 (1961).
11. See Bradley, *Church-State Relations;* Smith, *Public Prayer;* Jorgenson, *The State and the Non-Public School;* and Charles L. Glenn, Jr., *The Myth of the Common School* (Amherst, MA: University of Massachusetts Press, 1988).
12. Thomas Vitullo-Martin and Bruce Cooper, *Separation of Church and Child* (Indianapolis, IN: Hudson Institute, 1987), pp. 86–87.
13. See Burton A. Weisbrod, *The Nonprofit Economy* (Cambridge, MA: Harvard University Press, 1988), pp. 33–41.
14. Ibid., pp. 48–53.
15. National Assessment of Educational Progress, "Reading and Mathematics Achievement in Public and Private Schools: Is There a Difference?" Report No. SY-RM-50 (Denver, CO: Education Commission of the States, 1981), p. 1.
16. James S. Coleman, Thomas Hoffer, and Sally Kilgore, *High School Achievement: Public, Catholic, and Private High Schools Compared* (New York: Basic Books, 1982), pp. 59–60. Reprinted by permission of the publisher.
17. Lee M. Wolfle, "Enduring Cognitive Effects on Public and Private Schools," *Educational Researcher* (May 1987): 3–11.
18. Karl L. Alexander, *Comparing Public and Private School Effectiveness: Evidence and Issues,* Executive Summary (Baltimore, MD: Johns Hopkins University, October 1984), p. 8. See also Martha J. Chang and Robert J. Bickel, "An Analysis of the Comparative Effectiveness of Public and Private Schools Using SAT Data," Paper presented at annual meeting, American Educational Research Association, Chicago, IL, April 2, 1985.
19. Richard J. Murnane, "Comparisons of Public and Private Schools: Lessons from the Uproar," *Journal of Human Resources,* vol. 19, no. 2: 269–270.
20. An excellent statement of it is James C. Coleman, "Families and Schools," *Educational Researcher* (Aug.–Sept. 1987): 32–38.
21. James S. Coleman and Thomas Hoffer, *Public and Private High Schools: The Impact of Communities* (New York: Basic Books, 1987), pp. 96–148.

22. See Diane B. Gertler, *Subject Offerings and Enrollments in Grades 9-12 of Nonpublic Secondary Schools,* OE 24012-62 (Washington, D.C.: Government Printing Office, 1962); and Grace S. Wright, *Subject Offerings and Enrollments in Public Secondary Schools,* OE 24015-61 (Washington, D.C.: Government Printing Office, 1961).

23. Coleman and Hoffer, *Public and Private High Schools,* p. 52.

24. Ibid., pp. 135–140.

25. "Teachers in Elementary and Secondary Education," Photocopy. Center for Education Statistics, Washington, D.C., 1987, p. 7.

26. Some evidence to this effect can be found in Donald A. Erickson, "Disturbing Evidence about the 'One Best System,'" in Robert B. Everhart, ed., *The Public School Monopoly* (San Francisco: Pacific Institute for Public Policy Research, 1981), pp. 393–422; and in "Choice and Private Schools: Dynamics of Supply and Demand," in Daniel C. Levy, ed., *Private Education: Studies in Choice and Public Policy* (New York: Oxford University Press, 1986), pp. 82–112.

27. Coleman asserts this position very effectively in "Families and Schools."

28. The NTU supported a 1986 voucher initiative in the District of Columbia. The initiative lost by an overwhelming margin.

29. For example, Friedman has asserted over national television that "it has been demonstrated that private schools can be conducted for half the cost of public schools." Milton Friedman, panel discussion entitled "Resolved: We Should Move Toward Privatization, Including the Schools," on Firing Line, May 2, 1986, quoted in *Educational Choice,* (June/July 1986): 6.

30. Weisbrod, *The Nonprofit Economy,* pp. 130–141.

31. *Congressional Record,* November 16, 1983, pp. S16293.

32. Dennis J. Encarnation, "Public Finance and Regulation of Nonpublic Education," in Thomas James and Henry M. Levin, eds., *Public Dollars for Private Schools* (Philadelphia, PA: Temple University Press, 1983), pp. 175–195; and Daniel J. Sullivan, *Public Aid to Nonpublic Schools* (Lexington, MA: D.C. Heath, 1974).

33. Marc Bendick, Jr., "Education as a Three-Sector Industry," in Burton A. Weisbrod, ed., *The Voluntary Nonprofit Sector* (Lexington, MA: Lexington Books, 1977), pp. 101–142. It appears, however, that Bendick's procedures substantially underestimated public school costs, so the statement quoted may not be accurate.

34. Bendick, "Education as a Three Sector Industry," p. 128.

35. See Weisbrod, *The Nonprofit Economy,* pp. 38–51.

36. National Center for Education Statistics, *Background and Experience Characteristics of Public and Private School Teachers: 1984–85 and 1985–86, Survey Report* (Washington, D.C.: Office of Educational Research and Improvement, U.S. Department of Education, October 1988), p. 1.

37. Daniel J. Sullivan, "Comparing Efficiency Between Public and Private Schools," TTC-15 (Stanford, CA: Institute for Research on Educational Finance and Governance, 1983), pp. 29–30. See also

Sullivan's *Public Aid to Nonpublic Schools* (Lexington, MA: D.C. Heath, 1974).

38. Clint Bolick, *Changing Course* (New Brunswick, NJ: Transaction, Inc., 1988), pp. 104–105.

CHAPTER 8

1. Recent developments concerning choice within public schools are discussed in Richard F. Elmore, "Choice in Public Education," in William L. Boyd and Charles T. Kerchner, eds., *The Politics of Excellence and Choice in Education* (Philadelphia, PA: Falmer Press, 1988), pp. 79–98; Frank J. Esposito, *Public School Choice: National Trends and Initiatives* (Trenton, NJ: Office of Forms and Publications, State of New Jersey, 1988); Joe Nathan, "Results and Future Prospects of State Efforts to Increase Choice Among Schools," *Phi Delta Kappan* (June 1987): 67–73; and William Snider, "The Call for Choice, A Special Report," *Education Week*, June 24, 1987, pp. C1–C24. Policy statements supporting choice within public schools include National Governors Association, *Time for Results: The Governor's 1991 Report on Education* (Washington, D.C.: National Governors Association, 1986); President's Commission on Privatization, *Report of the President's Commission on Privatization* (Washington, D.C.: Government Printing Office, 1988); and Chester E. Finn, Jr., Assistant Secretary and Counselor to the Secretary, U.S. Department of Education, Testimony on Choice in American Education before the President's Commission on Privatization, December 22, 1987. Other analyses include John E. Chubb and Terry M. Moe, *What Price Democracy? Politics, Markets, and American Schools* (Washington, D.C.: Brookings Institution, 1989); Richard M. Murnane, "Family Choice in Public Education: The Roles of Students, Teachers, and System Designers," *Teachers College Record* (Winter 1986): 169–189; William Lowe Boyd, "Balancing Public and Private Schools: The Australian Experience and American Implications," *Educational Evaluation and Policy Analysis* 9 (Fall 1987): 183–198; Mary Anne Raywid, "Family Choice Arrangements in Public Schools," *Review of Educational Research*, 55 (Winter 1985): 435–467; John McClaughry, *Educational Choice in Vermont* (Concord, VT: Institute for Liberty and Community, 1987); J. R. Hough, *Education and the National Economy* (London: Croom Helm, 1987), pp. 234–244; Denis P. Doyle, *From Theory to Practice: Considerations for Implementing a Statewide Voucher System* (Sacramento, CA: Sequoia Institute, May 1984); and William L. Boyd and Charles T. Kerchner, eds., *The Politics of Excellence and Choice in Education*.

2. *Minnesota Statutes 120.062*, enacted 1988 session. Previous legislation gave school districts of residence authority to veto transfers.

3. Arthur G. Powell, Eleanor Farrar, and David K. Cohen, *The Shopping Mall High School* (Boston, MA: Houghton Mifflin, 1985).
4. E. Levinson, *The Alum Rock Voucher Demonstration: Three Years of Implementation* (Santa Monica, CA: Rand Corporation, 1976).
5. See Tim L. Mazzoni, "The Politics of Educational Choice in Minnesota," in William L. Boyd and Charles T. Kerchner, eds., *The Politics of Excellence and Choice in Education,* pp. 222–223.
6. Susan Fuhrman, ed., *Choice in Public Education: Exploring a Strategy for New Jersey* (New Brunswick, NJ: Eagleton Institute of Politics, Rutgers University, 1988), p. 5.
7. The Reagan administration held a White House seminar on choice in public schools in January 1989. Administration officials clearly regarded choice in public schools as a step toward choice of public or private school. The Bush administration's support for the latter appears to be pro forma.
8. My discussion of the Vermont experience is based on McClaughry, *Educational Choice in Vermont.*
9. Henry M. Levin, "The Failure of the Public Schools and the Free Market Remedy," *Urban Review* (June 1968): 32–37.
10. In 1985 the Reagan administration proposed the Equity and Choice Act of 1985 (TEACH). This proposed legislation would have allowed parents of children selected for Chapter 1 programs to use their pro rata share of such funds to pay for tuition or compensatory services or both from private schools. TEACH was never reported out of congressional committees, and a revised version was submitted in 1986. The revised version, entitled the Children's Options for Intensive Compensatory Education Act (CHOICE), also failed to survive congressional committee hearings. Previously, Congress had rejected tuition tax credits fourteen times between 1966 and 1983. For an analysis of the Reagan administration's 1985 proposal, see Wayne Riddle, "Vouchers for the Education of Disadvantaged Children: Analysis of the Reagan Administration Proposal," *Journal of Educational Finance* 12 (Summer 1986): 9–35; and Bruce S. Cooper, "The Uncertain Future of National Education Policy: Private Schools and the Federal Role," in William L. Boyd and Charles T. Kerchner, eds., *The Politics of Excellence and Choice in Education,* pp. 165–182.
11. For a good analysis of the political obstacles to voucher plans, see Cooper, "The Uncertain Future of National Education Policy," 165–182, and Thomas H. Jones, "Politics Against Choice: School Finance and School Reform in the 1980s," in Boyd and Kerchner, *The Politics of Excellence and Choice in Education,* pp. 153–163.
12. For an example of how private schools' fear of regulation contributed to defeat of a California voucher initiative, see William Lowe Boyd, "Balancing Public and Private Schools: The Australian Experience and American Implications," *Educational Evaluation and Policy Analysis,* 9 (Fall 1987): 183–198, at 194.
13. The formation of the coalition was formally announced at a testi-

monial dinner for former Secretary of Education William J. Bennett, September 19, 1988, in Washington, D.C.

14. "Voters Like Vouchers," advertisement by *Times Mirror* in *New York Times,* May 8, 1988, p. E29.
15. Jones, "Politics Against Choice: School Finance and School Reform in the 1980s," pp. 153–163.
16. Mueller v. Allen, 463 U.S. 388 (1983).
17. *Act for Better Child Care Services of 1988,* S.1885, H.R. 3660, 100th Congress, 2d session.
18. *Congressional Record,* May 19, 1988, p. 60.
19. *Postsecondary Enrollment Options Act,* Minnesota Statutes 123.3514, 1985 Legislative Session, as amended in 1986 and 1987.

CHAPTER 9

1. The data on hospital chains in this analysis are taken from Richard B. Siegrist, Jr., "Wall Street and the For-Profit Hospital Management Companies," in Bradford H. Gray, *The New Health Care for Profit* (Washington, D.C.: National Academy Press, 1983), pp. 35–50.
2. Information about ETS is based on an interview with Gregory J. Anrig, President, October 6, 1987, publications provided by ETS, and professional experience with ETS personnel since 1969.
3. Information about Sylvan Learning Corporation, Huntington Learning Systems, and American Learning Corporation is based on visits to corporate headquarters and publications provided by the companies. The visits to Sylvan Learning Corporation and Huntington Learning Systems took place on days when I could participate in an orientation session for potential franchisees. The publications provided by these two companies included the detailed statements by franchisors required by the Federal Trade Commission.

CHAPTER 10

1. The discussion of compulsory education is based on William F. Aikman and Lawrence Kotin, *Final Report, Legal Implications of Compulsory Education,* NIE Project NEG-00-3-0161 (Boston: Massachusetts Center for Public Interest Law, May 17, 1976).
2. Pierce v. Society of Sisters, 268 U.S. 510 (1925).
3. Patricia Lines and Judith L. Bray, *What Is a School?* LEC-83-17 (Denver, CO: Education Commission of the States, December 1983), p. 1.
4. Christopher J. Klicka, *Home School Statute Chart of the 50 States* (Great Falls, VA: Home School Legal Defense Association, May 1987). This publication provides a state-by-state summary of the legal

status of home schooling. Actually, Iowa adopted a moratorium on prosecutions of home schooling pending new legislation on the subject.

5. Patricia M. Lines, "An Overview of Home Instruction," *Phi Delta Kappan* (March 1987): p. 514. This article is an excellent summary of the home schooling movement.

6. The preceding data is taken from Klicka, *Home School Statute Chart.*

7. Raymond S. Moore, "What Educators Should Know About Home Schools," Paper prepared for the Family Research Council of America and the U.S. Department of Education (Washington, D.C.: U.S. Department of Education, n.d.), p. 6.

8. Interview with Michael Farris, President and Founder, Home School Legal Defense Association, in *Education Update,* 10 (Fall 1987): 4–5. *Education Update* is published by the Heritage Foundation. Lines estimated that between 120,000 and 260,000 pupils were being schooled at home in 1985–86. See Lines, "An Overview of Home Instruction," p. 510.

9. 1986–87 NAESP platform. Reprinted by permission.

10. In 1986 the National School Boards Association adopted a recommendation that urged that private schools be held to the same standards as public schools. *Education Week,* September 30, 1987, pp. 11–12.

11. Lines, "An Overview of Home Instruction," p. 511. See also Sonia K. Gustafson, "A Study of Home Schooling: Parental Motivations and Goals," Senior thesis presented to the faculty of the Woodrow Wilson School of Public and International Affairs, Princeton University, April 1987.

12. Brian D. Ray, "A Comparison of Home Schooling and Conventional Schooling: With a Focus on Learner Outcomes," *Science*, Department of Science, Mathematics, and Computer Education, Oregon State University, 1986, pp. 5–6.

13. Earl W. Gladin, "Home Education: Characteristics of Its Families, and Schools," Ph.D. diss., Bob Jones University, Greenville, SC, 1987, p. 108.

14. Jane Ann Van Galen, "Schooling in Private: A Study of Home Education," Ph.D. diss., University of North Carolina, Chapel Hill, NC, 1986.

15. Gladin, "Home Education," p. 108. A recent study of all pupils educated at home in the state of Washington concluded that "private schools are losing proportionally more enrollment to homeschooling than are the public schools and the reason does not appear to be economics." Jon Wartes, "Report From the 1986 Home School Testing" (Woodinville, WA: Washington Home School Research Project, 1987), p. 16.

16. Various educational arguments for home schooling have been set forth in the publication by Lines, Gladin, and Moore cited above and in Raymond S. Moore, "Research and Common Sense: Therapies for

our Homes and Schools," *Teachers College Record* (Winter 1982): 355–377; David D. Williams, Larry M. Arnoldson, and Peter Reynolds, "Understanding Home Education: Case Studies of Home Schools," Paper presented at annual meeting of the American Educational Research Association, New Orleans, LA, April 1984; *Growing Without Schools,* a journal devoted to home schooling published by Holt Associates Inc., 729 Boylston Street, Boston, MA 02116. These publications include additional references or bibliographies on the subject.

17. Moore, "Research and Common Sense," p. 366. See also interview with Michael Farris, President and Founder, Home School Legal Defense Association, in *Education Update,* 10 (4) (Fall 1987): 4–6.

18. See the references cited in note 16 for summaries of the evidence on social and emotional development under home schooling.

19. See Lines, "An Overview of Home Instruction," p. 513, referring to data collected by Maria Della Bella in Connecticut.

20. Lines, "An Overview of Home Instruction," p. 516.

21. C. K. Rowley, "The Political Economy of British Education," *Scottish Journal of Political Economy* 16 (1969): 152–176.

22. See Milton and Rose Friedman, *Free to Choose* (New York: Avon Books), pp. 140–178, especially p. 171. Kolderie has aptly summarized the problem: "The universalist approach—making each public service available to everyone, at no charge, regardless of ability to pay—has simply become too expensive to be continued; and the subsidy this involves to those well-to-do citizens who do not need it now occurs at the expense of the poor who need it most. On the other hand, the selective approach—of targeting subsidies to the poor, and insisting from here on that those who can afford to pay should do so—may undercut the willingness of the middle class to support an adequate level of service for the poor. In theory, it seems insoluble." Ted Kolderie, *An Equitable and Competitive Public Sector* (Minneapolis, MN: Public Services Redesign Project, Hubert H. Humphrey Institute of Public Affairs, November 1984), p. 23.

23. See Otto F. Kraushaar, *Private Schools: From the Puritans to the Present* (Bloomington, IN: Phi Delta Kappa Educational Foundation, 1976).

24. For the primary sources of the data and an excellent summary of the decline in marriage as a social institution, see Bryce J. Christensen, "America's Retreat from Marriage," *The Family in America* (February 1988): 1–8.

25. Bureau of the Census, U.S. Department of Commerce, "America in Transition: An Aging Society," *Current Population Reports,* Series P-23, No. 128 (Washington, D.C.: Government Printing Office, 1983), p. 1.

26. Samuel H. Preston, "Children and the Elderly: Divergent Paths for America's Dependents," *Demography,* 21 (November 1984): 435–457; also "Children and the Elderly in the U.S.," *Scientific American,* 251 (December 1984): 44–49.

27. Stanley M. Elam, ed., *The Phi Delta Kappa Gallup Polls of Attitudes Toward Education*, 1969–1984 (Bloomington, IN: Phi Delta Kappa, 1984).
28. Statements about Arizona developments are based on telephone calls to Sun City officials in November, 1988.
29. See Myron Lieberman, "The Future of the Custodial School," *Phi Delta Kappan* (September 1976): 122–125.
30. For an analysis of declining birth rates among the middle class in all the western industrial democracies, see Benjamin Wattenberg, *The Birth Dearth* (New York: Pharos Books, 1988).
31. Elise Jones et al., "Teenage Pregnancy in Developed Countries: Determinant and Policy Implication," *Family Planning Perspectives* (March/April 1985): 53–63.
32. David L. Chambers, "The Coming Curtailment of Compulsory Child Support," *Michigan Law Review* (August 1982): 1614–1632; and *New York Times*, November 25, 1988, pp. 1, A20.
33. C. Emily Feistritzer, *The Condition of Teaching* (New York: Carnegie Foundation for the Advancement of Teaching, 1983).
34. Data provided by Public Service Research Council, Vienna, VA.

CHAPTER 11

1. For an excellent discussion of the issues, see Harold S. Luft, "Economic Incentives and Clinical Decisions," and Robert M. Veatch, "Ethical Dilemmas of For-Profit Enterprise in Health Care," in Bradford H. Gray, ed., *The New Health Care for Profit* (Washington: National Academy Press, 1983), pp. 103–124, 125–152. See also the exchange between Uwe Reinhardt and Arnold Relman in Bradford H. Gray, ed., *For Profit Enterprise in Health Care* (Washington: National Academy Press, 1986).
2. The analysis that follows draws heavily on Gray, *The New Health Care for Profit*, pp. 125–152; and Veatch, "Ethical Dilemmas."
3. *Current Opinions of the Judicial Council of the American Medical Association* (Chicago, IL: American Medical Association, 1981), p. 29.
4. American Medical Association, *Judicial Council Opinions and Reports* (Chicago, IL: American Medical Association, 1971), pp. 37, 48.
5. Bradford H. Gray, *An Introduction to the New Health Care for Profit*, pp. 1–3.
6. Veatch, "Ethical Dilemmas," pp. 134, 139.
7. A proposal to establish such a competitive system is set forth in Simon Harding, "Adam Smith in the Classroom," *Economic Affairs* (Oct./Nov. 1985): 27–32.
8. For example, Michael Krashinsky contends that education produces both public and private benefits, but that the costs and problems associated with monitoring the provision of public benefits in private schools renders voucher plans inadvisable. In his work, "government produces education itself because that is the cheapest way to ensure

that the right level of public benefit is produced in the schools." Historically, as pointed out in chapter 5, ensuring "the right level of public benefit" can be equated with forcing Catholics to attend Protestant-oriented public schools. Regardless, Krashinsky cites no evidence about the efficacy of regulation of public schools or its alleged superiority to competition as a means of protecting parents. See Michael Krashinsky, "Why Educational Vouchers May Be Bad Economics," *Teachers College Record* 88 (Winter 1986): 139–151; response by Edwin C. West and rejoinder by Michael Krashinsky, same issue, pp. 152–167.

9. See Myron Lieberman, *The Future of Public Education* (Chicago: University of Chicago Press, 1960), pp. 140–145. My views on most other aspects of private education have changed drastically since 1960.

10. Richard J. Murnane, "Comparisons of Private and Public Schools: The Critical Role of Regulation," in Daniel C. Levy, ed., *Private Education Studies in Choice and Public Policy* (New York: Oxford University Press, 1986), pp. 153–169.

11. The major proposal along this line is Task Force on Teaching as a Profession, *A Nation Prepared: Teachers for the 21st Century* (Washington, D.C.: Carnegie Forum on Education and the Economy, 1986). For criticisms of the Carnegie report, see Gene Geisert and Hilary E. Mumma, "Foundation Largesse for Union Ideology," *Government Union Review* (Summer 1987): 38–53, and Myron Lieberman, "A Botched Attempt at Educational Reform," *The World and I*, Sept. suppl. to *Washington Times*, pp. 86–92.

12. Several chapters in Gray, *The New Health Care for Profit*, elucidate this evidence.

13. See Myron Lieberman, *Education as a Profession* (Englewood Cliffs, NJ: Prentice-Hall, 1956), pp. 417–451.

14. See Myron Lieberman, *Public Sector Bargaining* (Lexington, MA: Lexington Books, 1980), for a detailed argument to this effect.

15. Ibid.

16. An excellent analysis of the problems associated with developing useful indicators of school performance is Richard J. Murnane, "Improving Education Indicators and Economic Indicators: The Same Problems?" Paper presented at the annual meeting of the American Educational Research Association, April 1987. The usefulness of Murnane's analysis is limited here by the fact that it is oriented to policymakers, not individual consumers.

17. *On Further Examination: Report of the Advisory Panel on the Scholastic Aptitude Test Score Decline* (New York: College Board, 1977).

18. Harold Howe II, "Let's Have Another Test Score Decline," *Phi Delta Kappan* 66 (9) (1985): 599–602.

19. Daniel J. Koretz, *Educational Achievement: Explanations and Implications of Recent Trends* (Washington, D.C.: Congressional Budget Office, 1987).

20. *New York Times*, May 10, 1987, p. F28.

21. William J. Bennett, Address to the National Catholic Education Association, New York, April 9, 1988.
22. Nathan Glazer, "The Future Under Tuition Tax Credits," in Thomas James and Henry M. Levin, eds., *Public Dollars and Private Schools: The Case for Tuition Tax Credits* (Philadelphia, PA: Temple University Press, 1983), pp. 87–100.
23. For a good discussion of this point, see Murnane, "Comparisons of Public and Private Schools," pp. 153–169.
24. The discussion of this approach draws heavily on Richard A. Epstein, *Medical Malpractice: The Case for Contract* (New York: Center for Libertarian Studies, 1979).

Index